A Study in Business Ethics

A Study in Business Ethics

BY

DR. (MRS) RITUPARNA RAJ

Himalaya Publishing House

MUMBAI • NEW DELHI • NAGPUR • BENGALURU • HYDERABAD • CHENNAI • PUNE • LUCKNOW • AHMEDABAD • ERNAKULAM • BHUBANESWAR • KOLKATA

First Edition	:	**1999**	**Reprint**	:	**2008**
Reprint	:	**2001**	**Reprint**	:	**2009**
Reprint	:	**2003**	**Reprint**	:	**2012**
Reprint	:	**2004**	**Reprint**	:	**2013**
Reprint	:	**2007**	**Reprint**	:	**2014**
			Reprint	:	**2016**

Published by : Mrs. Meena Pandey for **Himalaya Publishing House Pvt. Ltd.,**
"Ramdoot", Dr. Bhalerao Marg, Girgaon, Mumbai - 400 004.
Phone: 022-23860170/23863863, Fax: 022-23877178
E-mail: himpub@vsnl.com; Website: www.himpub.com

Branch Offices :

New Delhi : "Pooja Apartments", 4-B, Murari Lal Street, Ansari Road, Darya Ganj, New Delhi - 110 002. Phone: 011-23270392, 23278631;
Fax: 011-23256286

Nagpur : Kundanlal Chandak Industrial Estate, Ghat Road, Nagpur - 440 018. Phone: 0712-2738731, 3296733; Telefax: 0712-2721216

Bengaluru : Plot No. 91-33, 2nd Main Road Seshadripuram, Behind Nataraja Theatre, Bengaluru-560020. Phone: 08041138821, 9379847017, 9379847005

Hyderabad : No. 3-4-184, Lingampally, Besides Raghavendra Swamy Matham, Kachiguda, Hyderabad - 500 027. Phone: 040-27560041, 27550139

Chennai : New-20, Old-59, Thirumalai Pillai Road, T. Nagar, Chennai - 600 017. Mobile: 9380460419

Pune : First Floor, "Laksha" Apartment, No. 527, Mehunpura, Shaniwarpeth (Near Prabhat Theatre), Pune - 411 030.
Phone: 020-24496323/24496333; Mobile: 09370579333

Lucknow : House No 731, Shekhupura Colony, Near B.D. Convent School, Aliganj, Lucknow - 226 022. Phone: 0522-4012353; Mobile: 09307501549

Ahmedabad : 114, "SHAIL", 1st Floor, Opp. Madhu Sudan House, C.G. Road, Navrang Pura, Ahmedabad - 380 009. Phone: 079-26560126; Mobile: 09377088847

Ernakulam : 39/176 (New No: 60/251) 1st Floor, Karikkamuri Road, Ernakulam,
Kochi – 682011. Phone: 0484-2378012, 2378016; Mobile: 09387122121

Bhubaneswar : 5 Station Square, Bhubaneswar - 751 001 (Odisha). Phone: 0674-2532129, Mobile: 09338746007

Kolkata : 108/4, Beliaghata Main Road, Near ID Hospital, Opp. SBI Bank, Kolkata - 700 010, Phone: 033-32449649, Mobile: 7439040301

Printed at : M/s Sri Sai Art Printer Hyderabad. On behalf of HPH.

Dedication

This book is humbly dedicated to my respected Father-In-Law, Shri. Pijush Das & my most beloved Mother-In-Law, Smt. Hem Prabha Das; two figures in my life, who are epitomes of ethics in their own areas of operations.

CONTENTS

PREFACE

With the introduction of Business Ethics as a course of study in the MBA and PGDM courses in various Institutes and Universities of India, students were faced with the problem of not finding a text book to meet their needs, and teachers were faced with the problem of not finding adequate and relevant teaching and learning materials covering the entire syllabus prescribed for the course. Such a challenge also fell upon me when I had to teach this new subject in the MBA course of Tezpur University, a newly established Central University. Collecting materials from various sources became a major activity and designing case studies from real life industrial situations and discussion problems became a major challenge. However, the great satisfaction of a job well done was mine, when students not only of Tezpur University, but also of North Eastern Regional Institute of Management (NERIM), where I was the Dean (Academics) from 1998, approached not only me, but also the Secretary of the Institute, to provide funds for publishing a Text book on my class lectures and teaching materials. In the meantime, Himalaya Publishing House came forward to publish the Text book in this new area of study.

Recently, there has been an increasing awareness, and more importantly, an increasing interest in the field of Business Ethics. This is indeed very welcome trend! In fact, perhaps, there has not been any time in the history of business development where the concepts and an understanding of the nature of business ethics has been so urgently needed, never before had the need for ethical practices in business so widely felt! Business Ethics proves that businesses can be, and have been, ethical and still make profits. Till the last few decades, Business Ethics was thought of as being a contradiction of terms. The popular concept was that if it is business, then it cannot be ethical, and if it is ethical, it does not represent business at all. This amounts to saying that business can make profits only through immoral ways, by being unethical! Nothing can be more further from the truth. Thankfully such thoughts are not prevalent any more. There are examples galore where not only have ethical companies made profits, but more importantly, it is only ethical companies which discharged its social responsibilities, that have survived competition and turbulent changes through the years and have contributed to social welfare and have continued to flourish undiminished. Hence, today, more and more interest is being given by corporate houses and business leaders to the application of ethical practices in business dealings.

A business or company is considered ethical only if it tries to reach a trade-off between pursuing it's economic objectives and its social obligations, i.e., between its commercial objectives and its welfare obligations. What are obligations of a business is open to interpretations. The list of obligations that a company must perform is long and complex and hence are costly to the company; yet they must be discharged if a company wants to survive and grow in the long run and is not satisfied in making short term profits. While discharging its obligations to the society, the company not only fulfils its own duties, but also paves the way for a stronger and more ethical foundation.

In fact, considered from all angels, it is unethical NOT to make profits. It is unethical for a company to make losses. A company which cannot make profits and make losses, misutilises scarce national resources, cannot pay back creditors, upsets the economy, promotes inefficiency and, most importantly, cannot, at any cost discharge its social responsibilities, meet its welfare commitments and jeopardizes the future of its employees and drives them into the unemployment market. Such a loss-making company becomes nuisance and a burden to the economy and has no right to exist in the marketplace. Moreover, it has no business to force its employees into economic insecurity, which is highly unethical. Thus, instead of profits being contradictory to ethics, business ethics dictates that the first responsibility of business is to remain profitable and generate revenue for the shareholders and the society.

Why business ethics has assumed so great a part in our market economy is partly due to the fact that unethical decisions are not limited only to themselves, but affects a wide range of other situations and have widespread ramifications. One unethical action is like a pebble thrown into a pond of water, it produces endless ripples in the pond until the water of the entire pond gets disturbed by it. Similarly the single unethical action is not limited to the individual in the company who commits it, but spreads within the entire organisation; one unethical organisation affects the entire industry; and one unethical industry in turn, affects the entire economy and ultimately the entire nation.

Since business exists and operate within the society and is a part of a subsystem of society, its functioning must contribute to the welfare of the society. To survive, develop and excel, business must earn social sanction of the society wherein it exists and functions. Without social sanction, a business cannot earn loyal customers, cannot operate in the marketplace and will soon wither and die away. Thus, business can earn social sanction only through being ethical in its dealings, working for the welfare of the society and by discharging its social responsibilities.

Inspite of India having an ancient culture and philosophy about worklife, we in India have not yet managed to develop our own management styles in consonance with our own cultural ethos and have been systematically importing management systems and styles from foreign countries. While successful countries like the USA, UK, Germany, France and Korea are rediscovering Indian ethos, we in India are in the process of losing it. While the success of Japan in managing her economy and enterprise lies in 'Japanising' the management process within the framework of Japanese ethos, culture and value systems, Indian companies in the meantime, are nonplussed by the failure of the sure-fire and instant management success formulae from Harvard, Oxford or Tokyo, to take root in Indian soil.

Indian tradition and heritage, its culture and philosophy, its ethos and values are a treasure house, where the richest and the rarest of gems are stored. It is ours only for the asking. If we can apply even a few of these gems to the management of the modern organisation, we will be doing a great service, not only to ourselves, or to our organisations, but also to our future generations of entrepreneurs and managers.

Organisations which have ignored the Indian philosophy of work, have only achieved external development at the cost of internal growth and inner peace. In such organisations, the 'man' in the manager is lost - he amounts to nothing - he stands nowhere. There is loss of ethical and humane values in such organisations. The organisation itself is dehumanised. There is erosion of morals and principles. There is crises of confidence. There is no industrial peace and corruption reigns supreme. Executives suffer from stress and tension, while employees suffer from demotivation and frustration. Workers are demoralised and consumers are by-passed. Nature is exploited and human welfare is neglected. In such companies, wealth is amassed but the soul is lost.

In Indian philosophy, human capacity is much more important than Plant Capacity; quality of heart and mind is much more important than Quality Circles, and modernisation of man - both his thoughts and actions - are more important than modernisation of machinery. Mental peace and inner harmony is more important to build up a strong character which imbibes the basic and the best of human and ethical values.

That may be the reason why Arnold Toynbee, the Nobel Prize winning historian, states thus-

> "It is already becoming clear that a chapter which had a Western Beginning in business management, will have to have an Indian Ending, when the world adopts rich thoughts of Indian ethos and wisdom, if it is not to end in the self-destruction of the human race".

This book is an attempt to look at business ethics from the Indian perspective. Although Case Studies, Discussion problems and Market situations from the western countries have been incorporated into the text, however, the discussion is predominantly set in Indian ethos and the book is primarily based upon Indian ethical value system.

While writing this book, help was forthcoming from numerous quarters, mention of all of them may be impossible. However, I would be failing in my duty if I did not place on record some of them. My friends and colleagues in the various teaching institutes and universities of my association, helped me not only with their experiences, discussions, analyses, insights, viewpoints and wisdom, but also with their co-operation and their inspiration and encouragement. My junior colleagues and officials of North Eastern Regional Institute of Management (NERIM), with whom I share a special and warm relationship, have contributed with their enthusiasm and encouragement which went a long way to the writing of this book. My sense of indebtness and gratitude to Professor A.K. Choudhary of Gauhati University goes much beyond this formal acknowledgement.

Words fail me when I seek to acknowledge the help, support and advice that I received from my husband Sanjib Raj, Marketing Executive, Larsen & Toubro Limited, during my strenuous hours of work and his generous sharing of my multifarious responsibilities in several spheres during the writing of this book. Now I place on record my gratitude to him formally- Thanks, indeed !

I also take this opportunity to express my gratitude to my most revered and beloved mother , Mrs Biva Chowdhary, for her constant encouragement and blessings and filling my life with courage. Thanks are also due to Mrs Bhaswati Choudhury, Mr. Monohar Choudhury and Mr. Siddhartha Chowdhary - just their presence in my life makes my life beautiful !

I thank Himalaya Publishing House, and specially Mr. S.K. Joshi, for doing a fine job of publishing this book in record time.

Finally, I express my gratitude to my dear students, all of them, who have made my job of teaching them such a pleasure. I hope this book will benefit them and eliminate their frantic search for learning material on the subject - ultimately this book was written for them! I do hope that I am able to contribute meaningfully, through this book, to a subject so close to my heart.

Date - 10.8.1999

Place-Calcutta

Rituparna Raj

CHAPTER 1

1.1 AN OVERVIEW OF BUSINESS ETHICS

Recently, there has been an increasing awareness, and more importantly increasing interest in the field of Business Ethics. This is indeed a very welcome trend! In fact, perhaps, there has not been any time in the history of business development when the concepts and an understanding of the nature of business ethics has been so urgently needed, so urgently felt, never before had the need for ethical practices in business so widely felt.

After the epoch making effects of the Industrial Revolution on business and the subsequent framing of labour legislations for protecting employees and the laying down of their rights and duties in legal terms, there has been one area which has caused concern repetitively to both business academicians and business practitioners alike, and that has been the ethical way of conducting business.

Previously, it was thought that business ethics is a contradiction of terms. The popular concept was that if it is business, then it cannot be ethical, and if it is ethical at all, it does not represent business. Fortunately, there were people in the world, even at that time, significant people, who disagreed with this philosophy–the notable amongst them being our very own J.R.D. Tata– and it is mainly due to the efforts of these significant people that Business Ethics has reached the proper place in business that is due to it.

1.2 WHAT IS ETHICS

The word 'Ethics', which is Latin is called 'ēthicus', and in Greek is called 'ēthikos', has come from the word 'ethos', meaning character or manners. Ethics is thus said to be the science of morals; a treatise on this; moral principles; recognised rules of conduct.

(Blackie's Compact English Dictionary; R. Cunliffe & G. Payton; S. Chand & Co., Ltd., 1969)

The character of a man is expressed in terms of his conduct. Conduct of a person is a series of actions, which when taken together, can be termed as 'good' or 'bad'; 'right' or 'wrong'; 'moral' or 'immortal'. However, they may be amoral as well, which means that they are beyond the sphere of morality. For example, eating his lunch is an amoral conduct of a man. However, if he steals the lunch of another person to eat it, then that is immoral. Thus, 'right', 'wrong', 'good', 'bad', 'moral', 'immoral' are termed as **Moral Judgements.** Moral Judgement requires moral standards by which we judge human conduct. Thus, Ethics can also be termed as **the science of character of a person expressed as right or wrong conduct or action.**

1.3 Nature of Ethic

Firstly, the concept of Ethics deals with human beings only, because only human beings have been endowed with the freedom of choice and the means of free will. Only a human being can distinguish between good and evil, between right and wrong, between just and proper. Only a human being can distinguish between the end which he wishes to pursue and the means to gain that end. Hence, only for a human being, does the question of ethics, values and moral conduct arise.

Secondly, the study of Ethics has today become a set of systematic knowledge about moral behaviour and conduct. Hence, the study of Ethics is a science–a field of Social Science.

Thirdly, the science of ethics is a normative science. Normative sciences judge the value of the facts in terms of an ideal. Normative sciences are concerned not with factual judgements but with judgements of what 'ought to be'. Hence, Ethics is concerned with judgement of value or what **ought** to be. Ethics seeks to determine the nature of the norm, ideal or standard, and seeks to enquire into the fitness of human actions to this ideal.

Fourthly, Ethics deals with human conduct which is voluntary and not forced or coerced by persons or circumstances. That is exactly why injuring or even killing a person who has come to kill you is not considered a moral or legal offence, whereas a cold-blooded murder is considered to be the highest kind of moral and legal crime.

Ethics is basically an area dealing with moral judgement regarding voluntary human conduct. Moral Judgement requires moral standards by which to judge human conduct. These moral standards are the ultimate end or the highest good for all concerned. Ethics tries to set the standard for the ultimate end or the highest good to be persued. Moral standards are also related to moral obligations, or the duty to do what we consider to be 'right' and 'proper'. The primary objective of Ethics is to define the highest good of man and set a standard for the same. In doing so, Ethics has to deal with several inter-related and complex problems which are psychological, legal, commercial, philosophical, sociological and political in nature.

1.4 Objectives of Ethics

The objectives of ethics are manifold. Ethics–

- studies human behaviour and makes evaluative assessment about them as moral or immoral (a diagnostic goal);
- establishes moral standards and norms of behaviour;
- makes judgement upon human behaviour based on these standards and norms;
- prescribes moral behaviour and makes recommendations about how to or how not to behave (therapeutic goal);
- expresses an opinion or attitude about human conduct in general.

1.5 Business Ethics

Having discussed the nature and concept of Ethics, we can say that Business Ethics is nothing but the application of Ethics in business. Business Ethics proves that businesses can be, and have been, ethical and still make profits. As has been stated before, till the last decade, Business Ethics was thought of as being a contradiction of terms. Thankfully, not any more. Today, more and more interest is being given to the application of ethical practices in business dealings and the ethical implications of business.

It has already been stated that human beings have been endowed with the freedom of choice and the means of free will. He can distinguish between good and evil, right and wrong, just and proper. He can distinguish between the end he wishes to persue and the means to gain that end. Now, what is true for human beings is also true for business, because business are carried on by human beings only, and business organisations are nothing but formal structures for human beings to carry on their businesses. Moreover, businesses are thought of as being living, growing entities. Thus, businesses also have choices–a choice to maximise their profits and a choice to do good for the society in which they live and operate.

However, at most times, profit maximisation and discharging of social responsibilities at the maximum limit, cannot be carried on simultaneously. One is bound to affect the other. For example, Concern for Task (Productivity) and Concern for Human Beings (workers) are bound to pull each other in opposite directions. It is difficult, if not impossible, to maximise both together. A conflict arises in trying to achieve both simultaneously. Hence, many managerial choices represent **Managerial Dilemmas**, between the profit consideration (commercial concern) and the social consideration (welfare concern) of the organisation. Many managerial decisions have ethical implications and these decisions give rise to Managerial Dilemmas.

For example, ruining occupations of age-old inhabitants in a particular locality and their ethical way of life, by using advanced technology, is an ethical dilemma. Technological advancements have to come, have to be used; however, what to do with the people whose life and earnings are affected by the utilisation of advanced technology, is a question which is difficult to answer. Recently an award-winning regional language file of India, depicted the plight of an aged boatman whose occupation was to transport people and goods across the local river, as there was no bridge over the river. However, his occupation gets threatened when a bridge is built over the river.

This does not mean that technology advancement must not be utilised or that modern methods should not be welcomed. Certainly, they should. Science and technology should, by all means, be used to uplift and make better the lives of human beings all over the world, and specially in such backward regions as this boatman lived. However, consideration should also be given to see whether alternative means of arrangements can be made so that people are not unduly disturbed or that their trauma and upheaval is kept at a minimum. In case of the boatman, an ethical and effective solution lies in providing him with alternative employment on the bridge itself–as a security man, toll tax collector, etc..

Similarly, when Mergers take place between companies, or Acquisition of one company by a bigger company, where Job positions are duplicated, instead of employees losing their jobs for no fault of their, ethical solutions lies in Job Reassignment or Retraining for alternative Job Assignments.

A business or company is considered to be ethical only if it tries to reach a trade-off between perusing its economic objectives and its social obligations, i.e., between its obligations to the society where it exists and operates; its obligations to its people due to whom it can even think of persuing economic goals; to its environment, from whom it takes so much without it demanding anything back in return; and the like. What are the obligations of a business, is open to interpretations. The list of obligations that a company must perform is long and complex and hence, are costly to the company; yet they must be discharged, if a company wants to survive and grow in the long run and is not satisfied in making profits only in the short run. While discharging its obligations to the society, the company not only fulfils its own duties, but also paves the way for a stronger and more ethical foundation.

1.6 Business Ethics and Profits

Frequently the impression of most people is that ethics and profits are mutually opposed to one another, and that if a company is ethical, it can forget about making profits. People also frequently seem to believe that a profitable company must necessarily be unethical. This is like saying that a company can make profits only through unethical means. Nothing can be more further from the truth. There are examples galore, from the pages of history, where not only have ethical companies made profits, but more importantly, **it is only ethical companies which discharged its social responsibilities, that have survived competition and turbulent changes through the years and have contributed to Social Welfare and have continued to flourished undiminished.**

'Profit is a dirty word', said Jawaharlal Nehru, in the 1950's while referring to the public sector companies. Even private companies making profits were viewed with disdain by the public. Their dealings were suspect in the eyes of the upright moral citizens of that time. This was mainly because of the distorted view of business that society had during that time. With the wide spread interest in business activities since then, with the introduction of business and management education all over the world, and with the rapid widening of the market place and the astronomical growth of consumerism worldwide, the value of profit has been given its deserved place. Today, not only is profit not a dirty word, in fact, every company is expected to justify its existence in the marketplace, through the profit it generates. It has been felt that any company which cannot make profits even for its own operations has no right to exist in the marketplace and should be wiped out. A sick and loss making company is a liability and a burden to society–it cannot discharge its responsibilities to the society, it cannot meet its welfare commitment to its employees, indeed it cannot even compensate its workforce for their efforts, it cannot generate revenue for its shareholders, it cannot meet consumer demands adqeuately and cannot do all those things that a healthy responsible organisation is required and expected to do. Hence, profit is today viewed as a measure of the success of the company and its justification for sustained existence, growth and diversification.

In fact, considered from all angles, it is unethical, **NOT** to make profit. **It is unethical, for a company, to make losses**. Because, a company which cannot make profits and makes losses, misutilises scarce national resources cannot pay back creditors, does not make wealth for its shareholders, make huge liabilities, upsets the economy, promotes inefficiency and most importantly, cannot, at any cost discharge its social responsibility, meet its welfare commitments and jeopardises the future of its employees. Such a loss-making company becomes a nuisance and a burden to the economy and has no right to exists in the marketplace. Moreover, it has no business to force its employees into economic insecurity, which is highly unethical.

Thus, instead of profits being contradictory to ethics, business ethics dictates that the first responsibility of business is to remain profitable and generate revenue for the shareholders and the society. Rather, it is unethical, **not** to make profits. Hence, the first and foremost ethical obligation of every business is to make profits for its shareholders, for its employees, for its creditors and most importantly, for itself, so that it can discharge its social responsibilities and welfare commitments. But, how much profits to make, the means and methods of making it, and at what cost–that is the ethical question.

1.7 Relationship between Business & Ethics

The relationship between business and Ethics has long been debated. If Classical economists like Adam Smith and Milton Friedman were of the opinion that the only objective of business was profit maximisation and business had no right to 'meddle' with ethics, the Church, in pre-medieval times, was the spokesman and judge for all spheres of the society, including business. In medieval and pre-medieval period, the Church took upon itself to regulate the moral functioning of business, making moral declarations like–all businesses must remain closed on Sunday, the 'holy-day', when Jesus Christ was supposed to have taken a rest and it was morally 'correct' to stop working on sundays. These two are extreme views, known as the Unitarian View and the Separatist View. However, around the decade of 1950, Talcott Parsons, founded the Integration View which stated that neither was business an extension of morality and ethics nor can business keep itself absolutely aloof from the ethical practices of the society wherein it exists and operators. This view sought to integrate the two previous views presenting a more realistic picture.

The Unitarian View

This view is of the opinion that business is only a subset or sub-structure of the moral structure of the society. According to this view, business and morality cannot be separated and business must play by the rules of morality and ethics of the community which guides the activities of the community. This View was emphasised more by the Church in the European countries and the Church prescribed that business must exist only to do good for the society, and it had no other role to play apart from serving society and unshering in social welfare. This View stated that business must conduct its affairs purely through altruist motives and that profit was a dirty word.

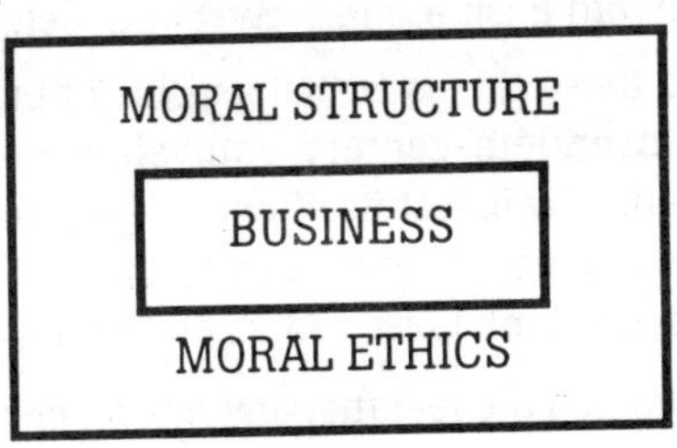

The Separatist View

Dramatically opposite to the Unitarian View, classical economists like Adam Smith and Milton Friedman asserted that the only goal of business should be profit maximisation; and that ethics and morality plays no part in business conduct. In fact, Milton Friedman, the celebrated economists, who won the Noble Prize for Economics, in 1976, hold the view that business should go on with the business of producing goods and services efficiently, and leave the solution of social problems to government agencies and concerned individuals. In short, managers should focus on what they know best–that is how to make profits. It was

Friedman who forwarded the classical view that the only responsibility of business is to earn profits, and he goes on to say, in his book, 'Capitalism & Freedom' (Chicago, 1962), thus–

> "There is one and only one responsibility of business–to use its resources and engage in activities designed to increase its profit so long at it stays within the rules of the game, which is to say, engages in open and free competition, without deception or fraud. Few trends could so thoroughly undermine the very traditions of our free society as the acceptance by corporate officials of a social responsibility other than to make as much money for their stockholders as possible. This is fundamentally subsersive doctrine."

Adam Smith and Friedman were of the opinion that business should be left alone to play by the rules of the prevalent market system, and the introduction of ethics would make an imbalance of the market dynamics. The Separatist View is of the opinion that business too has its own set of principles like 'reduce production costs,' 'optimise labour' and so on, and these principles are all related to the marketplace and have nothing to do with moral principles.

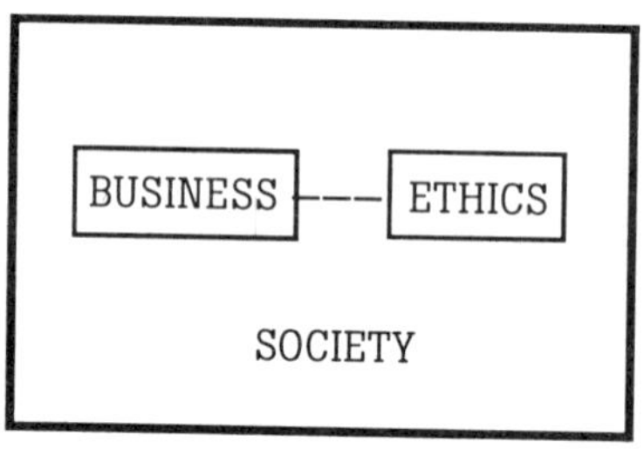

Playing the business game by the market rules will ensure that the 'individual hand of the market' would generate social welfare to community.

Theodore Levitt, the well-known psychologist, believed that if ethics and morality were allowed to enter the realms of business, then there is a danger of business values ultimately dominating over social values. He expressed thus, in his famous article, 'The Danger of Social Responsibility', (Harvard Business Review, Sept.-Oct., 1958)–

> "The danger is that all these things (social aspects of business functioning) will turn the corporation into twentieth-century equivalent of the medieval Church. The Corporation would eventually invest itself will all–embracing duties, obligations, and finally powers–ministering the whole man and moulding him and society in the image of the corporation's narrow ambitions and its essentially unsocial needs"

Many intellectuals expressed the fear that any replacement of altruism for self-interest will, therefore, be fatal to the efficiency of the system. Managers should manage only in the interests of the shareholders and shareholders should be put in the position where they decide how their wealth and resources will be used. They believe that business should not have any responsibility beyond obeying certain legal codes in achieving its economic and business goals.

The Integration View

This View was proposed by Talcott Parsons, wherein he sought to integrate ethical behaviour and business in a new area called Business Ethics. This View states that business is an economic entity and it has the right and the need to make profits, but, it must also discharge its obligations to the society where it exists and operates. Profits is certainly not a dirty word, but, neither is morality and ethics in business. This View states that society consists of a number of subsystems, and business and morality are just two of these subsystems. Since all subsystems within the society are interlinked and interdependent, so also are business and morality interlinked. Business and Ethics overlap and hence many business decisions are guided by moral considerations. In fact, business itself is considered to constitute of ethics, as it does so much good to so many people and specially to the society it serves. Production of goods and services and making them available to consumers who need them and benefit from them, itself, constitute a noble deed towards social welfare. Thus, business constitutes of ethics in itself, even while it pursues profits.

A sick and bankrupt organisation is a social liability and can hardly contribute in the area of social responsibility. Hence the first responsibility of a businessman is to generate surplus for his business. At the same time however, he must do so ethically, carry on his business on morally sound principles and go out of his way to assume social responsibilities beyond the legal minimum.

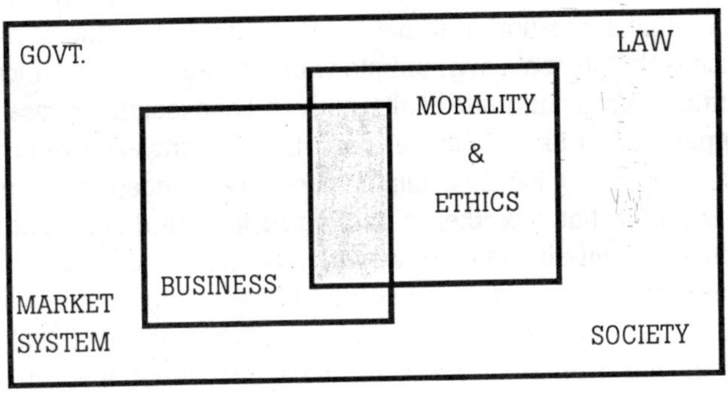

1.8 Nature of Ethics in Business

1. In business activities, most ethical questions could be of two types–Overt and Covert. **Overt** ethical problems like bribery, theft, sabotage, collusion, etc. are clear for everyone to see and are generally considered reprehensible. Most people deplore it and most businesses take care not to be so openly unethical. Hence, most problems in the business sphere are covert ethical problems. Covert ethical problems are more complex, not so transparent and generally defy ethical solutions. These types of problems occur in corporate acquisitions, marketing and personnel policies, capital investment, market war, etc. They are difficult to locate, to eliminate and are consequently much more dangerous and threatening to business.

2. For a decision to be ethical, it should possess the following characteristics. It should be–

a **Right** – that which is morally correct and due;

b **Equitable** – that which is just and equal;

c **Good** – that which brings in the highest good for all concerned;

d **Proper** – that which is appropriate and acceptable;

e **Fair** – that which is honest and due;

f **Just** – that justice is not only done, but is also seen to have been done.

3. Ethics is unstructured, i.e., it does not have a structured format or framework. It is abstract in concept. Hence, it does not have universal acceptance, mainly because–

a Ethics depend upon our moral standards;

b Moral standards depend upon our value system;

c The value system of people depend upon their background and childhood experience; and

d The background and experience of people are vastly different. Hence the ethical practices of people are also different.

4. Ethical decisions should express some obligations to others. If a decision merely results in benefits only to oneself, then that is not an ethical decision. The very concept of being ethical means that it results in some good for the larger society and not just for oneself.

1.9 Characteristics of Business Ethics

1. Ethical decisions differ with the individual perspective of different persons. Each person views the ethical question in terms of his or her own frame of reference. And this frame of reference is the person's own unique value system. Hence, ethical decision do not have unique solutions, but a multitude of alternatives. For example, In case of a Dam Building Project, the company loses Rs. 2 lakh per day, if operations are stopped. Being a labour intensive project, a number of locally available persons are engaged in the project. One day, during work, it is found that a worker is missing inside the dam. Work will definitely be stopped to search for the missing man. However, if the man is not found within a day or two, how long should work be stopped, inspite of the losses to the company, will depend upon the value system of the Manager and what, according to him, is the ethical thing to do. Given the same situation, but a different Manager, work will be stopped only upto what **that** Manager thinks is the ethical course of action, or work **may not** be stopped at all.

2. Ethical decisions are not limited only to themselves, but affects a wide range of other situations as well. Similarly, unethical decisions do not end in themselves, but have widespread ramifications. One unethical action is like a pebble thrown into a pond of water, it produces endless ripples in the pond, until the water of the entire pond gets disturbed by it. Similarly the single unethical action is not limited to the individual in the company who commits it, but spreads within the entire organisation; one unethical organisation affects the entire industry; and one unethical industry in turn, affects the entire economy and ultimately the entire nation.

Let us take the example on one individual who pays Rs. 1 lakh as bribe to secure a job which pays Rs. 2,000/- per month. If he wanted to get back his 'investment', that too without any interest and discounting his living expenses per month, he would require a minimum of 50 months, i.e., more than 4 years just to get back the gross 1 lakh rupees. Hence, he would be looking for opportunities to ask for bribes himself, from the very first day at work. The bribes that he takes, will compel others to take bribes and eventually the entire society gets engulfed in corruption. Moreover, the person giving bribe ends up with a distorted mentality about work and his morality gets eroded even before he starts performing in his job.

3. Most ethical decision involve a trade-off between costs incurred and benefits received. It needs to be clearly understood that costs and benefits, profits and responsibilities are two ends of a single spectrum. Both cannot be maximised simultaneously. If you want some benefits for your organisation or for yourself, you need to incure some costs or make some sacrifice. Similarly, maximum profits cannot go hand in hand with maximum social responsibilities or maximum welfare obligations. Maximum concern for task or productivity cannot go hand in hand with maximum concern for people. There has to be a trade-off, a compromise. And this compromise, where it is done, how it is done, results in a decision being ethical or unethical. One cannot get everything for nothing. Neither can one enjoy the beauty of spring without arriving at it through bitter winter. This is brought out wonderfully through the following poem–

> "Life is a Shylock, always it demands
> The fullest usurer's interest for every pleasure,
> Gifts are not freely scattered by its hand;
> We make return for every borrowed treasure.
>
> Each talent, each achievement, and each gain
> Necessitates some penalty to pay,
> Delight imposes lassitude and pain
> As certainly as darkness follows day.
>
> As you bestow on causes or on men,
> Of love or hate, of malice or devotion,
> Somehow, sometime, shall be returned again–
> There is no wasted toil, no lost emotion.
>
> The motto of the world is to give and take
> It gives to favours out of sheer goodwill,
> But unless speedy recompense you make,
> You'll find yourself presented with its bill.
>
> Where rapture comes to thrill the heart of yours
> Take it with tempered gratitude, remember,
> Some later time the interest will fall due,
> No year brings June that does not bring December.

Dr. Manoj Kumar Choudhury

4. The consequences of most ethical decisions are not clear. They are ambiguous in nature. Similarly, it is not often clear what the consequences will be of an unethical decision, either of an individual or of an organisation. The only certainty is that somewhere, sometime, somehow, something positive would result from an ethical decision and something negative from an unethical one. The consequences of both may not be immediate and may not be clear. In the previous example of paying a bribe to secure a job, even if you refused to pay the bribe and approached a higher official, your work may get done. On the other hand, even after paying the bribe, it is uncertain that you will either get the job done or your money back. Hence the consequences of ethical and unethical decisions are not guaranteed, may not be immediate and may not be crystal clear.

5. Every person is individually responsible for the ethical or unethical decision and action that he or she takes. Taking an ethical or unethical decision cannot be an impersonal

activity as it involves the person's individual and unique value system along with his moral standards. The same is the case with ethical or unethical actions. Every person has to take decisions, and whether these decisions are ethical or unethical, will depend upon his own conscience and upon what he is comfortable with. His own value system must justify his actions. For example, In case of Parliamentary Democracy, during a vote of confidence of a government, if the Prime Minister of the country pays bribes to a few independent MPs to buy their votes in the favour of the government, he is doing so, not for his own sake alone, but to save the entire government. In other words, the unethical action and decision of bribery, is taken on behalf of the entire government, and not merely on his own behalf. Yet, he alone is personally and individually responsible for the crime, and not his entire government.

In Hindu mythology, Ratnasur was a decoit who used to loot innocent travellers on their way through the jungle. Once a traveller asked him as to why he is committing such heinous crimes. Ratnasur replied that he is doing so on behalf of his parent, wife and children, to whom he wanted to give a comfortable and luxurious life. The traveller asked Ratnasur whether his parents, wife and children knew as to how he earned such luxuries for them. On being given a positive reply, the traveller once again enquired as to whether his near and dear ones, for whom he committed unethical crimes, would support his evil deeds and share his sins. Ratnasur immediately replied in the positive, saying that indeed they would do so. The traveller advised Ratnasur to go home and ask specifically of his parents, wife and children whether they would share his sins. When Ratnasur ran home to ask his relatives of the same, he received almost the same reply from everyone–his parent, his wife and his children. And this reply was–"As our provider, you are supposed to support us with your earnings. How you earn your livelihood is of no concern to us. As such, there is no question of us being a party to your evil crimes and we would never share your sins. You have committed those sins and they are yours alone; you yourself are responsible for them." On hearing these words, Ratnasur became shattered, but wiser now, he decided to take up penance to atone for his sins. And legend has it that this same Ratnasur later became sage Valmiki, who wrote the immortal epic Ramayana.

This is still true for our modern day Ratnasurs-the bureaucrats, the politicians, the academicians and all others, who resort to corruption on behalf of their family members, to provide them with luxuries which his or her salary cannot afford. These modern day Ratnasurs will also have to take individual and personal responsibilities for their unethical decisions and actions.

6. Ethical decisions are voluntary human actions. A person cannot escape his personal liability for his crimes by saying that he was forced to pay the bribe in order to get the job. All human beings have the freedom of choice and of free will. Even under compelling situations, many a man have refused to divert from the ethical way of life. Hence, no one can excuse himself or herself of his or her actions by citing force of circumstances or pressure of men for his or her unethical activities. Hence, all ethical or unethical actions are supposed to result from voluntary human actions and not from situations beyond their control.

1.10 Need for Business Ethics

Since business exists and operate within the society and is a part of a subsystem of society, its functioning must contribute to the welfare of the society. To survive, develop and excel, business must earn social sanction of the society wherein it exists and functions.

Without social sanctions, a business cannot earn loyal customers, cannot operate in the marketplace and will soon wither and die away. George A. Steiner, in 'Business & Society', (New York: Random House, 1975), says–

> "The managers of the biggest companies know that as a business gets larger, the public takes more interest in it because it has a greater impact on the community. The antennae of these managers are tuned to public opinion and they react to it. They seek to maintain a proper image of their company in the public mind. This leads to the assumption of greater social responsibilities."

No business, however great or strong or wealthy it may be at present, can exists on unethical means, or in total disregard to its social concern, for very long. Resorting to unethical behaviour or disregarding social welfare is like calling for its own doom. Thus, business needs, in its own interest, to remain ethical and socially responsible. As V. B. Day, in 'The Social Relevance of Business' had stated–

> "As a statement of purpose, maximising of profit is not only unsatisfying, it is not even accurate. A more realistic statement has to be more complicated. The corporation is a creation of society whose purpose is the production and distribution of needed goods and services, to profit of society and itself. Each element of that statement is needed if the whole is to be accurate; you cannot drop one element without doing violence to the facts."

Business needs to remain ethical for its own good. Unethical actions and decisions may yield results only in the very short run. For the long run existence and sustained profitability of the firm, business is required to conduct itself ethically and to run its activities on ethical lines. Doing so would lay a strong foundation for the business for continued and sustained existence. All over the world, again and again, it has been demonstrated that it is only ethical organisations that have continued to survive and grow, whereas unethical ones have shown results only as a flash in the pan, quickly growing and even more quickly dying and forgotten.

Business needs to function as responsible corporate citizens of the country. It is that organ of the society that creates wealth for the country. Hence, business can play a very significant role in the modernisation and development of the country, if it chooses to do so. But this will first require it to come out from its narrow mentality and even narrower goals and motives.

1.11 Arguments against Business Ethical

Though it is done very, very infrequently now-a-days, some authors and philosophers, nonetheless, do tend to put forward the argument that businesses being economic entitles, should have nothing to do with morals (i.e., with what people do) or ethics (what people ought to do). They argue that businesses should assume no other responsibilities, other than to produce goods and services efficiently and to maximise profits for the shareholders. They believe that business being economic entities, only economic values should be their guiding principles and the sole determinant of their performances.

Milton Friedman, the celebrated Noble Prize winning economist, in his book, 'Capitalism and Freedom', (Chicago: University of Chicago, 1962) put forward his classical view that the only responsibility of business is to earn profits. He believed that–

> "There is one and only one responsibility of business–to use its resources and engage in activities designed to increase its profits so long as it stays within the rules of the game, which is to say, engages in open and free competition, without deception or fraud. Few trends could so thoroughly undermine the very traditions of our free society as the acceptance by corporate officials of a social responsibility other than to make as much money for their stockholders as possible. The is fundamentally subversive doctrine."

Friedman feared that if business ethics formed a part of corporate culture, ultimately the customer would be called upon to bear the cost of the ethical practices of the organisation, as Friedman erroneously assumed that such ethical practices would increase the prices of the organisation's products. He further believed the social responsibility of business is contrary to basic business functions. Moreover, he says that the business manager does not know, and does not need to know, where public interest lies. That is the concern of politicians, bureaucrats, concerned organisations and individuals and the state.

Today, business have found out that they **are,** in fact, responsible for social welfare, since they live and operate within a social structure. Without earning social sanction, no business can hope to survive, leave alone develop and flourish. And ethical practices do not necessarily increase the cost of production, in fact they tend to reduce costs. But, even if they do increase costs, short term sacrifices must be made for long term good.

Another personality, the famous psychologist, Theodore Levitt, expressed fear that if business started being concerned about ethics, then business values would come to dominate social values.

These views were put forward in the 1950s and the 1960s. Since then, there has been a radical change of views and the fears expressed by philosophers and psychologists about business ethics have largely remained unfounded.

People at that time feared that any altruism or ethical conduct or embracing of any moral philosophies by the organisation would lead it to sacrifice its efficiency and productivity; and the competitiveness of the marketplace would fade away. Nothing could be more far from the truth. Having realised this, more and more business organisations are today accepting business ethics as part and parcle of their daily business conduct. And to their astonishment and delight, they have found that being ethical and moral have given them an unique edge and advantage in the marketplace. Moreover, their employees, executives and managers have felt proud to belong to such organisations. For, goodwill, loyalty genuine pride, and above all, mental peace, cannot be calculated accurately in terms of money. And no organisation in India has been more ethical than the TATA group of companies, founded by Jamestji Tata and developed and nurtured by J.R.D. Tata. From the time of its establishment, the TATA House has always based their business activities on ethical principles. The quest for excellence, national pride and nationalist spirit and ethical practices were the legacy left behind by the founding fathers of the TATA group of companies.

The TATA Group of Companies–An example of Ethical Business Practice

The Tata Group of companies were established on nationalist feelings, to make India Industrialised, even during the pre-independence days. It sought to make India rank in the forefront of industrialised nations, within a short span of time. Hence, it was always founded in ethical practices. As J.R.D. Tata, in an interview to the Economic Times, once remarked–

> "If someone were to ask me, what holds the Tata companies together more than anything else, I would say it is our shared ideals and values which we have inherited from Jamsetji Tata".

He also goes on to add–

> "Once we got the best people, the people who shared our values and ideals, we left them free to act on their own. We did not fetter them–we encouraged them and gave them opportunities for leadership. That is how Russy Modi at TISCO, Sumant Moolgaokar at TELCO and Darbari Seth at Tata Chemicals developed leadership of their own. Just provide the opportunities for leadership and allow your people to exercise their own intelligence and skills in management and entrepreneurship. I think you may say that this is the style of Tata. It is not an original style I created, but one that was naturally there and in which I believed strongly and which I strove to maintain."

The Tata tradition is also one which is based on many ethical and lofty ideals. As Sarosh J. Ghandy in 'Human Values & the TATA Heritage' (From 'Human Values for Managers'– Edited by S.K. Chakraborty), remarked about the Tata tradition–

> "Looking back over the past hundred years, I realised that the Tata tradition has been built up by men of great strength and character. The value system on which this tradition is based has proved to be an extremely effective one."

Quoting Mr. Sumant Moolgaokar, he said–

> "Mr. Sumant Moolgaokar, widely regarded as the architect of the Telco, was a man of few words and rarely made speeches. He did make a speech however, when he received the Sir Jehangir Gandhy Medal for Industrial peace, when he spoke thus–
>
> "When men take pride in their skill or craft and strive to perfect it, they give scope to their 'creative' impulse where one man's gain is not another's loss. There is nothing new in this source of human satisfaction. It has long been established that people enjoy exercising their innate and trained abilities and that this enjoyment increases as their abilities become more complex. We can add nothing to the principle but we can certainly give it shape and make it come to life even in the industrial setting."

Ghandy goes on to add–

> "The determination to manufacture steel marked 'Made in India', was based on the value that modernisation was necessary. This Pioneering spirit was the moving force behind Mr. Sumant Moolgaokar when he started building mercedes trucks in India with the help of labourers hurriedly assembled from the peddy fields. That spirit has built more than a million of those trucks. It has fought and won against competition from Japan and the United States of America, by designing and manufacturing Indian trucks, sometimes at the rate of one new model per year. It was the same spirit that filled the hearts of the people in my teams when we produced three new models of Hitachi Hydraulic Excavators in Jamshedpur in one year, while the Asian Tiger, Korea had taken three years to manufacture just one model. Thus, organisational values contribute to the vitality and effectiveness or organisations."

Finally, he added–

> "If I were to say that Telco's position as the private company with the highest sales turnover in the country, or its world-class modernisation by its existing men, is supported by the strength of its value, it would imply that organisational values have been an effective means for our business objective. If I were to say that when a government wanted to nationalise Telco, its workmen protested against this, I would be claiming that organisational values have been ends in themselves. Whichever way we look at it, Telco feels stronger because of the values it practises."

Discussion Situation 1: Statement of a Business Executive (Finance)

"I work in a Computer Training Institute of national repute and I have been asked to do a study of the pricing of our computer courses. I have seen that while we price our computer courses very high, so as to build a reputation of quality in the market place, we do not strictly stick to our prices. When we find that a student is able to pay for the course, we immediately charge advance fees from the student. However, when we find a student reluctant to join immediately, we are supposed to tell him or her that a discount would be given if he or she joins within a particular time period. Sometimes the discount goes upto 50% in order to retain the student. Moreover, to students who are not from science or engineering background and who are uncertain about persuing a career in computers and come to us for guidance, we are supposed to give them an Aptitude Test in computers. Everyone who goes through the test is supposed to 'get' more that 75% and we are to tell them that their aptitude for computers is very high. This is the rule that has been laid down for us by the management. Once the student believes this, we are to tell him or her that due to his or her 'brilliant performance', a merit scholarship would be awarded. This merit scholarship is in the form of a course discount of about 30%. All these are done to 'hook' a student to the course. Thus, the end result of all these is that different students end up paying different course fees for the same course. Moreover many students without an aptitude and genuine interest in computers end up enrolling for these courses. Students who are studious and have a genuine interest in the course, but do not know about bargaining and who sincerely pay the fees before the due dates are compelled to pay much higher fees than those who dilly–dally and are not sincere in paying the fees regularly.

From the company's point of view, this makes business sense economically, because all other Computer Training Centres in our town are following the same practise. But I do not feel that all these are right practices and I feel guilty in 'cheating' the students this way. When I raised the matter in front of my boss, he said this was the usual practise everywhere and we are not, after all, forcing anyone to join the course or compromising on the quality of the course–neither on the study material, nor in the teaching, nor in the examinations. Students join our courses on their own free will and we have never received any complaint on any aspect of our teaching or examinations.

I know what he is saying is absolutely true. We give the best possible computer training available in our country. The reputation of our company is one of the best in the marketplace. Our students have been placed in prestigious organisations and are still getting lucrative job offers. It is only in the admission time that all is not as it should be. I know that if we do not resort to all these tricks, we shall be losing out to competition and may not even be breaking even to maintain our high overhead costs. The cost of our courses are very high and in a small town like ours, not many students can afford the prices of our courses. Moreover, we do not have the liberty to reduce the pricing of our courses, since they are regulated from our Head office at Mumbai, and are standard all over the country. But we have the tactical approval of Head Office to continue with what we have been doing to woo students. Not only does Head Office approve, but also unofficially encourages to do this in all small towns of the country.

Yet, I donot like what we are doing. When I left my Business Institute after obtaining my MBA Degree, I was determined to maintain my personal standards of ethics in everything I did. I made a promise to myself never to compromise on my moral principles, no matter what happens. Now, in my very first job, I feel I am doing something which is ethically wrong. Yet leaving the job is not the answer, firstly, because I do not want to appear to be a coward and run away at the very first sight of problems, and secondly, if I leave whoever comes in my place will have to do the same thing that I am doing now."–Discuss.

Discussion Situation 2: Statement of a Business Executive Trainee (Marketing)

"We are an Advertising Agency, but we act more as marketing consultants then as advertisers for most of our clients. We have experienced that when we design an advertising campaign on genuine market analysis and based on the whole scientific truth of the product, the ads tend to become incredibly dull, generally unimaginative and in effect totally ineffective. Hence we do not attract much customers.

We have been in financial doldrums due to our decisions to stick to the truth, no matter what happens. However, now when we need finances very desperately and the Agency is on the verge of closure, an internationally reputed pharmaceutical company is willing to give us their advertising contract, but on one condition. They want the Advertisement to have maximum pull, be more attractive to the buyer, even if the attraction is not based on the complete truth and the ad is misrepresented.

'First time available in India', is the heading they want on a product, whose remedy in traditional Homoeopathic and Ayurvedic medicines have been available in India from time immorable. 'Total and Reliable Cure for children' is the message they want for a cough syrup, but there is a small asterisk, not prominently visible, and at the bottom of the page a footnote explains that it is unsuitable for children below three years, who they call 'infants'. They also want us to advertise their slimming tablets with the message 'completely safe and no side effects', when their effectiveness is suspect and more importantly, the elimination of their side effects have not been proved. We desperately need their money, but it would mean compromising the ethical standards of our past reputation. Moreover, the public would believe the Ad. completely, when they see that it is designed and issued by us, because of the tremendous faith they have on our ethical reputation, from our past records. Thus, we are in a moral dilemma–is it ethical to play with the goodwill, and more importantly, the health of out public? Then again, is it ethical to play with the financial health of our company, go bankrupt and force our employees on to the street ?"–Discuss.

Discuss Situation 3– Statement of a Business Executive Trainee (HRM)

"I had joined this Steel Plant about 3 months back as an Executive Trainee (Personnel) and have been placed in the Head Office, about 5 kms from the factory. Just yesterday, I had to go to the factory for some work and it was the first time I had seen it while in operation.

And, my God, I got the shock of my life when I saw the working condition inside the factory. The noise, the heat, the fumes and the pace of work was terrible. I could not stand it even for half an hour and I wonder how these workmen tolerate it day after day, year after year.

After returning to my air-conditioned luxurious office at Head Office I voiced my concern to one of my colleagues. 'How do they physically stand it?', I asked her, She replied–'They get tough as time goes on. And moreover, when they cannot tolerate it anymore, they fall seriously ill once or twice a year. That's the usual routine that I've seen'. I was shaken by their condition and asked her if there was any way we could do anything about it. She advised me to just concentrate on my work, for I was too new and too small a fry to make any impact. Moreover, in India, the working condition in most factories are similar to ours.

She was right, I know. The funny thing is how the Factory Inspector has never compelled the management to do anything about it–or whether he too has ever visited the factory or has gone away after just visiting the Head Office and having had tea with the management.

I know I could put in a request to improve some of the worst condition, but I would have to fight to get it approved. I don't know whether I should make the effort–after all I have to think about my confirmation, which is due in a few months time. Moreover, will it have any impact or will the management, and my colleagues too, would think that I am acting too big for my boots. This Steel Plant does not have a Trade Union and neither an Officers Association, so who is going to fight for me when I fall out with the management and my confirmation and later my promotions get delayed? But what I am more worried about is, whether I shall make any impact at all, since none of my colleagues, and neither the workers themselves for the matter, seem too much concerned.

If I want to do anything, first I shall have to unite the workers, which means that I shall have to first and foremost educate them about their rights, which in itself is a massive and time-consuming task. And then where shall I find the time to perform my duties in my own job? And moreover, will it not be like sabotaging my own company and instigating my own workmen against their own management? But then again, how can I sit back and not do anything after what I have seen? Is it right to think of what harm may come to oneself when one takes up a social cause? Is it ethical to keep quite after all, and see workers fall ill one after another, during the year? Or is it more ethical to try to do something, even if it is sure to end in failure, try to make some difference in the lives of all these workmen, and in the process, try to regenerate some awareness and awakening to their own plight?"–Discuss.

Ethical Practices in Management–The above discussion problems are instances of ethical practices in management. Put yourself in the positions of these three Business Executives and decide what you would do under those circumstances. Ethical decisions are much more difficult to make when a person is directly involved in the situation. It is easier to state what is 'right' and 'wrong' when a person is not directly involved. However, ethical decisions are much more complex than merely deciding between 'right' and 'wrong' or between 'good' and 'bad'. There are certain amount of risk taking involved in making an ethical decision. For example, in the case of the Executive Trainee (HRM) in the third Discussion situation, if he decides to take up the issue of improving the working condition of the factory, he would probably be putting his budding career at risk. In case of the organisation also, there has to be a balance between economic profits and social obligations. For example, in certain countries bribe giving and bribe taking is a part of their business culture, and they are not considered as bribes or corruption, like in the Latin American countries, India, Pakistan,

Bangladesh, etc. So if a company operating in those countries decide not to pay any bribe, however small, will it be able to secure business for itself? An American or European company would be shocked to learn that it is expected to give bribes at every turn in these countries, but local companies understand the culture where bribes are both understood and expected.

Business Ethics does not intend to be a self-appointed watch guard and tell what is 'right', 'equitable', 'good', 'proper', 'fair', and 'just' for a company to do. Neither does it intend to dictate as to how business organisations should conduct their affairs. Instead it is left to the individual Manager's own moral standards of behaviour and ethical systems of belief. Ethics only tries to help individuals understand and come to terms with their own moral standards and ethical values. For it is time now, indeed, to change over from the past way of thinking about business conduct and formulate new ethical ways of conducting business activities. For in the past, the mark of a best salesman was the one who could sell refrigerators even to eskimos. Little has changed since. Even today, the mark of a good salesman is to sell refrigerators to snow house living eskimos. But today, let us ask ourselves–true, it is a mark of great salesmanship, but is it ethical?

Summary of the Chapter in Brief–

* Ethics is derived from the word 'ethos' meaning character or manners.
* Ethics makes Moral Judgements of human conduct.
* Ethics can also be termed as the science of character of a person expressed as right or wrong conduct or action.
* Nature of Ethics–Ethics deals with human beings only; the study of ethics is a science; it is a normative science; it deals with human conduct which is voluntary and not forced.
* Objectives of Ethics–a diagnostic tool; establishes moral standards and norms of behaviour; makes judgement upon human behaviour; prescribes moral behaviour; expresses opinions and attitudes about human conduct.
* Business Ethics is the application of ethics in business.
* Ethics consists of Managerial Dilemmas, between the profit consideration (commercial concern) and the social consideration (welfare concern).
* Business Ethics means trying to achieve a trade-off between economic objectives and social obligations.
* Ethics and profits are not mutually exclusive and in fact, it is unethical to make losses and go bankrupt.
* It is only ethical companies which discharge its social responsibilities that have survived competition and turbulent changes through the years and have contributed to social welfare and have continued to flourished undiminished.
* Business ethics dictates that the very first responsibility of business is to generate revenue for itself.
* Relationship between Business & Ethics–**Unitarian View**: Business and morality cannot be separated and business must play by the rules of morality and ethics of the community. Business must conduct its affairs purely through altruist motives

and profit is a dirty word. **Separatist View:** The only goal of business should be profit maximisation; and ethics and morality plays no part in business conduct. **Integration View** : Business is an economic entity and it has the right to make profits, but, it must also discharge its obligations to the society where it exists.

* Nature of Ethics in Business–Most ethical questions are either overt or Covert; For a decision to be ethical, it must be 'Right', 'Equitable', 'Good', 'Proper', 'Fair', 'Just'; Ethics is unstructured and abstract and hence does not have universal acceptance; Ethical decisions should express some obligations to others.
* Characteristics of Business Ethics–Ethical decisions differ with the individual perspective of different persons; they are not limited only to themselves, but affects a wide range of other situations as well; most ethical decisions involve a trade-off between costs incurred and benefits received; the consequences of most ethical decisions are not clear; every person is individually responsible for the ethical or unethical decision and action that he or she takes; ethical decisions are voluntary human actions.
* Need for Business Ethics –Since business exist and operate within the society and is a part of a subsystem of society, its functioning must contribute to the welfare of the society.
* Arguments against Business Ethics–Business being economic entities, should have nothing to do with morals (what people do) or with ethics (what people ought to do). This view has changed drastically over the years, and more and more companies are resorting to ethical means of conducting itself and of doing business.
* The Tata group of companies is an example of ethical business practice.
* Ethical Practices in Management–Business ethics does not intend to be self-appointed watch guard and state what a company should do or how it should conduct itself. Ethics only tries to help individuals understand and come to terms with their own moral standards and ethical values; selling refrigerators to eskimos is a show of great salesmanship, but is it ethical?

Expected Questions:

1. Describe what you understand by the word 'Ethics'? How does Ethics makes Moral Judgement about human conduct?
2. Explain the Nature of Ethics. What are the Objectives of Ethics?
3. Differentiate between Ethics and Business Ethics; Unitarian View and Separatist View, Overt and Covert unethical decisions.
4. Explain what you consider to be Managerial Dilemmas of business.
5. How can a firm try to achieve a trade-off between commercial objectives and social objectives?
6. Are ethics and profits mutually exclusive? Explain why or why not. Describe how a company can ethically make profits.
7. Do you consider it to be desirable that a company should rather be principled and go bankrupt, if necessary, than to make profits through unprincipled means?
8. Describe how a company can discharge its social responsibilities.

9. What, according to you, is social responsibility of business?
10. Discuss the Integration View of the relationship between business and ethics, Do you consider it to be a realistic view? Give reasons for your answer.
11. Discuss the nature of ethics in business.
12. Describe the characteristics of business ethics.
13. Explain the personal responsibility of every individual for the unethical decisions taken on behalf of others.
14. "Ethical decisions differ with the value system and the moral standard of others. Hence Ethical decisions do not have universal acceptance"–Discuss whether the statement is true or false.
15. Discuss how unethical decisions and actions are not limited only to themselves, but affect a wide range of other situations as well.
16. Write a short essay detailing the arguments for and against business ethics.
17. Why is business ethics unstructured and abstract?
18. Explain trade-offs between costs and benefits.

1.12 Evolution of Business Ethics as a Field of Study

Though the introduction of Business Ethics as a field of study in management courses is a rather recent development, nonetheless, the concern for ethical business practices and the concept of 'Ethics' have been concerning people since long. Way back in 1933, Alfred North Whitehead, in this essay about businessmen titled 'Adventures of Ideas' (quoted in the 'The Responsible Businessmen', Readings from **For Line**, edited by John A. Larson, Holt, Rinehart & Winston Inc., New York; 1966, pp. 285), said–

'A great society is a society in which its men of business think greatly of their function'.

In 1986, a conference on 'company philosophy & Codes of Business Ethics', was held at the initiative of Lord Mayor of London, where more than 100 representatives from the industry and other professions met to deliberate on the issue of Business Philosophy and Business Ethics. About a year later, a group was formed with the name of 'European Business Ethics Network', with a number of European business managers and academicians at its helm of affairs. This network gave a great fillip to the business ethics movement. Thus, this movement went from strength to strength, and gained enormous momentum, as more and more people all over the world became aware of the need and importance of business ethics.

The first European Business Ethics Journal to be published was called the 'Ethics Degli Affari', which was published from Milan in Italy in 1988. With the publication of this Journal, Business Ethics entered into the reals of business academicians, and the concept of ethics in business began to be widely discussed and debated, both within the business practitioners and the academic circle. In the same year, in 1988, when the Japanese government came forward to fund a cross-cultural study on corporate responsibility, to be carried out by the Hitachi Institute in Japan, the concept of Business Ethics found an academic base and it became accepted world-wide as a separate field of study. The need for and the importance of ethics in business was firmly established. (Source: Akhilesh Tuteja, 'A question of Ethics', Association of Indian Management Schools (AIMS)).

Similar incidents of growing acceptance of ethics as a part of business, came to be reported from all over the world. As time went on, business ethics as a term became more and more familiar. At present, the concept of ethical business behaviour and ethics of organisational life has acquired relatively more importance in public as well as in professional sphere, more so during the last one decade, from the 1990s. At the beginning of the 90s decade, there were very few conferences being held on the topic, information was negligible, the number of books on the topic was few and the topic was not seriously studied in management courses and little mention of it was made in management textbooks. However, within this decade, the scenario has changed considerably. Many high quality Journals on Business Ethics, sponsored by Institutions, Corporate Houses and Universities, both within India and abroad, have come up. Organisations dedicated to good corporate behaviour have been formed. Example can be given of the European Business Ethics Network and its national subsidiaries, as already mentioned. Consultancy firms as well as large accountancy and financial services have added business ethics to their portfolio of services. Corporate Houses are conducting market research into the ethical concerns of their customers and to improve their ethical profile and reputation, they are bringing out 'ethical products' like cosmetics with the message, 'not tested on animals', or cards and newspaper companies with the message, 'this card/newspaper is made from recycled paper', etc. Financial companies have also started to invest their client's money only in those companies which meet their desired and stated criteria of corporate good behaviour or have a reputation of being ethical since long.

In India, the credit for starting a trend of thought on business ethics, and the philosophy of social responsibility of business and its welfare obligations, goes to J.R.D. Tata. J.R.D. Tata deserves all praise for having started this great mission in India, not just by taking or discussing about it in conference and forums, but, in fact, implementing it and making it a part of the great Tata corporate culture. J.R.D. Tata introduced a Pension Scheme for employees and designed the 8–hour workday, much before legal enforcement for them came into being in 1948. J.R.D. Tata created a 'family philosophy' for its employees and stated, 'Every man has an innate desire to be useful to others and, in India, the cause of lifting our people is such a crying one that service is easier than in a completely industrialized country. We here, at Tata, are so obsessed with our people's poverty'.

What is specially heartening is to note that the concern for public good, as conceived by J.R.D. Tata, still permeate into the Tata Group of Companies even today. In 1993, Ratan Tata stated that, 'Ethics for Tatas means conducting business in a manner which is fair and just to employees, suppliers and shareholders, having a concern for the community in which one is operating. It would involve putting combined interests above personal gain or exploitation'.

The greatest tribute which Russy Mody, who was an intimate part of Tata Steel for more than half-a-century, could have paid to Tata, was to state that 'My values were fashioned by the House of Tatas. These were to so conduct your business that profit was not your only motive, but the happiness of those who worked in your business; a fair deal to customers who bought your goods and efficiency in your job'.

(Source: 1. Dr. G. Anjaneya Swamy, 'Organisations with a Heart'; Indian Management; February, 1998).

2. 'The Tata Group: Profits with Responsibility'; World Executive Digest: 1989)

Another Group of Industries that practised ethical dealings with the public as well as with their employees was the Hero Group of Industries. Established way back in 1940s with a corporate mission to 'provide excellent transportation to the common man at a price he could afford', this group subsequently found itself in the Guinness Book of Records in 1987, and maintaining it till 1996-97, as the world's largest manufacturer of bicycles. The founding father of this Group, Brijmohan Lall Munjal, asserts that the triumph of the Hero Group, was due to the undying spirit and commitment of the common workmen and the hundreds of skilled engineers of Punjab. This is not surprising, as the management of the group takes very good care of its workers and executives. Long before others did so, Hero gave its workers an uniform allowance, House Rent Allowance, and also Leave Travel Allowance. Further, they organised regular medical check-ups at company cost for not only their full-time, and permanent workers, but also migrant labourers working for them, and also for their parents.

As far as teaching and learning of Business Ethics as part of the management education curriculum is concerned, the distinction of having first offered business ethics as a course goes to Harvard Business School, way back in 1915. However, it was only in the mid 1980s, that this subject was first offered in various Business Schools all over the world.

In India, the course on Business Ethics was first offered by institutes like Xavier Labour Relations Institute (XLRI), Jamshedpur and the TA Pai Management Institute, Manipal. In fact, a Centre for Business Ethics, called' Business Ethics Foundation; was established at Xavier Labour Relations Institute (XLRI), which was inaugurated by Mr. J.R.D. Tata himself on March 4, 1991.

Premier management institutes like all the Indian Institutes of Management (IIMs) have also inculcated the concepts and principles of moral values and business ethics in the academic curriculum. The Centre for Human Values, at Indian Institute of Management (IIM), Calcutta, has been doing some pioneering and pathbreaking work on business ethics and Indian moral values.

By the mid 1990s most management institutes and universities in India had included Business Ethics as part of their course curriculum.. The initiative in this regard was taken by the All India Council for Technical Education (AICTE). Many management institutes and Universities in the western countries and more recently in India too, have been concentrating their efforts on the ethico-moral development of their young emerging managers.

According to one estimate, in the United States of American alone, today more than 500 courses on business ethics are on offer; 90% of the country's business schools now teach the subject. Globally, more than 20 dedicated research units now study the topic and a number of Journals exclusively on the area of business ethics are found in India and abroad.

However, most of the teaching on business ethics offered by these courses tend towards moral absolutism, and hence they lack appeal. Since no effort is made to understand the practical difficulties in using ethics in business, much less offer practical solutions for them, many business executives, and indeed many young budding emerging managers feel that there is little practical relevance of ethics to everyday business decisions where many a times 'right' and 'wrong' are by no means clear and are mostly managerial dilemmas. If ethics and the interests of the business conflict, manages are told by academicians that they must always do the right thing–if for no other reason than just because it is right. One recent treatise on business ethics put it as 'If in some instance it turns out that what is ethical leads to a company's demise, then so be it'. No wonder then, that such type of moral absolutism finds very few practical takers. In the real business world, few managers are ever going to sacrifice their companies on the alter of such altruistic extremism.

A manager who is struggling to run a business as ethically as possible wants and needs practical answers to his everyday ethical dilemmas. Increased interest in business ethics has helped to make managers aware of the need to be as ethical in their business dealings as possible. Thus, managers are searching for mechanisms to help resolve ethical dilemmas in the workplace. As a beginning, many firms (example, Fiat) have implemented ethical codes of conduct and have set up ethical figures, like Ethics Ombudsmen, Ethics Committees, etc., in the recent past.

Today, business managers, all over the world, have started to think beyond the pure profit maximisation objectives of business firms, advocated by Adam Smith and Milton Friedman. Modern business managers today are searching for methods and techniques of implementing business ethics and instilling moral values into business practices.

To this end, in 1992, February, Xavier Labour Relations Institute (XLRI), Jamshedpur, organised a National Conference of Company Directors, on the topic of Business Ethics. This national conference was aimed at reinforcing ethical awareness in Indian Industries and for providing a forum for discussion and debates on the subject as also to provide a platform for guidance to business managers on future directions on implementing business ethics in reality.

The XLRI and the Bajaj Institute of Management in India, have also followed the footsteps of Harvard Business School in setting up professional chairs in business ethics.

In Europe, the European Community had recently appointed a Commission to study in details the state of business ethics in Europe.

Thus, one finds that as time passes, the movement on business ethics is gaining more and more momentum all over the world. Today, a mass awareness has been built into the desirability and indeed the necessity of incorporating ethical practices in business conduct. In the future, this is bound to be more necessary than even before.

Chapter 2

Ethics & Worklife in Indian Philosophy

Worklife in Indian Philosophy

Inspite of Indian having an ancient culture and philosophy about worklife, we in India have not yet managed to develop our own management styles in consonance with our own cultural ethos and have been systematically importing management systems and styles from foreign countries. While successful countries like the USA, UK, Germany, France and Korea are rediscovering Indian ethos, we in India are in the process of losing it. While the success of Japan in managing her economy and enterprise lies in 'Japanising' the management process within the framework of Japanese ethos, culture and value systems, Indian companies in the meantime, are nonplussed by the failure of the sure- fire and instant management success formulae from Harvard, Oxford or Tokyo, to take root in Indian soil. The main crux of the issue is that there is absolutely no need for India to borrow from foreign lands what she can more easily get at home something much more value-based, internalised and much more fundamental. Indian companies will find in India itself, an ancient tradition and an unique heritage to draw from, all that they need for their management styles and practices. There are many cultural values which are shared by both Japan and India, and whereas these cultural values are the principal target of abuse and ridicule by the modern Indian elite, Japan has emerged as business leader of the world primarily because it has relied on these values and had 'Japanised' the management process within the Japanese ethos, culture and value system. Perhaps the secret of Korea's success also lies in the use of indigenous styles and practices, instead of foreign, alien imported styles and methods of management.

However in India, the trend appears to be against the use of anything indigenous and Indian. The zeal, specially amongst the educated Indians appear to be against Indianising management styles and practices, against the use of Indian culture and values, terming them as traditional and conservative, outdates and out of vogue, and not suited to the modern times . While the west is realising the importance and utility of ancient Indian philosophy, heritage and wisdom and are borrowing from it more and more, India herself is in the verge of rejecting it and borrowing more from the west. The techniques of meditation and the philosophy of yoga, are being more and more accepted within the educated circles of the western countries, and they have almost become a rage there.

Indian philosophy regards work as worship and the customer as God Himself. Serving the customer is equated with serving God. As Mahatma Gandhi has rightfully said, - "we are not doing the customer a favour by serving him, rather the customer is doing us a favour by giving us an opportunity to serve him". Such is the ethos and philosophy of Indian culture. Moreover service to the customer must be done with a detached mind, without craving for the fruits or results of the work done. According to the Bhagawad Gita, a detached mind is essential, because only a calm and serene mind without any attachment, can take clear decisions; and creativity, vision, innovation and new ideas can come only from a clear, focused and detached mind.

Organisations which have ignored the Indian philosophy of work, have only achieved external development at the cost of internal growth and inner peace. In such organisations, the 'man' in the manager is lost, he amounts to nothing- he stands nowhere. There is loss of ethical and humane values in such organisations. The organisation itself is dehumanised . There is erosion of morals and principles. There is crises of confidence. There is no industrial peace, and corruption reigns supreme. Executives suffer from stress and tension, while employees suffer from demotivation and frustration . Workers are demoralised and consumers are by-passed. Nature is exploited and human welfare is neglected. In such companies, wealth is amassed but the soul is lost.

In Indian philosophy, the individual is considered to be supreme. Nothing worthwhile and of lasting value is considered to be achieved by sacrificing the individual. Moreover, Indian philosophy stresses that if the individual is good, the world is good. ' If you are good, then the world is good' this is the motto of Indian philosophy. This motto tends to emphasis the importance of an individual's perception and attitude, on his moral conduct. If an Individual's perception of the world is good, then he too would try to do good, and consequently good results and everything good would come to him. If, on the other hand, an individual's attitude is that all men are evil and untrustworthy, he too would always act in a suspicious manner, concealing his activities, fearful of everybody, not being able to trust anybody, and hence he himself becomes untrustworthy. Thus, no good results occur and he finds unpleasant things happening to him. This reinforces his belief that mankind is evil and that the world is a horrible place to live in. Thus, by his own attitude, he has created the hell that he lives in. Hence the Indian saying is true even psychologically, apart from beings true morally. How much wisdom much ancient Indian philosophy holds for the modern man !

In Indian philosophy, human capacity is much more important than plant capacity, quality of mind and heart is much more important than quality circles, and modernisation of man- both his thoughts and actions- are more important than modernisation of machineries. Mental peace and inner harmony is more important to build up a strong character which imbibes the basic and the best of human and ethical values.

Indian tradition and heritage, its culture and philosophy, its ethos and values are a treasure house, where the richest and the rarest of gems are stored. It is ours only for the asking. If we can apply even a few of these gems to the management of the modern organisation, we will be doing a great service, not only to ourselves, or our organisations, but also to our future generations of entrepreneurs and managers.

Arnold Toynbee, the Noble prize winning historian proves a point when he writes–

> " It is already becoming clear that a chapter which had a Western Beginning in business management, will have to have an Indian Ending, when the world adopts rich thoughts of Indian ethos and wisdom, if it is not to end in the self-destruction of the human race".

2.1 Indian Ethos for the Worklife

1. Man's Unique Inner Resource

Indian ethos states that all human beings and indeed, all creatures, are but a spark of the Divine. Thus, all of us are brothers under the skin, in the soul, as we all belong to, and are a part of the same God. Indian ethos states that every soul on earth is a potential God, a part of the divine. Perhaps this explains the Indian ritual of praying to animals of various kinds as also to numerous plants, specially the 'tulsi' plant and 'pipal' tree. Even the Indus valley civilisation remains show that people there, at that time also, used to worship some animals. This is basically due to the acceptance of a potential God in every soul, be it man, animal or plant. This divinity in man can lead him to perfection in knowledge, wisdom and power. Due to this divinity, man has immense potential capacity for self-development and self improvement. With this capacity, human beings can achieve all seemingly impossible goals and overcome even monumental obstacles and difficulties. The partnership of God and man can bring about extraordinary and miraculous results, not only to himself, but also to his organisation, and to the society. This is the unique inner resource in man which can be harnessed to yield best results , with the combination of self- help and self effort. This philosophy of Indian wisdom provides an excellent incentive to people to perform one's duty to the best of one's capacity and capability. It motivates people to function, by reinforcing that he is not working alone. If his end is towards something good, and he is abiding by ethical means, then God is surely by his side, helping him to achieve success.

2. Holistic Relationship between Man and Nature

Indian ethos emphasises the holistic aspect between man and the cosmic. According to this philosophy , there is an intimate relationship between man and the Universe, between man and nature. This view states that all human beings and nature are interconnected and interdependent. Thus, the only law (dharma) of life is service to each other. If man plants trees, takes care of them - watering them in times of drought and providing shades during times of excessive rain or sun–and generally takes care to keep them healthy, then the trees, in turn, provide man with shade, firewood, building material, etc., apart from providing him with food, environmental protection and the like. If we analyse carefully, we shall see that everything in this Universe depends upon somebody else for their survival. Even for the simple act of cooking our food, we are dependent on so many people–the farmer, first of all, for his agriculture produce, the driller for the liquified petroleum gas in our cylinders, the artisen who has provided us with the pottery and other cooking utensils, etc. Thus, no one in this universe can live in isolation by ignoring and rejecting others. We are mutually interdependent and so shall we remain.

Indian ethos places emphasis on both spirit and matter. Both these are interlinked in the holistic approach. This means that man is permitted to enjoy both the internal as well as the external quality of life. That is why in the Indian philosophy there existed the 'ashrama' system of life. A child or 'balaka', was required to stay with his guru at his ashram in the middle of the forest and cater to the needs of the guru, apart from concentrating all his energies on acquiring knowledge, skills and values which he would find useful later on in life . The house-holds or the 'grihastha' was permitted to enjoy all pleasures of life, apart from providing for and taking the responsibility of his family. Later on in life, the individual was required to give up all these sensual and worldly pleasures, sacrifice his active way of life, retire to the forests or to some quite place to meditate and offer penance for the sins committed in his earlier life. Thus, both material as well as spiritual way of life is advocated, but each at the right time in life.

3. Cooperation with Each Other

Indian ethos stress upon cooperation amongst others at work and otherwise; integration, synthesis and team–sprit for peaceful co-existence and mutual interdependence.

Excessive competition, intra-organisation and inter-organisation, which is experienced by everybody in the workplace at present, have destroyed many a young mind and family lives, besides giving rise to stress, tension and frustration leading to alcoholism, excessive socialising, frightening loneliness, drug and sexual abuse, and even suicide.

Cooperation, mutual trust and respect, joint efforts and team spirit can lead to all round prosperity and success for everyone concerned, due to the synergistic effect of combined effort. Close interdependence, interconnection and integration of human beings, society, nature and business, can only lead to universal good of all concerned.

4. Self–Management

Indian ethos prescribe that a man should be able to control himself first, before he can control anybody else. Every manager must manage himself first, before he can even try to manage anybody else. He must know himself first – His strengths, weaknesses, his dreams and desires, his goals and ambitions, before he can be an effective manager. Proper control, harmony and integration between the body, mind, emotions, intellect and soul is the essence of self management.

Self analysis through introspection is essential to know and discover oneself. Only when one has self knowledge, can he undertake to manage himself. Introspection involves self examination of one's own thoughts, feelings, emotions, sensations and passions, as well as one's dreams and desires, goals and ambitions, strengths and weaknesses.

5. Yoga and Meditation

Yoga basically stands for excellence. Excellence at work can also be achieved through yoga. Similarly, meditation stands for concentration. Meditation means to reflect upon deeply on anything, or to contemplate upon something. This method has proved immensely beneficial to people in the workplace. Meditation helps one to focus so that the eye of wisdom can be opened. Meditation helps to solve many complex problems of the organisation demanding higher consciousness. A karma-yogi who practices the technique of meditation can end up with a calm and serene mind which is not perturbed and perplexed with every day worries of the workplace. Meditation results in a calm mind which helps one to focus on problems in a more clear frame of mind. In a calm mind, one can have flashes of intuition and creativity. Hence, one can achieve great benefits by calming and stilling the mind. If a problem is thought of deeply, repeatedly and often and the whole mind and the consciousness are concentrated upon the problem, (which amounts to meditation only) flashes of creative solutions come into the mind, which has resulted in many a great invention, innovative products and creative ideas and thoughts.

6. Dharma

Dharma in Indian philosophy means 'duty' and is almost synonymous with integrity and righteousness. Dharma stands for all those ideals, philosophies, purposes, influences, teachings and experiences, that shape our character. Dharma is spiritualism and is essentially divinity. Each organisation in Indian ethos is considered to be a living entity, having its own dharma and character . Thus , an organisation is supposed to inculcate within itself, all essential human and ethical values, like courage, fairness, justice, righteousness, self-discipline, fearlessness, etc. However, dharma, in the sense of one's duty, is different and specific for everyone in the organisation. The dharma (ethical duty) of the Chairman of the company would be different from the dharma of the office clerk. The only dharma common to both of them, and to all others in the organisation, is to perform one's own duty to the best of one's capacity. Every organisation is required to follow its own dharma, or pay the price for its loss of integrity. A soul-less company, is doomed to perish and die. Only when an organisation keeps within its own dharma, and does not violate it, does the organisation flourishes and grows.

7. The Spirit of Renunciation (The Spirit of Sacrifice)

The spirit of renunciation, also known as the spirit of sacrifice, of worldly goods and all material possessions, is advocated by Indian philosophy and ethos. The spirit of 'tyaga', is epitomised in Indian Philosophy as a very great virtue. One is called upon to renounce all inner cravings and sensual enjoyment of outer objects. The 'tyaga' philosophy is based on the belief that there is greater joy in overcoming a desire than in satisfying it. 'Renounce all so that you may enjoy all' –this is the message of the Isha Upanishad. The Bhagawad Gita, also advises one to renounce the attachment to the fruits of action, the rewards of work. Renunciation results in mental peace, inner growth and spiritual progress. Renunciation of the attachment to material things and the aims and values of a lower order of life, results in a rise to a higher level of consciousness. There are two levels of human consciousnesses. (a) The lower consciousness operating through our five sense organs with external world, and is sensual in nature. This also leads us to our desires and is called the lower mind; and (b) The higher mind or higher consciousness which is the vision of the inner mind. This consciousness is operated, not through sense organs, but through a purified mind, in silence, and in meditation. Values emerge effectively only from a purified mind, i.e.., from the inner mind or the higher consciousness. Thus, renunciation is the only way in which fundamental values of life enables one to transform lower consciousness into higher consciousness.

Spirituality, a refined state of the mind, is one of the resources of consciousness. Spirituality is not a matter of being religious, but it is the ability to transcend oneself, to see oneself from a distance in a detached way, to analyse one's action and intentions, and to correct them, if necessary. To make this possible , one has to embrace the spirit of renunciation of worldly goods, of sensual pleasures, and of material aims and objectives. One has to look at oneself and at the world in detached, non-emotional way. This is the essence of Indian ethos.

In conclusion, it seems apt to say that Indian ethos has many valuable messages for the modern day manager. However, we have not been able to take advantage of our ancient heritage and wisdom, when western countries are doing just that. In our search for the best, the persistent tendency has been to look everywhere, but within. An insight into our cultural milieu, norms, values and beliefs, will help us to evolve management styles and systems, which are based on solid foundations since they are best suited to the requirements of the Indian climate. Such systems and styles will assist in the process of collective maximisation of the diverse talents and resources available to us. Importing styles and systems, that are alien to the existing way of life, and thereby implicity imposing foreign values and norms of behaviour will only result in social and economic discord. Our ancient values and cultural norms are time-tested, and have guided many a man in power, during moral crises, to find ethical answers. Notable amongst them is Mahatma Gandhi, who resorted to the Bhagawad Gita to find answers, whenever he was in moral dilemmas. Albert Einstein, and Leo Tolstoy were two other people. It is high time now, for us too, to follow in the footsteps of these great people.

2.2 Indian Values for the Workplace

1. The Importance of Relationships in the Workplace

Indian families, unlike western ones, are characterised by extended childhood , where children live with their parents and are supported by them, for an extended period–girls, even working girls, more often then not , till they get married; and boys continue to live with their parents, even after their marriage. From birth, the Indian child is exposed to numerous relations, often sharing warm and close personal relationships with them. Given the close physical contact, alongwith overwhelming care and inordinate amount of love and concern from elders, emotional links with others becomes the core characteristic of the Indian personality profile. Thus, the individual comes to the work place with a strong need to relate to others. This is exemplified in the office where the subordinate calls the superior 'elder brother' or 'elder sister' (in case of women boss) whereas in the western countries, employees call each other 'Sir' or 'Mister' (as in the UK), or using first names (as in the USA) , even with an aged or superior employer.

Such needs in individuals greatly facilitates cohesive team building and an empowering and enabling organisational culture. That Indian employees are worst team players, where excellent individual results get converted to poor team performance, is a case in point of Indian companies not positively harnessing the team spirit of the Indian worker.

Due to poor handling of this need for relationship of the Indian worker by the organisation, the worker faces an identity crisis in the absence of intimate relationships, both vertically as well as horizontally. So, just to gratify and satisfy their need for emotional linkages in the workplace, such workers tend to form intensely loyal, informal groups, that get into power politics, form associations and unions and indulge in confrontations which result in intergroup conflicts; and individuals goals get prominance at the expense of organisational goals, which ultimately lead to poor team spirit, and poor team performance.

Taking care to develop, consciously, relationships amongst individuals within the workplace, can result in an organisational culture which helps individuals to release positive energies like empathy, togetherness, mutual understanding and help emotional support and great team building.

2. Respect for Elders

Indian culture puts a high value on experience and age. Indian culture teaches the individual to admire, respect and obey elders. One of India's greatest traditions constitutes reverence for older people, unlike in the western countries, where a greater premium is put on the productive work force. In the organisational context, the conjunction of the abilities of older and younger people should result in corporate excellence, where the older person offers his experience and guidance to the younger, and the mistakes of the younger person gets converted into learning experiences. Such a relationship within the organisation, proves to be of immense value. The younger person becomes more confident in his job due to the valuable inputs received from the older person; and the older person gets and receives youthful insights and the views and perceptions of the younger generation. Such a relationship results in the integration of experience and knowledge, where the older person plays a paternal role and focuses on the growth and development of the younger person.

3. Respect for Hierarchy and Status

In the Indian joint family system, a child learns very early in life, respect for hierarchical layers of people, their status within the family and their varying degrees of authority. Having come through a number of strict codes of behaviour in his family, the individual, in his worklife too, conforms to the rules and regulations of the organisation, displays high support for his superiors and low deviance and rebellion. If this value of tolerance and respect for seniors is well utilised in the workplace, then it results in smooth maintenance of organisational power and mutually supporting and empowering superior–subordinate relationship.

4. Need for Security

The Indian system of joint family, and the early parent–child relationships are so protection-oriented , that the Indian worker puts a very high premium on security, even in the workplace, and specially in his job. Though it does tend to make many individuals timid and risk-avoiders, and leads to bureaucratisation and delayed decision makings, it also results in smooth acceptance and implementation of decisions taken; as well as conformity with organisational norms, and smooth functioning of the organisation. In the workplace , such a need for security results in unquestioning acceptance of superior's authority and mutual superior-subordinate dependence. Such a sense of mutuality has many positive outcomes and much more work gets done without any disruption. When organisations make employees feel safe and secure on the job, then employees are much more motivated to put in their best efforts. When the cloud of insecurity hangs over the heads of the employees, then they feel fearsome, demotivated and a lack of confidence. That is the prime reason as to why many companies have today introduced the compensation system of a fixed salary along with commission. This makes the employee confident that he is assured of a salary, whatever happens, at the end of the month. That Indian workers tend to avoid work as soon as their jobs become confirmed, and they become secure, is an area for thought and analysis; the fault mainly may lie in the assessment and appraisal systems, and the system of transfer and promotion.

5. Simple Living & High Thinking

Indian culture highly values living by high ideals. In recent times, an illustration of this cultural imperative is Mahatma Gandhi, whose whole philosophy in life was simple living and high thinking. Though people in their worklife may not be expected to actually practise this, however its importance is predominant as far as expected leader behaviour is concerned.

A true leader is expected to follow this ideal, as he strives for lofty goals. He is expected to exhibit value-based conduct, and ethical and moral thoughts, during the pursuit of his goals, so that followers may feel a sense of pride while trying to emulate him.

At the individual level, congruence between the personal value of living by ideals, and the organisational level behavioural expectations, results in a psychological process of constant reflection and contemplation, clarity of one's goal and direction, ethical conduct, and a sense of dedication to one's purpose and mission in life. This, ultimately results in low vanity and ego, and even lesser exhibitionism and display. The individual starts being less oriented towards self, and more oriented towards the well-being of others in the organisation. Narrow infighting, rivalry, and petty office politics ceases and there is greater collaboration among people.

This value has a far-reaching impact on the organisation. Power games and inter-group rivalry within the organisation gets eliminated. Conflicts and destructive and meaningless competitions are reduced. A sense of dedication and commitment leads to a greater attempt to adjust to organisational demands and pressure. Leaders with vision, who work with this philosophy in mind, can help in generation clarity of vision, goals and purpose, sound organisational philosophy, besides increasing subordinate's motivation, their sense of direction and their dedication.

6. The Karta

The Karta finds mention in many Indian ancient texts and scriptures. The Karta is the head of the family whose members may be extended and joint. The Karta's authority over everyone within the family is unquestionable. A. Jolly, 'On Family (Hindu)', in 'Encyclopaedia of Religion and Ethics' (ed.) (Hastings, J; Volume 5. NY Scribner, 1920), states that the concept of the Karta has been described in the Narada Smriti, as the manager of the family with the power to influence every decision pertaining to the welfare of the family. The Karta, by his behaviour and functioning, evokes feelings of security, trust and dependability.

The nurturing, caring, dependable, sacrificing, yet firm, demanding, authoritative and strict dimensions of the Karta is valued by the individual right from childhood. Thus, such an individual accepts the ultimate authority and decisions of the Karta, even for major personal decisions like whom to marry and when to stop studies and get a job. Such an individual, even later on in life, keeps looking for a Karta to guide and lead him on. Thus, even in the workplace, this individual tends to look for a symbolic father figure–a Karta - for guidance and protection. If he finds such a Karta in his boss, then he willingly and unquestioningly, accepts his authority and gives his respect and reverence. The superior, in this case, has the subordinate totally in his hands and can mould and shape him according to his wish. If the superior takes the pain and makes the effort to mould him right, and shape his growth and development, then the subordinate is indeed lucky in finding such a Karta in the workplace. In such a case, the superior must have a nurturant attitude towards subordinates, for the Karta philosophy develops only with respect to subordinates. A person cannot become a Karta by himself, without his subordinates; just as a person cannot become a leader without having followers.

THE KARTA

⇓ Influence

THE INDIVIDUAL

⇓ Searches for in

THE WORKPLACE

⇓ Finds a Symbolic Karta in

THE BOSS

Positive	**Negative**
* Receives guidance & protection.	* May not take initiative to do things independently.
* Cordial superior-subordinate relationship.	* Subordinate does not question the boss and accepts all judgement unquestioningly.
* Superior can mould subordinate in a productive way so that subordinate becomes efficient and highly skilled.	* Superior can manipulate the growth and development of the subordinate.
* Respect and reverence of subordinate for the superior results in quick decision-making and efficient work.	* Respect and reverence of the subordinate for superior may be exploited and misutilised.
* Subordinate develops a highly loyal attitude for the superior.	* Misplaced loyalty and a wrong sense of it may lead subordinates to keep quiet even when the superior is wrong or unethical.

(Actually, in Indian philosophy, the Karta is taken to be highly moral , principled and ethical person who only has the welfare of the members under his guidance, in his heart. Moreover, a manipulative and unethical person does not fall under the concept of Karta)

7. Internal Orientation (Work is Worship)

While in the West, the quality of worklife has always been founded in the external environment, in the East, specially in India, the quality of worklife is dependent on the internal environment - that is, on the integrated inner structure of the worker. According to the Indian Philosophy, Quality of Worklife is not a function of pays, perks, cars, executive club membership or foreign travels. It is a deep and satisfying feeling that one is doing something worthwhile and what one is doing is making a difference to many people - fellow human beings. It is finding oneself within his work, a feeling of having served many, a feeling of purifying oneself through his work, a feeling that one's work is God itself, and having served the customer, he has served God.

Descartes had asserted, 'I think, so I exist'. In Indian philosophy, this is- 'I exist, so I think'. The West depends more on the brain - that analytical, logical and rational part of the human instrument; whereas in India, what is more valued is the mind - that intangible but ultimate and supreme part of the human body, more a psychological concept rather than a physiological one. However, more and more scientists are today acknowledging and accepting the existence of the human mind. The West cherishes the 'Personality' – the outward appearance, abilities and skills of human beings, their manners and mannerisms. All these are external. The East cherishes the 'Character' – the inner qualities, values and inner goodness of man. An outstanding personality without the inner goodness of character is meaningless and is hardly satisfying. For example, a person trying to develop his human relations skill (a personality trait), without having any real interest or concern for human welfare, will get exposed, sooner or later, for what he is. Similarly, a person trying to develop his communications skills (again a personality trait) without having the least concern about what others are trying to express, to what others are saying, and more importantly, trying to 'listen' to what others are **not** saying, will just end up polishing his exterior, while his interior remains as selfish as ever. It is very important to develop one's personality in today's professional times, no doubt about it; but along with it, one must focus one's attention also on character-building. For if personality is the building, character is the light within; If personality is built on 'sympathy', character is built on 'empathy'; If personality is 'passion', character is 'compassion'. Personality builds up the external man, while character builds up the internal man. Both are equally important for success in todays competitive age. Though people in the West tends to be demonstrative and extroverts, and rely more on the personality to get them across, Indian philosophy tends towards introvertism. Physical demonstration of love, affection, gratitude approval, through words and gestures, do not feature predominantly in the Indian Philosophy. Public display of emotions are not a part of a strong character. Thus Indian philosophy tends to be very internal oriented, where the internal being is much more important than the external being.

8. Importance of Wisdom

While the West strives to acquire more and more knowledge in the workplace, and everywhere else, the East believes that it is wisdom, which is more worthy of pursuit. Thus, while the West stresses on a knowledgeable worker, Indian philosophy strives to create a wiser worker. Knowledge results in skills; with more knowledge in the workplace, workers become better skilled in their work. But, wisdom is a result of values. Knowledge tells us what to do, but values tell us what to be. Learning to do (i.e. skills) is temporary and will change as soon as technology changes and new and better technology replaces the current one; whereas learning to be (i.e. values) are enduring and can never change. Values are enduring and unchanging over time. The organisation faces challenges from its workforce, not due to any lack of skills, but due to lack of values. **Mental quality is more important than mental capacity**. Mental capacity may come from the right **knowledge**, but mental quality comes from **wisdom**. Similarly, quality of the mind of the workforce is more important than quality circles to produce a quality product from within a quality organisation.

In modern times, more and more organisations are providing the worker with tangible and intangible articles to fulfil their need hierarchy, in the workplace. Worker's motivation is sought to be 'bought' through 'prestige' and 'position'; like a better designation, better perks, better fringe benefits and better pay package. The Indian philosophy does not attach great importance to these things. According to the Indian philosophy, the satisfaction of the worker in his job and the quality of his worklife depends upon his mental attitude. Rather it seeks to emphasise upon the worker's mental, emotional and social adjustment with the external realities in the workplace, without sacrificing his ethical values and moral conscience. This is the essence of wisdom, and this wisdom is sought by organisations, in worker's worklife.

9. Balance & Moderation

Balance and moderation is the essence of Indian life. Indian philosophy places a great value on balance of life. 'Moderation is the essence of life' – this is the traditional Indian philosophy. According to this philosophy, the individual is the foundation of the workplace and nothing of substance can be achieved at the cost of the individuals. As Mahatma Gandhi had said, "If the individual ceases to count, what is left of society ?" Balance or equilibrium is the keynote of Indian thought. Sythesis and harmony are stressed upon. Indian philosophy states that Indian workers seek to achieve self-actualisation through their work, however humble or low down the work may be. In fact, no work is considered lowly or unworthy of doing. All work is considered spiritual, all work is considered to be a means for purifying one's mind and ego; all work is considered to be a moral duty for the person concerned–his 'dharma', the efficient discharge of which purifies the soul and earns blessings for the next life. Indian philosophy prescribes moderations in our thoughts and actions. It seeks to create a balance between inner and outer life; between work and leisure. Though work is considered worship in Indian philosophy, it does not, at the same time, tell anyone to become a workaholic. Praying and meditation are prescribed as great means to cleanse the soul, yet it does not tell people to leave their families and go into the forest to pray and mediate. There must be a balance in everything. Serving other is wonderful, and must certainly be undertaken, yet Indian philosophy does not tell one to serve others at the expense of one's family or oneself. In fact, Indian philosophy states that one's duty is first towards oneself and one's family. Running away from one's responsibilities, even to pray or meditate, is considered to be a very great sin. Thus, Indian philosophy tries to create a balance–too much of even a good thing is bad–this is motto.

10. Rights and Duties

The talking of duties automatically brings about the question of one's rights. Not so in Indian philosophy! Indian philosophy does not consider anything as matter of right, but states every thing, for even the highest person in the land to the poorest of the poor, only in terms of duties. 'Rights' have no place in the Indian philosophy. This however, does not imply that the rights of individuals are neglected or ignored. When everyone discharges their duties as prescribed, everyone's rights too get automatically fulfilled. When a teacher discharges his or her 'duty', the 'right' of the student to acquire quality education gets automatically satisfied. When a post office clerk attend to his duty at his appointed time, the right of the customer to avail of prompt service is automatically met. If a manufacture does his duty of producing and selling a quality and defect-free product, the 'right' of the consumer to receive value for money is fulfilled. It is only when people attend to their duties, that other's rights get fulfilled, and not before, and not vice-versa. With the correct performance of duties, with the emphasis on internal attributes of the worker, rather than on the externalities of the work situation, a wiser worker is developed where the quality of work life gets fulfilled within the mind of the worker and not from external factors.

2.3 Quality of Worklife in Indian Philosophy

Quality of worklife is an area which has been receiving quite a lot of attention during the present time, hence a discussion of quality of worklife from the Indian perspective, is necessary. There is a high difference between Quality of Worklife as seen from the Western perspective and from the Indian perspective.

There must be quality in one's life. Every one expects and accepts that. But, a difference must be made between Quality of Life and Quality of Living. Quality of Living is based on material possessions and the external aspect of life. Quality of Life, on the other hand, is based on inner happiness and satisfaction, and are based on one's philosophy and values. Quality of Life cannot be bought with money, though Quality of Living is based on how much money one has. Quality of Living is also termed as the standard of life. Money can make one's life comfortable, and at times may also bring happiness, but it cannot bring in mental peace and inner satisfaction. Lack of money brings in unhappiness, but too much of it also does not assure happiness in life. One must possess enough to meet one's needs; the average man is not happy in stark poverty, but, it must be understood and accepted that quality of life does not depend merely on one's wealth.

Similarly, Quality of Worklife does not only depend on one's position in the organisation, nor on the trappings of power and prestige that comes with the job. Quality of Worklife is more of a mental attitude; the inner satisfaction of having done one's work according to the best of one's ability and capacity, of not having to fulfil one's ego or false sense of pride by resorting to petty office politics and power manipulations, by achieving a sense of joy from a job well done, a sense of pride and dignity in one's job, however small or insignificant it may be; of trying to grow on the job and achieve success, not to exhibit or display, but more for one's growth and self-development. According to Indian philosophy, the quality of one's worklife does not depend on the external environment, or on the incentives of the job, but depends on the internal environment– on the integrated inner structure of the worker. As has been said before, quality of worklife is not a function of pays, perks, cars, executive club membership or foreign travels. It is a much more deeper feeling that provides one with the motivation not only to perform the job well, but also to excel at it, to achieve self-actualisation and to grow and develop on the job. It is to become, in the process of doing one's job, a better person – a better human being. When the opportunities for achieving all these are present on the job and in the workplace, then one's quality of worklife is said to be high.

Quality of worklife provides one with a deep and satisfying feeling that one is doing something worthwhile, that one is creating value and excellence for one's company, one is contributing to the general welfare of humanity, and that one is making some changes to the lives of those within one's area of influence, and that one's presence in the company is making some difference to the company.

Discussion Problem

Mr. Prasad has a confectionary shop where he sells various cakes, breads and pastries. Now, since Mr. Prasad does not have a bakery of his own, his shop acts more as an outlet for the products of various other bakeries. Since Mr. Prasad's shop is located on the fringe of a residential area, most people buy their requirements late in the evening, while returning home from work. But by that time, the cakes and pastries become stale, as they are usually provided to Mr. Prasad's shop by the various bakeries, late at night the previous day. Hence his sales were not good. Moreover, Amar, Mr. Prasad's sales boy always tells the truth to customers when asked about the freshness of the cakes and pastries. As sales continued to fall, Mr. Prasad decided to add another outlet to his shop, that of a Xerox machine. For this, he hired another young boy by the name of Anil. Anil was a smart lad who was good at his job. One day, Anil offered a solution to Mr. Prasad about his confectionary shop. He urged Mr. Prasad to decorate the stale cakes and pastries with icing and other flavours to camouflage their staleness and sell them as new, at a higher price. Mr. Prasad acted on his suggestion and soon sales began to increase. Sales began to soar so much that Mr. Prasad had to place bulk orders to all the bakeries that provided him with cakes. Now Mr. Prasad was in a moral dilemma; he was not comfortable with what he was doing , whereas he saw no solution to his problem of falling sales. He considered the situation from all angles, and analysed all factors to decide to what to do next.

The Factors were

1. Sales have been increased on the unethical means provided by Anil. However, it is ethical to make profits in business;
2. If customers find out, they would avoid Mr. Prasad's shop and he may even have to lose his Xerox business;
3. Sales had decreased when Amar had been ethical and honest, and the confectionary shop was almost going bankrupt. It is unethical to make losses in business and go bankrupt;
4. Though sales were going down, people in the locality knew that Mr. Prasad and Amar were honest and ethical in their dealings, and they were held in great esteem. People had trust in them both. They had won the goodwill of the people of that residential area, and the great esteem that people had for Mr. Prasad led him to do great business with his Xerox machine;
5. If he closed his confectionary shop and concentrated only on his Xerox outlet, he had the following problems–
    a) all his investments in the shop would go down the drain and he stands to lose a great deal of money;
    b) His Xerox outlet alone would not be able to generate enough revenue to support himself and his family comfortably;
    c) Right now he had no money to invest in anything else;

d) Amar, the honest and ethical lad, who had served Mr. Prasad loyally for so many years, would be thrown out of a job and would find no means of supporting himself immediately ;

e) There was no question of firing Anil; firstly, because he was good at his job; but secondly, and, more importantly, since he has come to know how sales of the confectionary shop had increased, he might leak out the secret to people in the area after leaving the job.

Discuss the problem of Mr. Prasad, his moral dilemma, and his future course of action, taking into account, all the factors outlined above.

PART-II

The Concept of Ethics in Worklife According to The Bagawad Gita

The Bhagawad Gita cites numerous instances of how moral values and ethics can be incorporated in one's worklife. Contrary to the belief that Indian (or Hindu) philosophy subscribes to the view that one should renounce all work, worldly pleasure and one's duties, and should retire to the forests to mediate, the Gita clearly directs all men to carry out their duties according to the best of their capacities. In fact, according to the Bhagawad Gita, running away from one's designated duties instead of fulfilling them, is a great sin. The Bhagawad Gita says that anyone who runs away from his obligations, his duties, his problems and the challenges facing him, is a great coward, worthy only of ridicule and shame.

The Bhagawad Gita is the message of the Lord to his much beloved and trusted friend, in the middle of a battlefield. In the battle of Kurukshetra, the Pandava and the Kaurava clans met each other to fight; who were cousins by birth, but warring enemies by circumstances. Arjun was the chief warrior of the Pandavas, who stood for right and truth, against the Kauravas who epitomized all that is evil and unethical. So the battle of Kurukshetra was a battle between good and evil. Though Arjun was a courageous and valiant warrior, yet he could not reconcile himself to the fact that he would have to fight and kill his cousins and kins to win the battle of Kurukshetra. Thus, when Arjun became distressed and disheartened after seeing all his cousins and seniors on the battlefield of Kurukshetra, and wanted to surrender without fighting, rather than killing his relatives, Lord Krishna, unrevealed to Arjun, the mystries of human life and human work. For the modern day Arjuns also (the business managers), the message of the Lord, given probably in the 10th century B.C., still holds enormous relevance to modern business enterprises. The Pandavas, feeling a sense of injustice burning like an inferno in their hearts, was determined to fight for justice, for upholding moral values and for the good of mankind. On the other hand, the Kauravas had no noble motive to fight for. They know that they had done wrong, and that they were fighting for something over which they had no moral right. Even Dhidarastra, the father figure of the Kauravas, could himself feel that the Kauravas lacked the spirit of motivation arising out of a sense of fighting for justice and for upholding certain moral values and ethics. Even Karna, one of Kaurava's most valiant warriors, was consumed in his heart of hearts, with a sense of guilt for having supported a cause unethical and wrong.

Management, whether of a kingdom, a war or a business organisation has to be founded on some mission and exist on a philosophy, ethical conduct, a strong moral standard and an inbuilt value system. Only such factors can motivate its people to fight for organisational causes and goals. This sense of standing for something ideal and noble, inspires and enthuses employees to give their wholehearted cooperation for the cause of the organisation, and to do their best. On the other hand, if people feel that the organisation to which they belong, is unethical ; misleads and exploits the public, they too would be caught in a moral dilemma, like Karna. They would carry out their work, no doubt, but only because they are employed by the organisation, and for no other reason. In their inner most hearts, they would be guilty and ashamed to identify themselves with their organisations. And as such, the zeal to work, the enthusiasm and the consuming passion to achieve organisational excellence, would be missing in them. With such a workforce, who work only because they are employees of the organisation and nothing more, no organisation can hope to excel in the market place or become trend setters. For that, organisations need to have a workforce with a burning desire, a passion to perform and excel. And that can come only when the organisation is ethical.

2.4 Ethics in Worklife from The Bhagawad Gita

Chapter II of The Bhagawad Gita

Text-2 – The Supreme Personality of Godhead said : 'My dear Arjun, how have these impurities come upon you ? They are not at all benefiting a man who knows the value of life. They lead not to higher planets, but to infamy'.

Text-3– 'O son of Pratha , do not yield to this degrading impotence. It does not become you. Give up such petty weakness of heart and arise, O chastiser of the enemy'.

In this society, all people live within social structures. These social structures may be a tribe, a race, a clan or a village. Every individual within a particular social structure has to play out his or her specific role within the social norms of that social structure. For example, the Kshatriya race to which Arjun belongs, has the duty to fight for the well-being of the rest of the society. A Kshatriya, right from childhood, is trained in the tactical skills of fighting the enemy and practising how to protect the society. By refusing to fight, Arjun would be neglecting his duty and letting down the prestige and the reputation of the Kshatriya tribe.

Just as in the social structure, so also in managing an social structure, it has to be ensured that every individual carries out his or her specific activities in a planned and pre-determined way. Every organisation must ensure that all employees perform their designated duties so that the organisation can function smoothly. Every individual in the organisation has a specific role to play, the neglect of which affects the overall efficiency, functioning and well-being of the organisation. The Bhagawad Gita also reinforces the same, when it prescribes that every person should discharge his or her duties according to the prescribed norms of social and group behaviour.

TEXT - 7 Arjun tells Lord Krishna :

'Now I am confused about my duty, and have lost all composure, because of miserly weakness. In this condition, I am asking you to tell me for certain what is best for me. Now I am Your disciple and a soul surrendered unto you. Please Instruct me'.

This verse clearly shows that Arjun was facing a moral dilemma, between what he knew was his duty (i.e., fighting the enemy, which means his cousins), and what he considered to be immoral conduct (i.e., killing his cousins and other relatives in discharging his duty, in order to win the war). Arjun was an epitome of all virtues. If Arjun himself could become so confused and in conflict in distinguishing between what is 'moral' and 'immoral' then it is quite natural for an ordinary man to become mentally confused about his duties while functioning in a hostile and corrupt world. When Arjun, the all-knowing and the almighty, who has Lord Krishna himself as his closest friend, could acknowledge his inability to act in such a situation, and seek guidance from the Lord, then there is even more reason for an ordinary manager to face managerial dilemmas during his business activities. The manager too needs 'guidance', and soul-searching many a times, when he has to choose between his commercial considerations and his ethical considerations. The Bhagawad Gita provides such guidance to a confused manager facing managerial dilemmas. Even Mahatma Gandhi acknowledged that he used to turn to the Gita whenever he was confused and frustrated, and always found the right answers from the Gita. Like Gandhiji, the modern manager can also find comfort and solace, and more importantly, the right answers to his dilemmas, if he accept the Bhagawad Gita as a message from the Lord. However, what will eventually guide him in his day to day business activities, will be his value system and moral standards, his principles and his philosophy of life.

Text 14– 'O son of Kunti, the nonpermanent appearance of happiness and distress and their disappearance in due course, are like the appearance and disappearance of winter and summer seasons. They arise from sense perception, and one must learn to tolerate them without being disturbed'.

Text 15– 'O best among men (Arjun), the person who is not disturbed by happiness and distress and is steady in both, is certainly eligible for liberation'.

In business organisation also, the swing of fortunes should not unduly disturb the mind of the business manager. Being a business venture, there is bound to be both profits and losses in the business, from time to time. Profits and losses are temporary and should not perturb the minds of manager. What is permanent and are enduring to the organisation are basic principles of moral values which are fundamental and do not change. When institutions and organisations are build on these values and ethical principles, then these institutions and organisations leave behind them the imprints of their good work and their contribution to the welfare of the society. In such an organisation, there is no conflict in the mind of the employee, for he has to perform only his own prescribed duty in an ethical manner.

Text 33– 'If however, you do not perform your religious duty of fighting, then you will certainly incur sins for neglecting your duties, and thus, lose your reputation as a fighter',– Thus spoke Lord Krishna to Arjun.

Text 34– 'People will always speak of your infamy and for a respectable person, dishonour is worse than death'.

The Bhagawad Gita repeatedly speaks of the need for an individual to perform his prescribed duty. In fact, one's prescribed duty is considered equal to a religious duty, the performance of which leads one to satisfaction and purity of the soul, and whose non-performance brings dishonour, which is considered to be worst than death.

The most profound message given by the Bhagawad Gita is the prescription of the way in which one's duties must be performed. The most important knowledge about work is given by the last few stanzas of this Chapter (chapter II) of the Gita, which says–

Text 47– 'You have a right to perform your prescribed duty, but you are not entitled to the fruits of action. Never consider yourself the cause of the results of your activities and never be attached to not doing your duty'.

Prescribed duties are those activities which one is designated to perform to fulfil his specific role in this world, and are acquired in this material life. Contrary to prescribed duty is capricious work, which are mere actions without the sanction of authority; and not performing one's prescribed duty amounts to inaction. One who is attached to the result of his work is also the cause of the action. Thus, he enjoys of suffers the result of such actions.

This is the most profound message of the Bhagawad Gita. A worker has the right only to perform his prescribed duty, never to the fruits of his action. This philosophy is prescribed only to deliver the worker from undue misery should his work fail, or from undue esctasy, should his work succeed. A man has to work ceaselessly throughout his life. All work is either met with success of failure. If in case of success, the worker feels deliriously happy, and in case of failure, he feels dejected and morose, then throughout his whole life, the worker will be subjected to a see-saw swing of emotions; being happy and unhappy by terns, as success and failure comes to him in turns. If, on the other hand, the worker performs his duty to the best of his ability, and once the work is over, he leaves the result to the Lord (or to fate), because the result of the work is beyond his control, then he is forever serene and does not experience swings of emotions. Only the work we perform is within our control, the results of the work is beyond our control. Hence, a wise man does not unnecessarily worry and fret over what is not within his control. Rather his view is that–'I have done my best; Upon God I leave the rest'. These are the reasons why the Bhagawad Gita has advised man not to consider oneself entitled to the fruits of action.

Text 48– 'Perform your duty equipoised, O Arjun, abandoning all attachment to success of failure. Such equanimity is called yoga'.

Text 55– The Supreme Personality of Godhead said :

'Partha , when a man gives up all varieties of desire for sense gratification which arise from mental contention and when his mind, thus purified, finds satisfaction in the self-alone, then he is said to be pure transcendental consciousness'.

These two verses illustrates the meaning of Yoga and Transcendental Consciousness. Yoga denotes a state of mental equanimity, where nothing can disturb the mind. A state of pure transcendental consciousness, is a state of the purified mind, free from the desire for sense gratification. Both these two states describe two extremely superior mental states which can exist in the organisation, in one's worklife.

Text 56– 'One who is not disturbed in mind admist the threefold miseries or elated when there is happiness and who is free from attachment, fear and anger, is called a sage of steady mind'.

A steady mind is another mental state which is highly desirable in one's worklife, to retain one's equilibrium and equantimity, and to insulate oneself from all fears, doubts, worries, confusion and anger, and proceed in the narrow path of honesty and ethics.

Attachment means accepting things for one's own sense gratification and detachment is the absence of such sensual attachment. Success of failure, a person without attachment is always steady in his determination.

Text 57– 'In the material world, one who is unaffected by whatever good or evil he may obtain, neither praising it nor despising it, is firmly fixed in perfect knowledge'.

In the material world, there is always the possibility of good and evil, because this world is full of duality. A person working in a business organisation, is also bound to face uncertainty regarding what is moral or immoral. However, only when one is not agitated by material upheavals and is unaffected by good and evil, can he make a correct choice when faced with a managerial dilemma.

Text 60– 'The senses are so strong and impetuous, O Arjun, that they forcibly carry away the mind even of a man of discrimination who is endeavouring to control them'.

This verse gives a measure of how difficult it is to remain ethical, whether in social life or in worklife, when one's senses are assaulted by cut-throat competition, petty jealousies and office politics, rivalry and consumerism in the marketplace. The path to good and right is slippery and narrow, and distractions exist at every turn and they attract and assault one's senses, and demand gratifications. That is why the Gita says that such alluring invasion of the senses carry away the mind of even a man of discrimination.

Text 61– 'One who restrains his senses, keeping them under full control and fixes his consciousness upon Me, is known as a man of steady intelligence'.

If the last verse showed how difficult it is keep one's mind steady in the face of temptations for sense gratifications, this verse provides a method to remain steady and in control of one's senses. And this method is to fix one's consciousness upon the Lord, surrendering oneself completely to the mercies of the Lord.

Text 62– 'While contemplating the objects of the senses, a person develops attachment for them and from such attachment lust develops, and from lust anger arises'.

Text 63– 'From anger, complete delusion arises and from delusion bewilderment of memory. When memory is bewildered, intelligence is lost and when intelligence is lost, one falls down again into the material pool'.

These two verses outline the process whereby a person is lead into unethical means, and consequently to doom and ruin. However, the last two verses of this Chapter II, illustrates the way by which a person may escape from such ruin and doom. These two verses are found in Text 70 & 71 .

Text 70– 'A person who is not disturbed by the incessant flow of desires that enter like rivers into the ocean, which is ever being filled but is always still–can alone achieve peace and not the man who strives to satisfy such desires'.

Text 7– 'A person who has given up all desires for sense gratifications, who lives, free from desires, who has given up all sense of proprietorship and devoid of false ego–he alone can attain real peace'.

The relevance of the message in Chapter II of the Bhagawad Gita to a modern business organisation is immense, as it deals with one's worklife. Any organisation which desire to survive and prosper, must necessarily be founded on some basic principles or ethics, or else it parishes very fast. The tangible proof of this is seen in the continued success of value-based organisation in the marketplace. Values are the soul of organisation–the industructible, the intangible–that transcends time and age, and remains unchanged, even with the changes within and outside the organisation. In a highly unpredictable world characterised by rapid changes, that which is totally unchangeable and constant, are values. With a beautiful analogy, the Lord explains that the human body is like our clothes. When the clothes become old and dirty, the soul too changes its clothes, i.e., it enters another body. The soul itself is unchangeable and indesrubtible. Similarly, the values of an organisation , which is the soul of the organisation, are also unchangeable and industructible. They do not change-however, with the change of time, with the change of the environment, and consequently, with the change of the organisation, a new interpretation of the value system become necessary. Forever true, and forever relevant, values form the corner stone of effective management of mankind. They cannot be compromised with, nor can they be partly true. **A Half truth is a full lie. Just** as Gandhiji had said, 'Values cannot be compromised with. I have never known water to be diluted'.

An acceptance of certain fundamental core values does wonders for any business organisation. It removes confusions and conflicts amongst managers, unites employees together cohesively, enthuses them to work productively; employees feel a sense of pride to belong to such an organisation, bestows on the organisation clarity of vision, and an ability to progress happily towards supreme goals which remains universal, though the paths leading to them may be different. In such organisations, neither do employees strive for personal enhancement at the cost of the organisation, nor does the organisation strive for organisational enhancement at social cost.

Steadfastness in discharging one's duties without seeking credit for the end results, undistraced by transit worldly attractions, a rational and calm mind, are the valued possession of a business manager. The sense of such a manager are stable, and he is focused towards the fundamental purpose of the enterprise an d proceeds towards it unwaveringly through good times and bad.

The Lord has never advocated renunciation of work, In fact, He says that not performing one's prescribed duties is a cardinal sin. If everyone were to renounce work, would society and would family life survive? On the other hand, working judiciously, honestly, sincerely and compassionately, creates a thriving economy in the community. Where everyone prospers Organisational Prosperity is found only where employees regard work as worship. Selfless work, where one performs for organisational prosperity and achievement, even at the cost of personal gains, results in self-actualisation. 'Work is worship', Gandhiji reminded his countryman, and it is indeed true that God resides in work; the purest form of worship is in discharging one's duty in life dedicatedly, selflessely and with utmost trust in the ultimate mission. True salvation in everyday life, is not achieved through renunciation of work, but rather with performance of work-rarely without.

Chapter-III Karma-Yoga

Karma Yoga deals with the discharging of one's prescribed duty. In this chapter, the Lord explains two kind of procedures of doing work-Sankhya-Yoga and Karma-Yoga or Buddi Yoga. Sankhya yoga is the analytical study of the nature of the intangible and is the subject matter for persons who are inclined to speculate and understand things by experimental knowledge and philosophy. On the other hand, Karma-Yoga is liberation through the discharging of one's prescribe duty. Both the Yogas are interdependent, as religion and philosophy. Religion without philosophy is sentiment only, or sometimes even fanaticism; while philosophy without religion in mere mental speculation.

Chapter III

Text 4– 'Not by merely abstaining from work can one achieve freedom from reaction, nor by renunciation alone can one attain perfection'.

The Lord reiterates that work or karma is the driving force of life, and none can attain freedom or perfection by abstaining from work or through renunciation. Moreover this work done by men has to be ethical. To live, to exist, to survive, work is a necessary prerequisite. The Lord says 'Those who do not work, do not even have a present, leave alone a future. What good is a life which has never striven towards a worthy moral goal? Moreover a distinction should be made between ethical work and work which is useless, or work which is downright 'immoral'. The overriding consideration of our work should be for the larger good of mankind, and not for mere sense gratifications, or for short term personal benefits. We can create our own heaven or hell through our actions. When we strive for a lofty goal, which is an upright and moral one as well, we are filled with a sense of heavenly bliss, which itself is God.

Text 5– 'Everyone is forced to act helplessly according to the qualities he has acquired from the modes of material nature, therefore, no one can refrain from doing something not even for a moment'.

It is not a question of embodied life, but it is the nature of the soul to be always active. The body is only a dead vehicle to be worked by the spirit soul, which is always active and cannot stop even for a moment. As such the soul has to be engaged in the good work of human welfare, otherwise it will be engaged in occupation dictated by illusory energy.

Text 8– 'Perform your prescribed duty, for doing so is better than not working. One cannot even maintain one's physical body without work.'

In verse after verse the Lord reiterates the importance of performing one's prescribed duty. Without work it is not possible even to maintain oneself physically, leave alone emotionally and spiritually.

Text 21– 'Whatever action a great man performs, common men follow. And whatever standards he sets by exemplary acts, all the world pursues'.

Text 22– 'There is no work prescribed for me within all the three planetary systems. Nor am I in want of anything, nor have I a need to obtain anything–and yet I am engaged in prescribed duties'.

Text 23– 'For if I ever failed to engage in carefully performing prescribed duties, certainly all men would follow My path'.

In these three verses, the Lord exemplifies how common men follow the conduct of the Leader. One who considers himself a leader of men, even if he is a boss, leading a team of employees under him, his conduct and behaviour is constantly being monitored by those who follow him. Hence, he must be careful at all times to indulge himself only with perfect exemplary action, within his sphere of influence, so that his followers can emulate his actions. The Lord has no need to work, yet He keeps Himself always engaged in work– discharging his prescribed duties–so that common men would also be inspired to perform their prescribed duties. Hence, essentially, the Lord advices leaders to lead from the front, with personal examples and in performing their prescribed duties, so that their followers may also be inspired to keep performing duties. The Lord states that there is no greater virtue than performing one's prescribed duties in total humility. The Lord also has a message for organisational managers–that common men, meaning the employees under them, follow whatever standards of performance and efficiency and excellence they set within their organisations, through their exemplary acts. 'Example is better than precept'–this saying is even more true in case of business managers.

Text 27– 'The spirit soul bewildered by the influence of false ego thinks himself the doer of activities that are is actually carried out by the three modes of material nature'.

Text 30– 'O Arjun therefore, surrendering all your works unto Me, with no claims to proprietorship, and free from lethargy, fight'.

Text 34– 'There are principles to regulate attachment and aversion pertaining to the senses and their objects. One should not come under the influence of such attachment and aversion, because they are stumbling blocks on the path of self-realisation.

Those who are ignorant and vain thinks of themselves to be the doer of activities that are actually designed to be, even before the birth of the individual. We are all like puppets in the hands of Lord. We are only here to discharge our prescribed duties. However, in discharging our duties, we should not consider ourselves to be the doer of those activities since they are planned and designed to be from time immemorable. We are only the means in the Lord's scheme of things. Sometimes this is difficult for us to grasp with our limited brain power, and our myopic vision. But the Lord is all knowing–He knows the past, the present and the future; while we see only the present. We are just actors acting out our parts in the Lord's design of the world. Hence, it is not advisable for us to think of ourselves, and indeed it is arrogant too, to be the doer of our activities. Thus, the Lord tells Arjun that the war of Kurukshetra would have taken place anyway, since it was designed in the Lord's scheme of things. Moreover this was planned by the Lord way before Arjun was even born. And Arjun was born with this end in mind. Hence, Arjun should not think of himself as the one who is responsible for the battle of Kurukshetra, as it was bound to happen anyway.

In verses 30 and 34 , the Lord shows the way in which one's prescribed duties could be performed. One should work with no claims to proprietorship and freeing oneself from lethargy and procrastination. As has been stated before, if a person succumbs to attachment and aversion pertaining to the senses and their objects, then that person will always be subjected to a see-saw swing of emotions between elation and despair, between hope and distress. Such swings of emotions will act as stumbling blocks on the path of self-realisation, and the true worth of the person will always remain unrealised.

Text 35– 'It is far better to discharge one's prescribed duties, though faultily, than another's duty perfectly. Destruction in the course of performing one's own duty is better than engaging in another's duties, for to follow another's path is dangerous'.

In this verse, the Lord explains the virtue of performing one own's prescribed duties only, although it may be performed faultity, than to discharge duties that are not one's own. Even in an organisation ,everyone is involved in performing their specific duties. If a person fails to perform his own duties, and starts performing other's duties, the resultant chaos and confusion can well be imagined. Hence, this instruction of the Lord is a lesson in sound management.

Text 36– Arjun asked–'By what is one impelled to sinful acts, even unwillingly, as it engaged by force?'

This question is pertinent, because we find ourselves drawn towards sinful situations, sometimes even without being aware of those situations. Similarly, in an organisation, many a man does not realise when he has been drawn towards unethical and sinful activities. And it is very rarely that realisation dawns upon the person in time for him to save himself from such unethical and sinful activities.

Text 37– 'The Supreme Personality of Godhead said: It is lust only, Arjun, which is born of contact with the material mode of passion, and later transformed into wrath, and which is the all-devouring sinful enemy of this world'.

When lust is unsatisfied, it turns into wrath; wrath is transformed into illusion and illusion continues the material existence. Therefore, lust is the greatest enemy of the living entity. In an organisation, this lust takes the form of lust for money, for promotions which results in more power, positions, prestige and importance, and when this lust for money, power, position, prestige and importance does not get satisfied, then, it turns to wrath. This wrath then takes the form of anger, jealousy, bitterness, envy, passion, etc., which leads man to commit terrible and inhuman crimes against their own co-workers in the workplace.

Text 38– 'As fire is covered by smoke, as a mirror is covered by dust or as the embryo is covered by the womb, the living entity is similarly covered by different degree of this lust'.

Test 39– 'Thus the wise living entity's pure consciousness become covered by his eternal enemy in the form of lust, which is never satisfied and which burns like fire'.

Test 40– 'The senses, the mind and the intelligence are the sitting places of this lust. Through them lust covers the real knowledge of the living entity and bewilders him'.

Text 41– 'The working senses are superior to dull matter; mind is higher than the senses; intelligence is still higher than the mind; and he (the soul) is even higher than the intelligence'.

The Lord first explains how this lust is born, develops and slowly makes our mind its home. But the Lord also shows us the way out of the grip of this lust. And the way out is to exercise our intelligence and control the senses, which is the residence of this lust.

Chapter V (Karma Yoga: Action in Krishna consciousness), Chapter VI (Dhyana Yoga) and Chapter XVIII (Attaining the Supreme), contains messages which pertains to management of an organisation, as well as to worklife. These messages are as relevant today, as they were hundreds of years ago, to the modern business manager. Hence some of them are being produced here.

Chapter V Karma Yoga : Action in Krishna Consciousness

Text 2– The Personality of God head said : 'The renunciation of work and work in devotion are both good for liberation. But, of the two, work is devotional service is better than renunciation of work'.

Text 3– 'One who neither hates nor desires the fruits of his activities is known to be always renounced. Such a person, free from all dualities, easily overcomes material bondage and is completely liberated'.

Text 4– 'Only the ignorant speak of devotional service as being different from the analytical study of the material world. Those who are actually learned say that he who applies himself well to one of those paths, achieves the results of both'.

Text 5– 'One who knows that the position reached by means of analytical study can also be attained by devotional services and who therefore sees analytical study and devotional service to be on the same level, sees things as they are.'

Text 7– One who works in devotion, who is a pure soul and who controls his mind and senses is dear to everyone and everyone is dear to him. Though always working, such a man is never entangled'.

Text 20– 'A person who neither rejoices upon achieving something pleasant nor laments upon obtaining something unpleasant , who is self intelligent , who is unbewildered and who knows the science of God, is already situated in transcendence.'

Text 24– 'One whose happiness is within, who is active and rejoices within and whose aim is inward is actually the perfect mystic. He is liberated in the Supreme and ultimately he attains the Supreme'.

Text 26– 'Those who are free from anger and all material desires, who are 'self-realised', self-disciplined and constantly endeavouring for perfection, are assured of liberation in the Supreme in the very near future.'

Chapter VI Dhyana-Yoga

Text 5– 'One must deliver himself with the help of his mind, and not degrade himself. The mind is the friend of the conditioned soul and his enemy as well'.

Text 6– 'For him who has conquered the mind, the mind is the best of friends, but for one who has failed to do so, his mind will remain the greatest enemy'.

Text 7– 'A person is considered still further advanced when he regards honest well wishers affectionate benefactors, the neutral mediators, the envious, friends and enemies, the pious and sinners all with an equal mind'.

Text 16– 'There is no possibility of one's becoming a yogi, if one eats too much or too little, sleeps too much or does not sleep enough.

Text 17– 'He who is regulated in his habits of eating, sleeping, recreation and work can mitigate all material pains by practising the yoga system'.

Text 30– 'For one who sees Me everywhere and sees everything in Me, I am never lost, nor is he ever lost to Me'.

Text 36– 'For one whose mind is unbridled, self-realisation is difficult work. But he whose mind is controlled and who strives by appropriate means is assured of success. That is My opinion'.

Chapter XVIII Attaining the Supreme

Text 5– 'Acts of sacrifice, charity and penance are not to be given give up; they must be performed. Indeed sacrifice, charity and penace purify even the great souls.'

Text 6– 'All these activities should be performed without attachment or any expectation of result. They should be performed as a matter of duty. That is my final opinion'.

Text 7– 'Prescribed duties should never be renounced. If one gives up his prescribed duties because of illusion, such renunciation is said to be in the mode of ignorance'.

Text 8– 'Anybody who gives up prescribed duties as troublesome or out of fear or bodily discomfort is said to have renounced in the mode of passion'.

Text 9– "O 'Arjun, when one performs his prescribed duty only because it ought to be done and renounces all material association and all attachment to the fruit, his renounciation is said to be in the mode of goodness'.

Text 10– 'The intelligence renouncer situated in the mode of goodness, neither hateful of inauspicious work nor attached to auspicious work, has no doubts about work'.

Text 11– 'It is indeed impossible for an embodied being to give up all activities. But he who renounces the fruits of action is called one who has truly renounced'.

Text 18– Knowledge, the object of knowledge and the knower are the three factors that motivate action–the senses, the work and the doer the three constituents of action'.

Text 23– 'That action which is regulated and which is performed without attachment, without love or hatred and without desire for fruitive results is said to be in the mode of goodness'.

Text 24– 'But action performed with great effort by one seeking to gratify his desires and enacted from a sense of false ego, is called action in the mode of passion'.

Text 25– That action performed in allusion, in disregard of spiritual injunctions and without concern for future bondage or for violence or distress caused to others is said to be in the mode of ignorance'.

Text 26– 'One who performs his duty without association with the modes of material nature, without false ego, with great determination and enthusiasm and without wavering in success or failure is said to be a worker in the mode of goodness'.

Text 27– 'The worker who is attached to work and the fruits of work desiring to enjoy those fruits and who is greedy, always envious, impure and moved by joy and sorrow, is said to be in the mode of passion'.

Text 28– 'The worker who is always engaged in work against the injunction of the scripture, who is materialistic, obstinate, cheating, and expert in insulting others and who is lazy, always morose and procrastinating is said to be a worker in the mod e of ignorance'.

Text 35– 'That determination which cannot go beyond dreaming, fearfulness, lamentation, moroseness, and illusion-such intelligence determination, O Son of Partha, is in the mode of darkness'.

Text 39– 'And that happiness which is blind to self-realisation, which is delusion from beginning to end and which arises from sleep, laziness and illusion is said to be of the nature of ignorance'.

Text 49– 'One who is self-controlled and unattached and who disregards all material enjoyments can obtain, by practice of renunciation, the highest perfect stage of freedom from reaction'.

Text 56– 'Though engaged in all kinds of activities, My pure devotee, under My protection, reaches the eternal and imperishable abode by My grace'.

Text 57– 'In all activities, just depend upon Me and work always under My protection. In such devotional service, be fully conscious of Me'.

Text 58– 'If you become conscious of Me, you will pass over all the obstacles of conditioned life by My grace. If, however, you do not work in such consciousness but act through false ego, not hearing Me, you will be lost'.

Text 61– 'The Supreme Lord is situated in everyone's heart, O Arjun, and is directing the wanderings of all living entities, who are seated as on a machine, made of the material energy'.

Text 70– 'And I declare that he who studies this sacred conversation of ours, worships Me by his intelligence'.

Text 78– 'Whenever there is Krishna, the master of all mystics, and whenever there is Arjun, the supreme archer, there will also be certainly, opulence, victory, extraordinary power and morality'.

End of the Bhagawad Gita

Conclusion: The Bhagawad Gita contains many messages for the management of an organisation as well as for improving the quality of worklife, which are as relevant today as they were thousands of years ago. Many of its verses are directly significant for the modern manager who may be confused about his direction, and struggling to find an answer to ethical/dilemmas.

The three attributes of Ask (A- Attitude, S - Skills, K - Knowledge) have assumed crucial significance in the functioning and the efficiency of organisations. However even with the abundance of knowledge and skills readily available to any organisation today, these are no good until and unless they are backed by the right attitudes. Senses may be controlled with effort, but attitudes are more difficult to change, since they are fashioned from one's childhood and background, and are reinforced in adult life by one's past experiences.

The Lord reiterates that work or karma is the driving force of life, and this work has to be ethical. To live, to exist, to survive, work is a necessary prerequisite. The Lord says 'Those who do not work, do not even have a present, leave alone a future'. What good is a life which has never striven towards a worthy moral goal? However, a distinction has to be made between 'ethical' work, work which is useless and work which is downright immoral. The overriding consideration of our work should be for the larger good of mankind and not for sense gratification only, or for short term personal benefits. We can create our own heaven or hell, here on earth itself, through our own actions. When we strive for a lofty goal, which is an upright and moral one as well, we are filled with a sense of heavenly bliss, which itself is God.

In different verses, the Lord stresses that the work of man must strive to form and find manifestations of goodliness in whatever form or shape one finds it in. Only then, will one be able to bring about welfare in the organisation, directly of indirectly; immediately or ultimately. Even with all the constraints of organisational life, and the pressures of business life, managers should strive devotedly to conduct their business activities ethically, whatever be the end result. This will promote harmony and synthesis in the organisation. Managers who resort to unethical means to grab immediate results are successful only for a very short while. The rolling wheels of time, make them and their organisations insignificant in a very short span of time.

To exist in the marketplace, and to do good for society, necessitates an organisation to have a Mission Statement that spells out what it attempts to achieve - its vision, mission and its value system. This Mission Statement ranges over time and visualises all the good that the organisation strives to do, all the social obligations it attempts to fulfill, all the welfare commitments it resolves to meet. Many organisations are not capable of surviving in the marketplace because their goals are myopic, their mission short-lived. The Japanese Consumer Electronics giant Mitsubishi has spelt out a 500 year Mission Statement. The organisation will undergo great changes within these 500 years, its activities will change course, its existing products will become obsolete and new products will be launched to replace them, its management and employees will leave and die, but its mission will remain unchanged and true, over time. What sterling qualities of moral values, ethics, genuine consumer concern and an insatiable quest for excellence and perfection must have gone into designing this Mission Statement for a 500 year long period!

The Lord has adviced in the Bhagawad Gita, that one is born into this life only to play his part, as has been designed for him, within his role ; hence one must perform his prescribed duties with utmost devotion, sincerity and humility. The Lord further advises one to perform one's prescribed duties, even if faultily, than to perform someone else's duties perfectly. Before one acts, there is some impetus, which is called inspiration. Then work takes the form of action. First one has to undergo the psychological processes of thinking, feeling and willing and that is called impetus. When the inspiration is there and the worker is there, then actual activity takes place by the help of the senses, including the mind, which is the centre of all the senses. The sum total of all the constituents of an activity are called the accumulation of work.

God resides in whatever is excellent; God is found in whatever is perfection. Those organisations which steadfastly strive for excellence in quality, in service and in genuine consumer concern, are examples of moving towards God. Ethics is not concerned only with the end, ethics affects the means as well. The concepts of 'Total Quality Management', 'Zero -Defect Products', 'Consumer's Delight', Family Organisation'; are actually tools to achieve excellence and thereby God. These are ethical techniques in business conduct. Backed by the right attitude, i.e., to provide consumers and all concerned with the organisation, with the best possible, and not just to make profits or win marketplace wars, is what takes us nearer to God. This is essence of work which the Lord imparts to eagerly listening Arjun, in the Bhagawad Gita.

> "When doubts haunt me, when disappointments stare me in the face and I see not one ray of hope on the horizon, I turn to Bhagawad Gita and find a verse to comfort me; and I immediately begin to smile in the midst of overwhelming sorrow. Those who meditate on the Gita will derive fresh joy and new meanings from it everyday"
>
> – Mohandas Karmachand Gandhi.

Source : 'Bhagawad Gita As It is', Bhaktivedanta Book Trust, by His Divine Grace A.C. Bhaktivedanta Swami Prabhupada, 1995)

Summery of the Chapter in Brief

* India has always been borrowing management styles and systems from foreign lands, instead of developing her own management styles in consonance with her own cultural ethos; and drawing from her rich heritage and tradition as well as her ancient value-based culture.
* Indian philosophy regards work as worship, and the customers as God Himself. Serving the customer is equated with serving God.
* Organisations which have ignored the Indian philosophy of work, have only achieved external development at the cost of internal growth and inner peace.
* In Indian philosophy, the Individual is supreme. If the individual is good, the world is good.
* In Indian philosophy, human capacity is much more important than Plant capacity, Quality of Mind and Heart is much more important than Quality Circles, and modernisation of man is more important than modernisation of machineries.
* Indian tradition and heritage, its culture and philosophy, its ethos and values are a treasure house, where the richest and the rarest of gems are stored.
* 'It is already becoming clear that a chapter which had a Western Beginning in business management, will have to have an Indian Ending, when the world adopts rich thoughts of Indian ethos and wisdom, if it is not to end in the self- destruction of the human race' –Arnold Toynbee.
* Indian Ethos for the worklife – Man's unique inner resource; Holistic Relationship between man and nature; Co-operation with each other; Self-Management; Yoga and meditation; Dharma; the spirit of renunciation.
* Indian values for the workplace: The importance of relationship in the workplace; Respect for Elders; Respect for Hierarchy and Status; Need for Security; Simple Living & High Thinking ; The Karta; Internal Orientation; Importance of wisdom; Balance & Moderation; Rights and Duties.
* Quality of living is based on material possessions and the external aspect of life. Quality of life, is based on inner happiness and satisfaction, and are based on one's philosophy and values.
* Quality of Worklife is more often a mental attitude; the inner satisfaction of having done one's work with the best of one's ability and capacity.
* Quality of worklife depends on the inner environment–on the integrated inner structure of the worker.
* The Bhagawad Gita, a conversation between the Lord and His much beloved friend Arjun, contains many lessons on sound management, that is as relevant today as it was when it took place, thousands of years ago.

Expected Questions

1. Discuss the Indian management styles and systems in consonance with her own cultural ethos.

2. Discuss the salient features of Indian philosophy and their relevance in managing a business organisation.
3. What is Quality of worklife ? Explain with an Indian perspective.
4. Discuss the relationship between ethics and worklife in Indian philosophy .
5. Examine the message of the Bhagawad Gita in today's organisational context.

Chapter 3

Attitudes, Beliefs, & Life Positions

3.1 Concept of Attitudes

Attitudes are pre-disposed, evaluative feelings of people about objects, people or events. Attitudes express either favourable or unfavourable feelings about something. They are evaluative statements and express one's way of thinking. Attitudes are formed right from our childhood experiences, our background, our learning situations, and are reinforced in adult life. On the other hand, perception is the process of becoming aware of situations and interpreting our sensory impressions, in order to give meaning to our environment.

To initiate the process of perception, firstly, we must have an external environment. This is easy, because we always have an external environment, anyway. Secondly, our senses must receive some message (or inputs) from the external environment. We have five sense organs, but apart from them, we also have our intuition, which is known as the sixth sense organ (or the 6th sense). All of us are continuously receiving messages through our sense organs, unless one is handicapped or has a disability like being blind, dumb or deaf . After receiving these messages from the sense organs, the brain organises and interprets them to give meaning to them according to our frame of reference.

For example, we 'see' a friend on the road, and 'Call Out' (speak) a greeting. But the friend does not acknowledge the greeting, i.e., we do not 'hear' him answering us, or 'see' him smile to us in return. According to our frame of reference (of course our mood at that time, how good a friend he is, how far was the distance, between us, the distractions on the road, etc.; all play a part, we may 'perceive' any one of the followings:

1. The friend is trying to ignore us.
2. He did not 'see' us or 'hear' our greeting.
3. He does not want to talk to us.
4. He is busy and is in a hurry.
5. He is upset and did not see us.
6. He is worried and has other things on his mind.
7. He is preoccupied with other thoughts.
8. He did not recognise us.
9. He wants to break our friendship
10. Some thing on the road distracted him.

Which of these perceptions we 'select' depends upon our attitude to friendship, friends and life in general. Individuals behave in a given manner, based not on the way their external environment actually is, but on what they 'see' or 'believe' it to be. Because individuals act on their interpretation of reality, rather than on reality itself, it is clear that perception is a critical determinant or our dependent variable.

Consider the following situations--

1. Employees perceive the work situation to be demotivating, even when management has just spent a huge amount of money trying to improve it.
2. Management of a company considers paying bribes to secure a contract as competitive strategy, because corruption is a part of the Indian system.
3. Employees consider the organisation in which they work as ethical or unethical based on their own perceptions and attitudes.

Basically, most of what a person perceives, or 'believes to be true', is based on the attitudes of the person concerned. Hence, perception and attitudes are personalised, individual beliefs and feelings, and it is very difficult to change them through advice and discussions. It is the person concerned who has to feel that what he believed to be true, is in fact, not true at all, and only a misrepresentation of reality.

Attitudes governing ethical behaviour

Human behaviour, to a large extent, is based on 'what a person perceives' rather than on 'what is reality'. People behave according to what they perceive as appropriate for the situation, and this perception is based on what their attitude is towards that specific situation or event.

A person's attitudes develop right from his childhood, and arise mainly from experiences and conditioned learning, and partly from one's value system. These attitudes are developed over a period of time, and they become fairly rigid by the time the person becomes an adult. Attitudes are dictated by the family one belongs to, one's social environment, their experiences and their learning examples. Our attitudes need to be objectively understood and analysed, because they are the foundation of what we consider worthwhile to achieve in life. For example, a person who perceives money and wealth to be of great value and his attitude towards them is that they are to be achieved at any cost, will leave no stone unturned to make money and wealth. He may even go through life equating money with happiness, and success with amassing wealth. For him, money and wealth may be ends in themselves, and no means too difficult or too unethical, to achieve them. Faulty attitudes, developed through faulty programming of the mind results in our attributing distorted meaning to success, power, achievement and happiness. And when we strive to meet our distorted standards of success, achievement and happiness, we find ourselves inadequate, helpless and unable to meet our standards, and hence we resort to unethical ways and means to achieve them.

One of the commonest distortion of the meaning of happiness and success is the firm conclusion by many people all over the world, that material possessions, money and power are the factors that bring in happiness, and is the measure of one's success as a person. Having formed this attitude from childhood, such people spend most of their lives trying to acquire them. Hence, we find children choosing careers which are more 'paying', employees seeking positions which are more 'lucrative', and managers striving for placements which are more 'powerful'. But just how much of material possessions, money and power would

would result in a man's happiness cannot be ascertained, and a person finds that the amount he has amassed is not enough, because they have not yet resulted in his happiness. So he feels that he would be happy if he collects some more. But this too does not result in the happiness that he is looking for. So he thinks that more is not enough, and wants yet some more. The person keeps on chasing after money and wealth in his pursuit of happiness and yet he finds that what he has collected does not result in happiness. In his frenzy, he does not stop to think that maybe it is his chase for money and wealth, ironically, which is making happiness elude him. Thus, the chase goes on and on in life, the person seeing his goal receeding even as he collects more and more, through fair means or foul. Ultimately, in the process, instead of getting the happiness he seeks, he ends up pulling himself and his near and dear ones, into the pit of frustration, disappointment and the resultant misery. Ironically it is because he sought happiness, by chasing after money and wealth, that happiness continued to elude him throughout his life.

When a person forms an attitude that material possessions, money and power are to be achieved anyhow in life, and that these are inevitable for successful living, then the person is forming an attitude only about the end he seeks to achieve. The means to acquire this end is never taken into consideration. Hence though the end is given an exaggerated value, the means are considered to be of negligible value. Thus, the person forms an attitude that he requires money and power for his happiness in life, but does not consider the means he would utilise to secure this end. The means of such acquisitions become unimportant later on in life. And whether it is in business or in public life, the result of such an attitude is widespread unethical practices in general and corrupt activities in particular.

Wrong Attitudes resulting in unethical behaviour

1. To achieve success in life, one has to be manipulative, calculative and manoeuvring.
2. If I have not achieved material success and do not belong to the 'right' social circles, then I have not achieved true success in life.
3. If I have acquired wealth and other possessions, it is important to exhibit them, so that I have something to show for my success.
4. If I want to come up in life, I must be careful to see that my colleagues do not look too good in the eyes of my boss.
5. Envy, Jealousy and competition in worklife is normal and must necessarily exist in every organisation which wants to succeed.
6. Getting promoted is basically a matter of scheming and making strategies and then being lucky.
7. It is only wishful thinking to believe that I can influence what happens in my life.
8. Making a lot of money is largely a matter of getting the right breaks in life.
9. Mortality and ethics must be bent at times to be successful in business.
10. Anyone who thinks that he can trust others in business, is asking for trouble.
11. The best way to handle people is to tell them what they want to hear and what pleases them.
12. It is difficult to get ahead in life without cutting corners here and there.
13. It is safest to assume that all people have a vicious streak in them and it will come out sometimes.

14. If I teach my subordinates all I know, one day, one of them might replace me.
15. I should go out of my way to cultivate friendship with powerful and influential people.
16. There is nothing wrong in taking credit for something I have not done in the organisation, if it furthers my cause.
17. In order to get ahead in life, it is necessary to keep self-interest above the interests of the organisation.
18. If my life does not work out the way I have planned it, will be devasting.
19. The more I achieve, the better person I become.
20. I must stay at the right side of my boss, no matter what happens or how he behaves.

Right Attitudes resulting in ethical behaviour

1. My success and happiness in life is not dependent on how much wealth I amass.
2. I must follow the dictates of my conscience and be at peace with myself under all circumstances.
3. My worth as a person is not dependent on how much I achieve in life.
4. I prefer my identy to come from my professional expertise, and all the good I do, than from my designation or the post I hold.
5. Even if I thought it would help my career, I would refuse a hatchman assignment.
6. One should take action only when one is sure that it is ethically correct.
7. There is really no necessity for me to take credit for someone else's work.
8. There is no need for me to malign the capabilities of my competitor. Let his or her record speak for itself.
9. I have no right to use my subordinate or colleagues to further my career.
10. I do not need to use gossip for personal advantage, either in my professional life or in my personal life.
11. Most people are basically good and dependable and can be mostly trusted.
12. When you ask someone to do something for you, it is best to give the real reason for it, than to give reasons that carry more weight in their eyes.
13. There is no excuse for doing something ethically wrong; everyone has other options.
14. Promotions are earned through hard work, perservance and fair-play.
15. A person's earning power is dependent on his or her expertise, ability and hard work.
16. The results that I have achieved are all due to my own efforts; luck has nothing to do with it.
17. I am the master of my own fate, along with God's guidance.
18. I am personally responsible for my own actions-whether they are ethical or unethical.

19. My worth as a person does not fluctuate with the amount of wealth I acquire.
20. To me, means are as important as ends, since it is impossible to achieve a worthy goal with unethical means. Unethical means can get only unethical ends.

It is essential, and very important, to conduct periodical self-analysis, to discover what out attitudes are, how they have been formed, how they govern the way we see things and how we behave based on how we see things. How we 'see' a situation, how we perceive it, governs the way we behave. Hence, how we see has to change if we want to change our behaviour. This would mean that we have to change how we perceive things. If we correct our perception, we shall be able to correct out attitudes. It is more difficult to change our attitudes than to change our perception. Since perception is dependent on out sensory impressions, we are able to change how we 'see' things. But attitudes are programmed from our childhood and by the time we become adults, they have a firm hold on us. Hence, in order to change our distorted attitudes, we shall have to first change our perceptions. With the change in perception, slowly and gradually, but finally and ultimately, our attitudes would also change.

3.2 Beliefs & Ethical Behaviour

One's beliefs are the foundations of one's value system. Beliefs are ideas or principles that people hold dear and give ordinance to. Most people and organisations believe in ethical values like integrity, honesty, justice, modesty, industry, simplicity, excellence, courage, patience, etc. These are called **Character Ethics**, meaning that these are basic principles of effective living, and these are internal qualities qualifying the inner goodness of man, arising out of their character rather than out of their external personality. People can achieve true success and genuine happiness only when they integrate these beliefs into their basic character.

Many people put in genuine efforts to improve their Personality. This is wonderful and greatly needed in a competitive and result-oriented world. However, at the same time, not enough people put in enough effort to improve their character or on character building. They would rather polish their exterior rather than build their interior. This is because they feel that the exterior can be seen by all, whereas the interior cannot be seen and hence is of no use. They could not be more far away from the truth. It is the interior that is of more lasting value and more fundamental. Books like 'Win Friends in 30 minutes', 'Influence People to do what you want them to do', 'Win over the Boss', are only an attempt at manipulation and getting people to do what you want them to do. Even if it means that they do not want to do it, or worse still, making them do it unconsciously without them being aware of what they are doing. Such manipulative tactics do not succeed, and hardly ever produce positive results. Many other books are only attempt to change the cover of a person, without changing the core values and beliefs of the person. These techniques rarely ever change the person to make him a better human being. They may succeed in changing the person only superficially, while the human inside, as the person he is, remains as selfish or as dishonest as ever. These techniques end up being a sort of polish to give a shine to the people-oriented skills of the person at the best; and just stop at being manipulations at the worst.

If a person uses these techniques and tactics to get others to like him, or to influence others, then he is not being guided by ethical beliefs. Soon people will discover the insincerities in him, and all his techniques, even if he used them with the best of intentions, will be perceived as manipulations. Intentions are no good if the basic moral beliefs are missing. People are not judged by intentions, they are judged by their actions-and actions or behaviour is guided by one's beliefs. **What we are communicates more than what we say or do.**

If people have internalised wrong beliefs, then however much they use effective human relations techniques, they would not be able to create genuine human concern, and sooner or later, the challenges of life will cause true motives to surface. Techniques and strategies are only means to achieve an end. However, if your destination is wrong, using techniques and strategies will only make you reach the wrong place sooner. On the other hand, if your character is strong, but you have some personality flaw, like say, lack of communication skill, even if you face problems with people while dealing with them, still people will believe in your primary goodness, and will learn to trust you for what you are, and not for what you say or do not say. When your character is strong, but your personality is weak, then it is like going in the right direction, but without the help of techniques and strategies. Your pace will be slow, others on the same road will leave you far behind, but at least, one day you will reach your destination. All these depend on what kind of a person you are on the inside. Like Emerson once said, "What you are shouts so loudly in my ears, that I cannot hear what you say."

Consider the following verse–

"You should build a better world," God said;
I questioned, "How? The world is such a wondrous place,
so complicated now,
And I so small and useless man,
There's nothing I can do."
But God, all wise and kind replied,
"Just build a better you."
Beliefs may be–'I am only one, yet I am one.
I can't do everything, yet I CAN do something.
What I can do, I WILL do.'

Beliefs of Mahatma Gandhi

A principle is a principle and in no case can it be watered down because of our incapacity to live it in practice.

It is beneath human dignity to lose one's individuality and become a mere cog in the machine.

Government of the people, by the people and for the people, cannot be conducted at the bidding of one man.

Truth resides in every human heart, and one has to search for it there; and be guided by truth as one sees it. But one has no right to coerce others to act according to his views of the truth.

A person cannot do right in one department of life, whilst he is occupied in doing wrong in another. Life is one individual whole.

Religions are different roads converging upon the same point. What does it matter that we take different roads so long as we reach the same goal?

Beliefs of John D. Rockerfeller, Jr.

I believe that every right implies a responsibility; every opportunity an obligation; every possession, a duty.

I believe that the world owes no man a living, but that it owes every many an opportunity to make a living.

I believe that thrift is essential to well-ordered living and that economy is a prime requisite of a sound financial structure; whether in government, business or personal affairs.

I believe in the sacredness of a promise; that character-not wealth or power-is of supreme worth.

I believe that the rendering of useful service is the common duty of mankind, and that only in the purifying of sacrifices is the dross of selfishness consumed, and the greatness of the human soul set free.

3.3 Life Positions & Ethical Behaviour

All human beings begin life at birth, being totally dependent on others-physically, emotionally and financially. We are nurtured and sustained by others and it is this nurturing that keep us alive and let us grow into adulthood.

Then gradually as we grow up, first from infancy to childhood, then into adolescence and finally into adulthood, we become more able to take care of ourselves and we become more independent-physically, emotionally, mentally and finally financially. Thus, we become inner-directed and self-reliant.

At a later stage, for example, when we enter into worklife or have a family of our own, we realise that our basic nature is of interdependence. We cannot achieve anything much alone. We need to work in teams, we must be part of a group, we must start and sustain relationships with others. Thus we enter the state of Interdependency. An interdependent person is still self-reliant and capable, but takes-and-gives himself meaningfully from and to others.

At the stage of dependency, we take and follow the values, beliefs and principles of our seniors, whether they are our parents, our grand-parents, our older siblings or an aunt or uncle who brought us up. As we grow up and become intellectually independent, and finally enter the state of interdependency, we being to question some of the values, ethics and principles learnt from our parents and seniors and reinforce them with our own experience from life. Thus, we evaluate the values and beliefs learnt in our childhood, supplement them with our own unique experience, and form our own conclusions. Thus, is formed our own unique value system, our own beliefs and our own moral standard, which will later dictate all our actions and govern our behaviour.

Thomas A. Harris in his book, 'I'm OK-You're OK' has described Eric Berne's Transactional Analysis, wherein all individuals are known to operate from three ego states. The first ego state which is developed in a tiny individual from birth to the age of 5 years is called the Child Ego State. Herein the individual records his own internal feelings and his response to external events. Since this ego state is based mostly on the individual's feelings, all emotions are governed by this ego state. Thus, feelings like curiosity, excitement, happiness, joy, sadness, impulsiveness, etc. originate from the Child ego state. Consequently, laughter, crying, tantrums, shouting, yelling, whispering, etc. are said to be governed by this ego state.

The second ego state to develop is the Parent Ego State. In this state, the child becomes old enough to understand and obey the instructions of the parents and seniors. Hence, in this stage, the child imbibes all the rules and regulations, philosophies, rituals, beliefs, values, ethics of the family he or she is born into without questioning or analysing what he or she is

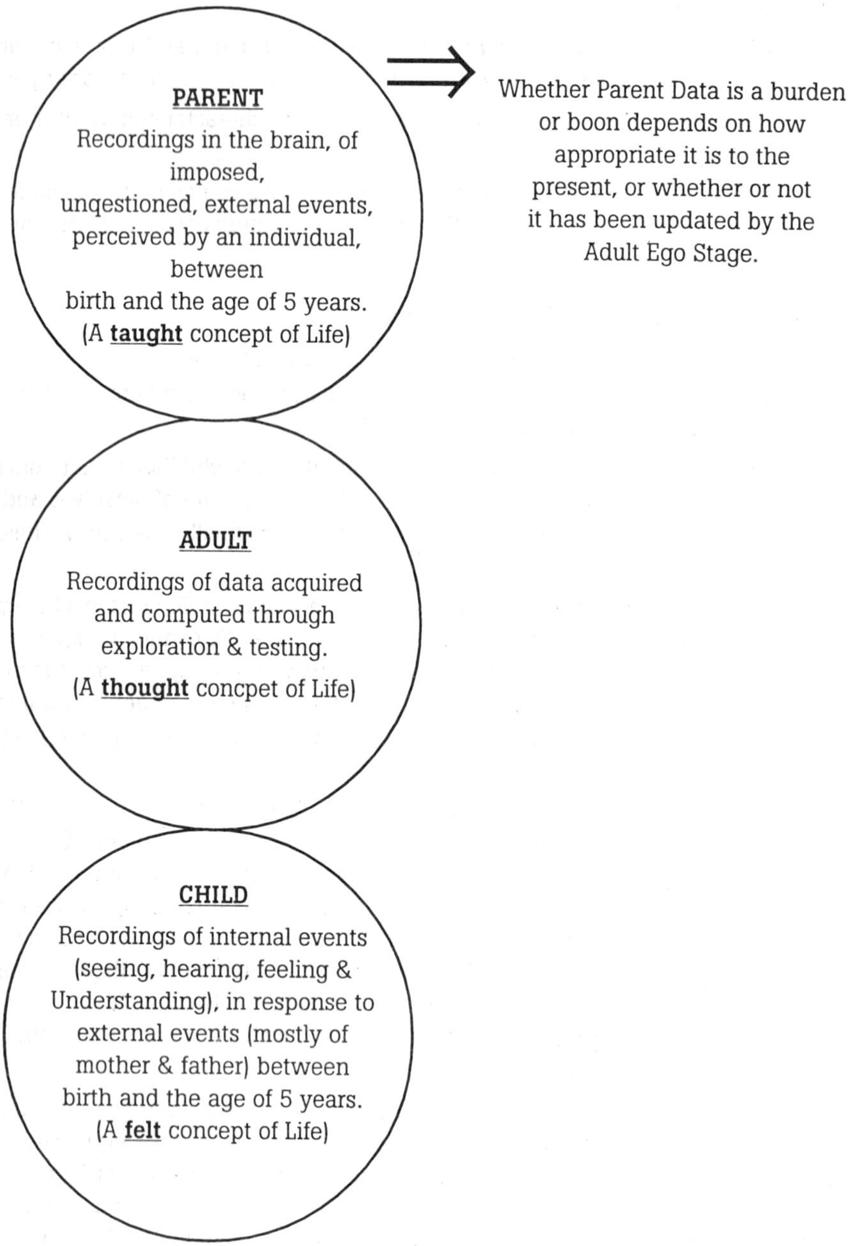

Source—Thomas A. Harris, 'I'm OK– You're OK–, Sterling Paperbacks, New Delhi, 1989.

learning. He or she merely learns whatever is taught, and this learning, without editing, becomes a powerful influence throughout life.

When the child grows up and starts questioning, reasoning and analysing most of what he has learnt during childhood, than another ego state, called the Adult Ego State is born. It is through this ego state that a person learns to form his own opinion through questioning the validity of the learnt concepts. Thus, all forms of logic, analysis, reasoning and questioning arises from the Adult Ego State. This ego state puts a balance between the Child ego state on one hand, and the Parent ego state, on the other. It is only when a person operates through his Adult ego state, that the person is said to be psychologically nature.

This Parent-Adult-Child Ego states help us to easily explain the nature of the value system in each individual. When the individual is in the Child Ego State, it has only the I-Me-Mine attitude to life. What his parents and seniors teach him constitutes his Parent Ego State. If the value system of the family he is born into is very high, and parents and seniors are very strict about ethical norms, then the individual also learns to imbibe such value system within himself. His upbringing and experiences in childhood helps him to mould his attitudes towards life. Thus, the moral standards of the family a person is born into plays an important role in setting the moral standard, and later the ethical behaviour of the person and what he finds morally correct. However, as soon as the Adult Ego State is developed, the person is able to analyse and think things over for himself, and he becomes capable of forming his own judgements. Thus, as soon as the person is able to reason and analyse things for himself, i.e., with the development of the Adult Ego States, the person forms his own unique set of beliefs, and his own moral standards develop, coinciding with, or completely different from that of the family. That is the reason why even with several siblings belongings to the same family, each has his own moral standards and sense of ethics, or why one out of several siblings, has a completely different moral standard from that of his family. Hence, we may find that although a man was born into a morally loose and ethically weak family, he himself has a very strong and upright moral character. This situation can also be reversed. A person belonging to a morally upright family may possess very weak ethical standards of behaviour. He may have experienced early in life that it pays to tell lies, cheat and commit unethical acts. These experiences may have become reinforced in adult life, and so the person internalises these values into his value system and acts them out throughout his life, until and unless something happens to reverse these beliefs.

Throughout the ages, people have been known to possess a duel nature. On one hand, he can be kind, on the other, he can commit such gruesome crimes as can only be imagined, if the need arises. If he is capable of loving, he is also capable of hating (sometimes even the same person, but at different times). He can be ethical in some areas, at the same time, he can be unethical, in others. Hence human nature is always at conflict- the baser animal instincts with the higher humane qualities. And man behaves ethically, or unethically, sometimes also on impulse, depending upon which side of his nature has the upperhand at that moment. As Somerset Maugham had said–

> 'There are times when I look over the various parts of my character with perplexity. I recognise that I am made up of several persons and that the person that at the moment has the upper hand will inevitably give place to another. But which is the real me? All of them or none?'

None-the-less, man's ethical or unethical conduct is not expressed always as an impulse of the moment, but it generally follows a certain set pattern based on his values system, which is again based on his family background, his upbringing, and his life experiences. For example, if his family members never objected of his telling lies in his childhood, but looked on indulgently at his habit of telling lies, or even passed it off as a joke, then his Parent Ego State, will record that telling lies is not such an objectionable habit. Later on in life, he may find out that telling lies pays off in school and saves him from many a tricky situation, his belief that telling lies is OK gets reinforced, and he may think of it as a part of daily living, and may consider it as smartness as well. Thus, telling lies become a part of his nature, a **well in-grained** habit, and he not only does not consider falsehood as unethical, but he may even boast of the times he escaped unscathed with his lies, and may even come to except and accept falsehood from others. On the other hand, there were people like Mahatma Gandhi for whom falsehood was one of the greatest sins possible, and his belief that a person's whole life must be spent in the pursuit of truth. For him, truth was everything. He saw truth as beauty-Satyam Shivam Sundaram. For him, truth was the means and the end as well. Thus, this illustrates that different people give different worth to different qualities and values. Moses valued Justice above everything. Plato valued Wisdon, Jesus Christ valued Love, whereas Gandhi valued Truth.

The 4-Life Positions

Thomas A. Harris, in his classic book 'I'm OK - You're OK', has described four life positions of individuals. These 4 possible life positions, held with respect to oneself and others, also help us to describe the attitudes and beliefs, and consequently the ethical behaviour with each life position.

Life Position 1- 'I'm not OK - You're OK'

In this life position, the person feels that he is not alright, he considers himself inadequate and inferior in some way, while the rest of the world (i.e. his immediate world could be his family members and his workplace) is alright. This is the universal position of early childhood, when the infant finds that he is dependent on others for everything (including love and affection), and he cannot do anything himself. This is the logical conclusion from the situation of birth and infancy. Everybody has a **NOT OK** Child in himself- the permanent recording of having been a child. In this position, the person feels at the mercy of others. He feels a great need for stroking (i.e., love and affection in early childhood, and recognition and praise in later childhood), which is the psychological version of the early physical stroking. The Adult in this position thinks-'What must I do to gain other's strokes or their approval?'

Beliefs of this position

1. I am inferior to others in some way.
2. My self-esteem is totally dependent on my appraisal by others.
3. I am too insignificant to challenge, question or rebel against other's judgement of me.
4. I must exist at the mercy of others.
5. My identity comes from others-those who like me.
6. It will be terrible if others do not like me.

Attitudes of this Life-Position

1. I must win the approval and liking of my superiors, colleagues and subordinates, to stay on in this organisation.
2. I must 'make' everyone feel that I am a pleasant and friendly person, and must go out of my way to win them over.
3. It will be simply awful if my boss, my colleagues or my subordinates do not like me.
4. Disapproval by anyone I meet means that he or she hates me.
5. If I want to come up in life, I must see that my colleagues do not look too good in the eyes of my boss.
6. The best way to handle people is to tell them what they want to hear, and what pleases them.
7. If I teach my subordinates all I know, one day, one of them might replace me.
8. I should go out of my way to cultivate friendship with powerful and influential people.
9. The more I achieve, the better person I am.
10. I must stay at the right side of my boss, no matter what happens or how he behaves.

Implications for Ethical Behaviour

People operating from this life position, suffer from a severe inferiority complex, and they break and bend all ethical rules just to be on the 'right' side of those who matter. They resort to manipulation and flattery to win the approval of others. They are insecure with their own positions and roles in the organisation and thus they resort to calculations and schemes to make themselves look good in the eyes of the boss, and their colleagues not too good. When they themselves become the boss or the manager, they would like to be surrounded by their own coterie of 'yes-man' who does everything at their bidding, just to make their ego feel good. Such bosses and mangers are terribly insecure, and hence they cannot give credit where it is due, and rather would try to keep all recognition to themselves. They are fearful of capable and intelligent subordinates, and may resort to underhand dealings and unethical tactics just to keep them down. When they feel they are being overshadowed, or that their positions in the organisation are being threatened by more capable and efficient people, then organisational ethics or personal ethic do not matter much to them. Since they operate from the position of **I'm NOT OK**, they will try everything in their power to hide the not-OK in themselves, while being fearful of the OK ness of others.

Life Position 2- I'm not OK - You're not Ok

People in this life position conclude quite early in life, in fact sometimes by the second year of life, that there is something wrong with both himself and the world. In adult life, a person operating from this life position stops developing, since one of its primary functions- i.e., getting strokes- is thwarted. A person in this life position gives up hope. He simply gets through life, and ultimately may end up in a mental institution in a state of extreme withdrawal, with regressive behaviour which reflects a vague, archaic longing to get back to life as it was in the first year of his life, during which he received the only stroking (literally) he ever know.

Beliefs of this position

1. Both you and I are not alright, and there is something wrong with both of us.
2. Both you and I are helpless to change our positions.
3. What happens to you and me will happen, and no one can change their destiny.
4. There is no use trying to improve our situations.
5. This world is a lousy place to stay in.

Attitudes of this Life-Position

1. Envy, Jealousy and Competition in worklife is normal, and must necessarily exist in every organisation.
2. Getting promoted is basically a matter of being lucky.
3. It is only wishful thinking to believe that I can influence what happens in my life.
4. It is safest to assume that all people have a vicious treat in them, and it will come out sometimes.
5. Anyone who trusts others is asking for trouble.
6. Everybody's self-interest is more important to him than the interests of the organisation.
7. It is no good trying to do something good in the workplace, because ultimately the boss will take all the credit. All bosses do.
8. I am incompetent fool in the organisation, and my colleagues and the boss is no better.
9. Nothing good is going to happen in this organisation. People don't deserve it anyway.
10. What will happen, will happen.

Implications for Ethical Behaviour

People operating from this life - position have no faith in themselves or in others. This makes them extremely suspicious, and they view everything in life negatively. They put a lot of value on fate, luck or destiny, and thus put in no effort to better their positions in life. Being suspicious of others, they cannot trust anyone, not even those who come forward to help them. Since they operate from the position 'you're not OK', they feel even those who want to help them must have some evil motive for wanting to help. It is very difficult for such people to differentiate between right and wrong. Since they believe that all people are untrustworthy, evil and bad, they do not relate to anyone, and consequently become extremely withdrawn from life. It is very difficult for anyone to help them out of this position because whoever wants to help is also regarded as 'you're not OK'. They may inflict all sorts of harm to themselves as also to others without being aware of it, because they feel that they and the others are not worthliving.

Life Position 3 – I'm OK – You're not OK

A child who is brutalized long enough by the parents he initially felt were OK, will switch positions to this third and potentially criminal position: I'm OK – You're not OK. A battered child while he is healing experiences a sense of comfort alone, and by himself alone, and he senses that he will be alright if his oppressors leave him alone. He feels that he is alright by himself, it is only the others who are not alright.

Beliefs of this position

1. I am somehow better that you are.
2. You are the cause of any mess that I find myself in.
3. It is your fault that I ache and pain.
4. I am superior to you and you are inferior to me.
5. My actions are justified in whatever I do.
6. I can control people and situations, and bend them to my advantage.
7. None has right to question my behaviour.

Attitudes of this Life Position

1. To achieve success in life, I have to be manipulative, calculative and manoeuvring.
2. If I have acquired wealth and other possessions, I must exhibit them, so that others respect and fear me.
3. Morality and ethics do not pay any dividends in life.
4. It is difficult to get ahead in life without cutting corners here and there.
5. There is nothing wrong in taking credit for something I have not done if it furthers my cause.
6. In order to get ahead, it is necessary to keep self-interest above the interests of the organisation.
7. There are many fools in this world just waiting to be taken advantage of.
8. There is nothing wrong in taking advantage of foolish people who cannot look after themselves. They would take advantage of you too if you only allow them.
9. If you can take advantage of other, it only shows how smart you are.
10. Most people are basically foolish, corrupt, evil and bad.

Implications for Ethical Behaviour

The early history of many psychopaths reveal that they were subjected to gross physical abuse, and consequently they occupy this life position. When a child is battered in early life by adults who are superior and stronger than him, he is traumatised; but although he has experienced brutally, he has also experienced survival. Thus, as he grows older he begins to strike back. He knows that this is the only way to survive – to act tough and strike someone down before he can strike you down. He has seen toughness and knows how to be tough. He also has permission (in his Parent Ego State) to be tough and to be cruel, because he has seen adults being cruel when he was a child. So the permission to be cruel is recorded in his Parent Ego State. Hatred sustains him although he may learn to conceal it with a mask of measured politeness. He goes through life refusing to look inwards. He is unable to be objective about his own complicity in what happens to him. It is always 'their' fault. Incorrigible criminals occupy this position. They are persons without a conscience who are convinced that they are OK no matter what they do, and the total fault in every situation lies in others. The ultimate expression of this position is homicide, **felt** to be justifiable by the killer. The person operation from this position suffers from stroking deprivation. Such a person may develop a routine of 'yes-man' who praise and stroke him heavily. Yet he knows that they are not authentic and honest strokes, because he himself had set them up to produce his own source of stroking. The more they praise him, the more despicable they become, and more he holds them in contempt, until he finally rejects them all in favour of a new group of 'yes-man'

People operating from his life position will be a law unto themselves in the organisation. Careful not to break the law openly and not to flaunt rules publically, they will resort to all sorts of manipulations and office politics. They will have no qualms about taking advantage of others, or making scapegoats of their colleagues and subordinates in order to get their own way. They will always be power centres and make and break groups and teams.

Life Position 4 – I'm OK – You're OK'

The first three positions are made unconciously, quite early in life and by the third year of life, one of these positions become fixed in every person. This decision to choose one position is perhaps one of the first functions of he infant's Adult Ego State, and is based on emotion or impressions, without the benefit of external, modifying data. The 4th position, however, is a conscious and verbal decision. The first three positions are based on feelings- this 4th position is based on thought, faith and the wager of action. We do not drift into this new position - it is a decision we make to consciously accept this life position. Children can be helped early in life to find that they are OK by repeated exposure to situations in which they can prove to themselves, their own worth and the worth of others.

Beliefs of this position

1. I am a part of this world, and I have as much right to exist and develop here as anybody else.
2. There is mutual interdependence between me and the people I love and work with.
3. My job or work is only one part of my being, and I have a much higher integrated life beyond the workplace.
4. I have been sent to this world with a higher mission, and I must live out my life as worthy of my having existed here.
5. The purpose of my life, as of everybody else's, in this world is to see that we do as much good as possible during out stay here.
6. Mutual interdependence between man and man, between man and nature, and between nature and the animal kingdom is the rule, rather than the exception.

Attitudes of this position

1. My success and happiness in life is not dependent on how much wealth I amass, or an anybody else, but on myself.

2. I must follow the dictates of my conscience, and be at ease with myself under all circumstances.
3. My worth as a person is not dependent on how much I achieve in life.
4. One should take action only when one is sure it is ethically correct.
5. There is really no reason for me to take credit for someone else's work.
6. I have no right to use my subordinates or colleagues to further my career.
7. Most people are basically good and dependable.
8. There is no excuse for doing something ethically wrong.
9. I am the master of own fate.
10. My worth as a person does not fluctuate, it stays constant.

Implications for Ethical Behaviour

A person operating from this life position is basically at peace with himself and with the rest of the world. He envys nobody because he knows that he can achieve all he wants by means of his capability and hard work. He is not overlay bothered by what others think of him, because he knows that his true worth does not come from people's opinions, but from his own conduct and his inner goodness. Consequently, he has not 'incentive' for resorting to unethical behaviour. As far as possible, without surrendering his conscience, he tries to be on good terms with all persons. He does not compare needlessly with others, for he knows that comparing himself with others will only make him vain or bitter, for there will always be greater and lesser persons than himself. He tries to achieve his cherished ends through just means. As a result, such a person has very little reason to stoop to immoral conduct or ethical behaviour.

Conclusion

Thus, it stands to reason that a person's ethical behaviour at the workplace, and in life in general, is governed by what life position be or she operates from. If he operates from Position - 1 (I'm not OK - you're OK), he suffers from an Inferiority Complex, and his behaviour is governed by the complex. Consequently, he would be looking for opportunities to make himself look good in the eyes of those who matter, just to overcome his insecurities, and to win the approval of others. He would try to please everybody, and in so doing, he may not be aware when he has crossed the limit of ethical conduct and has started behaving unethically. If a person operates from Position - 2 (I'm not OK - You're no OK), he would be of a suspicious nature, eyeing everyone and everything with suspicion. Consequently he would consider the baser human qualities like envy, jealousy, anger, lust, passion to be quite normal and even acceptable. It will be difficult for him to trust anyone and all his behaviour would be governed by his suspicious nature. If a person operates from Position 3 (I'm OK - You're not OK), then he suffers from a massive Superiority Complex, and may also possess criminal tendencies. His behaviour is bound to be tough and even cruel, although he may be polite and well-mannered on the outside. No rule or value would be too sacred for him to violate. If he operates from Position - 4 (I'm OK - You're OK), then he would be a well-adjusted, ethically correct individually, who is conscious of his role in this world. His philosophy is to co-exist peacefully, with everyone else, each helping the other in times of need.

Reference : I'm OK - You're OK' ; Thomas A Harris, Sterling Paperback ; New Delhi.

Discussion Situation

Mr. I.K. Prasad is the Chief Engineer of the State Electricity Board, and Mr. Prasad has a reputation of being 'soft' on his employees, due to which, it was rumoured, many of his employees do not exactly stick to the rules and regulations of the organisation. When Mr. P. Kumar joined the Board as an young engineer, just after his engineering degree, he was appalled to see how many people casually broke the rules of the Board, and got away with it. Time and again, he had tried to impress upon Mr. Prasad to take disciplinary action, at least against the workmen and the staff, but to no avail. Mr. Prasad would just ignore his complaints, saying that he did not yet have enough experience to understand the implications of these things.

One day, Mr. Prasad and Mr. Kumar were travelling together long distance, on some official duty. Suddenly, Mr. Kumar happened to notice one of their truck drivers stopping at a point on the highway and taking up people into the truck, who were waiting near the roadside.

'That's Balwant, Sir, cried Mr. Kumar, 'he's picking up passengers from the roadside in his truck, and taking money from them'.

Mr. Prasad too turned around and spotted Balwant doing exactly what Mr. Kumar had noticed. Just at the same time, Balwant too turned around and spotted his Board's car with 'Chief Engineer' written in the car plates. But because of the white curtains in the car, he could not be sure whether the occupants in the car had noticed him or not.

'Stop the car immediately, driver', shouted Mr. Kumar, 'I say, stop immediately; we have to catch him red-handed'.

'No, keep going', said Mr. Prasad urgently to the driver, 'Pretend not to have seen him'.

'But, Sir - why ? We had a good chance to catch him red handed. We have known it since a long time that Balwant uses his truck to make a little money on the side', exclaimed Mr. Kumar, as their car sped away.

'Clam down Kumar, calm down', replied Mr. Prasad patting Kumar's knee. 'I too know that whenever Balwant has to transport goods long distance, he uses the return trip to pick up passengers from he roadside. I also know that you see it as going against the rules. I know it *is* against the rules. But think analytically. How much salary does Balwant get from the Board ? Even after 10 -12 years of service, his services have not yet been confirmed. He earns around Rs. 2,600/- per month. He has two children apart from his aged parents who live with him. Can anyone today support a six-member family on less than Rs 3,000/- per month ? It is not out of choice that Balwant, or anyone else for that matter, breaks rules. Would you or I not have been tempted to do just what Balwant had done, had we been in his place ? And how much do you think he earns from these passengers ? 100 rupees ? As you have seen, these passengers are all daily-wage labourers or poor people, too poor to even pay the bus fare, and waits for some like Balwant to give them a ride for a pittance. Moreover, what harm is Balwant really causing to the Board ? The truck would have anyway come empty in its return trip. It is not that Balwant is causing some additional expenses to the Board by his action. Just now you wanted to stop the car. Had I stopped the car to catch him, or had even given an indication that I had seen him, I would have had to take action against him. I would have been compelled to at least call him to my office tomorrow and warned him not too repeat what he has done today, or to even give him a notice asking him for a written explanation. Then he would have had to stop what he has been doing or I would have had to take stronger action like terminating his services or suspending him. Now, he feels safe that no one has seen him. You know Kumar, you have to be humane when dealing with people. People like Balwant has not received much from our society, nor from the Board where he has been working for so many years. Management must be founded not only on values like honesty and truth and righteousness, but also on qualities like tolerance, sympathy and compassion. People like Balwant needs a little bit of empty and compassion from people like us to stay alive in this world. Now I think you will understand why I did not allow you to stop the car'.

'But, still Sir', said Mr. Kumar firmly, 'though I appreciate and understand your point of view, I cannot completely accept this philosophy. Don't you think Sir, that this kind of leniency on our part will lead to indiscipline and chaos in the organisation ? Balwant's case may be genuine Sir, but tomorrow someone else may take advantage of your kind nature and cheat the Board. Instead of letting Balwant break the rules of the Broad, isn't there any other way in which we can help him ? After all, Sir, it is unethical to break rules'.

Questions

1. Do you believe Mr. Prasad, the Chief Engineer is correct in his belief ?
2. What kind of value system is Mr. Prasad trying to build in his Board ?
3. Do you feel that Mr. Kumar is more ethical of the two ? Would the ethical culture of the organisation improve when someone like Mr. Kumar becomes the Chief Engineer ?
4. What sort of ethical behaviour do you think the employees of this organisation are encouraged to display ?
5. Do you think, it is really unethical to break rules ?
6. What would you have done had you been in Mr. Prasad's place? In Mr. Kumar's place ?

Summary of the Chapter in Brief

* Attitudes are pre-disposed, evaluate feelings of people about objects, people or events. They are evaluative statements and express one's way of thinking.
* Perception is the process of becoming aware of situations and interpreting our sensory impressions, in order to give meaning to our environment.
* Human behaviour, to a large extent, is based on 'what a person perceives' rather than on 'what is reality'.
* Attitudes develop right from childhood, and arise mainly from one's experiences and conditioned learning, and partly from one's value system.
* Wrong attitudes may result in unethical behaviour, whereas right attitudes result in ethical behaviour.
* Beliefs are ideas or principles that people hold dear and give ordinance to. One's belief are the foundations of one's value system.

* Character Ethics are basic principles of effective living, and these are internal qualities qualifying the inner goodness of man, and arising out of their character rather than out of their external personality.
* People should put adequate effort at character-building, along with Personality building, because what we are communicates more than what we say or do.
* Human beings go through three life positions in their relationship with others - dependency, independency and interdependency.
* All human beings are known to operate from three ego states - the Child the Parent and the Adult ego state.
* The Child ego state contains the recordings of internal events (seeing, hearing, feeling and understanding), in response to external events (mostly between mother and father), between birth and the age of 5 years . It is a **felt** concept of life.
* The Parent ego state contains the recordings of imposed, unquestioned external events, perceived by an individual, between birth and the age of 5 years. It is a **taught** concept of life.
* The Adult ego state contains the recordings of data acquired and computed through exploration and testing. It is a **thought** concept of life.
* There are four possible life positions of human beings, which are held with respect to oneself and others.
* Life Position 1 is I'm not OK - You're OK', where the person feels himself to be inadequate or inferior to others in some way, while the rest of the world is alright. In this position the person's behaviour is focused only on getting others to like and appreciate him, and to make other's look not too good.
* Life Position 2 is I'm not OK- You're not OK', where the person concludes quite early in life that there is something wrong with both himself and the world. A person in this life position just gives up hope and may ultimately end up in a mental institution in a state of extreme withdrawal, with regressive behaviour. They view everything negatively and with suspicion, and this negative feeling and suspicion is the basis of all their behaviour.
* Life Position 3 is I'm OK - You're not OK', where a brutalized child feels that he is alright, while his oppressors are not alright. This is a potentially criminal position. His behaviour may stem from cruelty that he feels for the world. His hatred and bitterness towards the world makes him unethical and cruel in his dealings with people.
* Life Position 4 is I'm OK - You're OK', where people accept themselves and the world as alright. This life position is a conscious and verbal decision. People operating from this life position are at peace with themselves and the world, and consequently has very little reason to stoop to immoral conduct or unethical behaviour.

Expected Questions

1. What are attitudes? Discuss how attitudes of people can affect their behaviour.

2. Explain the difference between Perception and Attitude. Does Perception affect Attitude?
3. Give a few examples of right Attitudes and wrong Attitudes concerning the workplace.
4. What are Beliefs ? Explain how Beliefs of people affect their ethical conduct.
5. What are Character Ethics?
6. Discuss the various Life Positions of people and their ethical implications.

Chapter 4

Part I Overview of the Ethical Value System

Everything we see, hear, say, imagine or do can be divided into two main categorie - i.e., the way situations **are**, and the way situations 'ought' to be. How situations ought to b is what gives rise to 'values'. One of the first important lessons to learn in ethics, is to see lif **as it is**, without our perceptions and attitudes distorting it to fit in with what we **want** to see Once we recognise what life actually is, only then we can go about moulding situations t what it 'ought to be' or to value based situations. The Indian system of values prescribe tha whatever be the ethical dimensions of a situation, it must be able to hold society togethe However, in the process, whatever holds the society together should not destroy the individual of the society. For if individuals are destroyed, what remains of society?

In chapter III , it was discussed as to how perception of a person affects his behaviou All of us react, not to reality itself, but to our own interpretation of reality. Our behaviour i affected, not by a particular situation, but how we see and what we see in the situation When we see a person frown, we may see the person as being angry (at us or at someon else), or we may see it as an insult to us, whereas the reality may be that the person i suffering from a terrible headache and is finding it difficult to keep his face straight-an hence the frown. It has to be accepted that we see the world, not as **it is**, but as we ar feeling at that moment, as we are thinking, and more importantly, as we **are** - or as we ar conditioned to see things. When we describe the world around us, and the people in it, w in effect describe ourselves, our perceptions, our attitudes, our morality, and our ethica value system.

Stephen R. Covey, in his highly acclaimed book, 'The 7 Habits of Highly Effectiv People', (Published by Simon & Schuster, 1990), states that individual value systems aris out of the 'Inside - Out' approach. 'Inside - Out' means to start first with self; even mor fundamentally, to start with the most inside part of self - with one's paradigms, one's characte and one's motives. For example, if one wants to be trusted by others, he has to first b trustworthy. There's no other way, no other technique, no other strategy or tactic - to ge others to trust you if you are not trustworthy. Similarly, if you want to have friends - first b friendly; if you want to be loved, first be loving - that's all there's to it - there's no other way If one wants the secondary greatness of recognised talent, he has to focus first on primar greatness of character.

Covey, in his Inside - Out approach, says that private victories precede public victories that making and keeping promises to ourselves procedes making and keeping promises t others. This approach says that it is futile to put personality ahead of character, to try t improve relationships with others, before improving ourselves.

Many people believe that values mean a moral standard of behaviour. However, values are different from moral standards or norms of human behaviour. Moral standards or norms are specific expectations about concrete behavioural patterns. They serve as the criterion for judging the moral quality of human behaviour. They express a criterion for what ought to be done. Values, on the other hand , are moral general in nature. They are deeply embedded in the people's subconscience, and manifests themselves in their behaviour. These values are abstract representations of what people believe to be right, good, just and worthwhile to pursue. When certain values are internalised by an individual as his personal values, they go beyond the zone of choice for the person concerned. His actions, based on those values then become spontaneous and continuous. Those values get reflected in his conduct. His compliance with these values become instinctive and automatic.

Values are sometimes also confused with Codes of Conduct. But values are different from codes of conduct. Codes merely represent rules and regulations - what 'to do' and what 'not to do'. But values go much beyond stating do's and don'ts. Values are what underline codes. Values and principles form the foundations of codes. To be effective, rules and regulation should be based on ethical values. And what is this value that we are talking about? **A Value is a sustained and assimilated mode of acting, thinking or merely being.** A set of basic values can help people to make decisions even in the face of uncertainty and in new situations which have never been faced before.

The expression of one's life, his behaviour and conduct, is just the expression of himself as a person - the expression of his value system. How a person behaves, what he does, his actions and conduct, merely express what is valuable to him, and what he considers worthy of pursuit.

When a person wants certain unassimilated values to become a part of his value structure, he must consciously and everytime the occassion arises, observe and exercise these values, until he is convinced that they have become assimilated as a part of his personal value system, and the expression of these values become a sort of spontaneous second nature to him.

For an individual to accept a particular value into his value system, he must first find out the worth of the pursuits off his life. He must examine what he considers worthy of pursuit, dear to his heart, valuable to him, and important to achieve. For example, if a person believes that personal freedom and liberty are worthy of pursuit , then he or she must make these become a part of his or her value system, to be striven for. Money, prestige, recognition, etc. are valuable only if it results in personal freedom and liberty, and not otherwise. When he understands this, the false estimation of their worth drops off and he begins to see them in their true perspective. No object, tangible (like money, material possessions) or intangible (like a tranquil mind, happiness) has a fixed worth. It is a person's value system that puts an worth onto these objects.

The values in an individual's value system are introduced and later reinforced over a life time of experience, but more particularly during growing up, formative years of the individual. During this period, various social institutions play important roles in inculcating values in the individual. The major institutions that provide the basic sources of values for a person during his formative years are - **first**, the family one is born into; **second**, the school, (along with its teachers and its discipline system) and other educational and extra - curriculum bodies like sports clubs, debating, painting, singing, dancing schools, etc.; **third**, one's religion; and **fourth**, the society or community one belongs to. The values fostered by each of these institutions reinforces the values taught by the others, and together they form the value system of the individual.

Values should be treated as qualities to be acquired. Otherwise, values merely reduces to rules and regulations about do's and don'ts. Values should be a part of one's daily living, and not called upon to act only in emergencies and in difficult situations. They should have relevance to one's behaviour and conduct in normal times too. If people were told to speak the truth, but the relevance of truth in life is not explained and not understood by the person, then telling the truth merely becomes a 'to do' rule and the worth of telling the truth is not discovered by the person.

Values not only enhances the quality of life of the individuals of the society, but they make the society, and thereby the world, a better place to live in. Value-based actions and decisions ensure the welfare of all people belonging to the society. When our actions spring from high ethical values, we display all the desirable qualities of a good human being, worthy of our place in the world.

The universal recognition that we are responsible for the other members of the society, and that we must have a standard of moral behaviour in our relationships with these members, requires some ethical value systems to make them operational. For the last thousands of years, man has attempted to set moral standards and to establish ethical value systems to regulate their conduct. None of these ethical value systems are perfect, and they need modifications; however, some of them do have direct relevance to managerial decisions. Let's examine some of them-

1. The System of Universalism;

The theory of universalism is based on the duties or obligations of an individual in society. The duties or obligations of an individual is termed as **Deontology**. The approach of universalism states that the moral worth of an action of an individual should be judged by the intentions of the person performing the action, and not by the outcomes of the action. Even if the outcome is not as desired, but the intention of the person was good, then the action is to be termed as good action. The underlying philosophy of this concept is that good intentions should always result in good outcome, ultimately, if not immediately. Deontology is sometimes also referred to as ethics based on the 'act' and whether or not the act is 'right'.

Personal duties and obligations of an individual are universal. No one can escape from discharging these duties and obligations, without adverse repercussions. Hence this deontological theory is termed as universalism. It focuses on individuals not as means but as ends in themselves, worthy of dignity and respect. Thus, only when a code of behaviour can be universally applied, should it be considered ethically correct.

Immanuel Kant (1724-1804) proposed the Categorical Imperative, which helps to evaluate an individual's moral conduct. According to it, one should act only in ways that one would wish all others to act, faced with the same set of circumstances, and also to treat others with dignity and respect. That basically follows the tanent that we should not do anything which we would not like to be done to us in similar circumstances. 'Do unto others as thou would have others do unto thou', said Jesus Christ, almost two thousand years ago. What is morally right for oneself must be morally right for others as well. Everyone's value is equal. Hence, no one's rights should be subordinated to those of others.

While praiseworthy in theory, the universalism approach finds itself in difficulty during practical application. It depends to a large extent, for its interpretation, upon the situation that the individuals finds himself in. Not all people may be agreed upon the same moral standards. Similarly, it would be difficult for an organisation to think of its people - its employees - as ends in themselves, rather than as means in the pursuit of corporate excellence. Again, though some people may prescribe to the time rate system of payment, others may believe that the piece rate system where everybody is paid by results, would be more equitable. Then it would be difficult to reconcile these two benefits, as everybody's belief is of equal importance according to the system of Universalism.

The System of Utilitarianism

This approach to ethics comes from **Teleology**, which is concerned not with an act itself, but with the consequence of the act. Thus the emphasis is upon the outcome of individual actions, and not on the intent of the individual. That is why this is sometimes referred to as 'ends - based' ethics or as 'consequentialism'.

A special version of teleology is **Utilitarianism**, which aims at creating the greatest degree of benefits for the largest number of people while incurring the least amount of harm possible. Thus, utilitarianism is concerned with maximising 'welfare' for the society. According to it, an action is 'good' if it results in benefits for society, and it is bad if it leads to damages or harms the society.

The Utilitarianism ethical system was originated by the British thinker Jeremy Bentham (1748-1832). It found support among most of the influential philosophers in its time, who held that the moral worth of an individual's conduct can be determined by the outcome or consequences of that behaviour. In situations where the outcomes can be measured in financial terms, the utilitarian system has great merit.

However, the Utilitarian system has certain limitations also. As a determinant of moral action, this system fails to provide a balance between the benefits of the majority against the sacrifices of a minority. Doestoevsky in his book titled, 'Brother karamazov', asked what would be the moral action of the society, if the happiness of the whole human race forever, should lie in the sacrifice of only one person, a completely innocent child, who should be slowly tortured to death. Such an action would obviously be morally 'wrong' despite its great benefits to a huge majority.

Moreover, Utilitarianism prescribes 'the greatest good for the greatest number'. In most cases, it is very difficult to reconciled 'greatest good' with the 'greatest number' of people. There has to be a trade-off somewhere. And the degree to which this trade-off will be possible, is not provided by Utilitarianism.

3. The System of Distributive Justice & Social Contracts:

The theory of Distributive Justice, which is founded by the single value of Justice, was proposed by John Rawls. Justice is thought to be the most likely outcome of an ethical process of decision making. All rules and laws must, necessarily, first and foremost, be just.

When people get together, as they always will, in forming societies and in cooperating with one another to get things done, two outcomes are possible. From such group activities, emerge two outcomes - conflict or collaboration. Collaboration results when people believe in the **synergy** effect - that joint activities yield greater benefits than the sum total of these activities taken separately. On the other hand, conflicts result when people do not receive a just distribution of the benefits yielded through their activities. Professor Rawls, a member of the faculty of Harvard University, believes that the base of all distribution systems should be just and the primacy of justice in the basic structure of our system of society requires greater equality. These distributive systems should result in compensating benefits for all and particularly for the least fortunate members of our society. This is also the idea of Social Contract. The moral value of an action, according to this approach, can be determined by the degree of cooperation it generates within the members of the society. If it leads to greater cooperation among the members of the society, then that action is termed morally 'good', and if it results in lesser cooperation and more conflicts, then it is termed as morally 'wrong'. The essential feature of this system is transparency and full participation of those affected in the decision making process. The only problem in applying this system to evaluate the moral worth of an action is that in this system, individual effort is down played, if not completely ignored.

4. Individual Freedom of Choice;

'Freedom', whether of an individual, a society or a country has great value, and freedom of choice refers to an individual being at perfect liberty to make enlightened choices of action, without being curbed either by another individual, a group or the society at large. Of course, these 'choices' must be within the law and the same freedom enjoyed by one individual in the society, must be extended to all within the society. Everyone should act to ensure greater freedom of choice by all in the society. All individuals must be allowed to make informed choices among alternative courses of action leading to their own welfare. This freedom of choice must be used in a wider context and with a broader meaning. For example, the right to work must not be limited to only providing work, but must also include the right to opportunities for promotion and advancement, the right to growth and development on the job. Similarly, the right to wages does not mean only the right to get a minimum amount of money, but also the right to have access to some basic standards of living through educational opportunities for one's children and medical assistance for the family.

5. The Legal System & Professional Codes:

The moral worth of an action can also be determined through the legal system. If an action of an individual is within the purview of the law, then it is considered to be 'right' but if the action is illegal, then it is considered to be 'wrong'.

Similarly, professional codes are also value-based norms of desired behaviour within a particular profession. For example, if a doctor does not violate the Hippocratic Code, then his actions are said to be within good moral standards.

Though this approach appears to be simple in theory, and easy to practice, it suffers from serious limitations. Law may be a convenient institutional means for implementing values. But if these laws are themselves a product of an unfair power game, if they are unjust and **unethical**, them adhering to these laws and following such laws would in fact, be unethical and against one's conscience. Moreover, ethics is not just legal laws. Ethics represents and encompasses much more than mere rules and regulations, and it is much more wider in scope than the legal system. The law prescribes only the bare minimum standard of human conduct within the society, while ethics is concerned not only with 'legal' actions, but with 'moral' actions. For example, the law states that homicide, i.e., killing people is a crime and needs to be restrained, and if committed, punished. Ethics is not merely concerned with people not killing each other – it prescribes that human beings should cooperate with each other to live higher and loftier sublime moral lives.

Similarly, a doctor following the Hippocratic Code is just doing the bare minimum for his patients. His legal obligations are covered as long as he stays within the Hippocratic Code, whereas his ethics will dictate that he should do everything in his power, even at great personal sacrifice, to bring about the welfare of his patient, to give him a new lease of life and to strengthen his will to live.

Reference :

1. 'The 7 Habits of Highly Effective People', Stephen R. Covey
2. 'Values/Ethics in Management – Relevance & Application', Naresh B Shah.
3. 'Ethical Choices in Business', R.C. Sekher
4. 'The Ethics of Management', Larue Tone Hosmer

Discussion Problem – An ethical Dilemma

A mother and her small son aged 6 years, went to the forest to collect firewood. While they were collecting firewood, suddenly a lion appeared and caught hold of the child. Hearing her son's cries, the mother ran to the spot and found the son between the two paws of the lion. The mother immediately rushed to the lion and kneeling down in front of it, folding her hands and with tears running down her cheeks, prayed to the lion thus – 'O Lord of the Jungle, O King of all animals, please spare my innocent son, he is all that I have in my life. He is my only child and will grow up to be my support in my old age'.

The Lion replied – 'Do not fear, O woman, I have taken pity on you. I shall spare your son, but only on one condition. If you can tell me truely what I shall do with your son, only then will I give you back your son'.

The mother, then, in her fright blurted out, 'O King of the Jungle, this means that truely you will never give me back my child'. To this, the lion replied, 'If you have spoken the truth, I cannot give you the child back, because that will make your statement false. But, if you have spoken falsely, then I cannot give you the child back, because you have broken our agreement to speak the truth. Therefore, I cannot give you the child back whether you have spoken truely or falsely.

The mother on hearing this, became embolden by her anger and thus replied, 'You had agreed to give back the child if I speak the truth. Hence, if I have spoken truely, you must now fulfill the terms of our agreement and give my child back to me. If I have spoken falsely, then you must give back my child first to prove that I had spoken falsely. Hence the child must be given back to me, whether I have spoken truly or falsely'.

Based only on the terms of the agreement between the Lion and the mother (and not taking into consideration whether a Lion has the right to eat a child), decide who is more ethically correct.

Summary of the Chapter in Brief:

* Everything we see, hear, say, imagine or do can be divided into two main categories- i.e., the way situations **are**, and the way situations ought to be.
* We see the world as we are feeling, as we are thinking and as we **are**.
* Our individual value system arises out of the 'Inside-Out' approach.
* Private victories precede public victories.
* Values are deeply embedded in people's subconscience and manifests themselves in their behaviour. They are abstract representations of what people believe to be right, good, just and worthwhile of pursue.
* A value is a sustained and assimilated mode of acting, thinking or merely being.
* The system of Universalism, based on Deontology, states that the moral worth of an action of an individual should be judged be the intentions of the person performing the action, and not by the outcomes of the action.
* The Categorical Imperative, proposed by Immanuel Kant (1724-1804), states that one should act only in ways that one would wish all others to act, faced with the same set of circumstances, and also to treat others with dignity and respect.
* The system of Utilitarianism, which comes from Teleology, is concerned not with an act itself, but with the consequences of the act, and also not with the intent of the individual committing the act.
* Utilitarianism prescribes 'the greatest good for the greatest number '.
* The system of Distributive Justice aims at a just distribution of benefits yielded through the activities of the people concerned.
* The idea of social contract states that the moral value of an action can be determined by the degree of cooperation it generates within the members of the society.
* Individual Freedom of Choices refers to an individual being at perfect liberty to make enlightened choices of action, without being curbed either by another individual, a group or the society at large.
* All individuals must be allowed to make informed choices among alternative courses of action leading to their own welfare.
* The Legal System and Professional Codes are also means whereby one can evaluate the moral worth of one's action.
* However, the law prescribes only the bare minimum standard of human conduct within the society, while ethics is concerned with 'moral' actions.

Expected Questions:

1. Discuss the Ethical Value System of an individual.
2. What are values and how do they affect human conduct? Differentiate between Moral Standards and Code of Conduct with Values.
3. Discuss the system of Universalism and the System of Utilitarianism, bringing out their differences, along with their relative merits and demerits.

4. Discuss - The system of Distributive Justice; Social Contract; Individual Freedom of Choice; The Legal system & Professional Codes.
5. Write a short essay on the different Ethical Value System.

PART II
CULTURE & ETHICS

Culture generally means the mode of life of a particular group of people, specially with reference to their pattern of life in society, their dress, rituals, beliefs, rules, regulations, conduct, behaviour, and ethical practices. Cultures of different nations are different, and sometimes different cultural practices can be found within the same nation or state. In India, of course, we have a multitude of cultures, each differing from the other in various ways , and diversity in cultural practices in each states is the norm rather than the exception. However, inspite of all this diversity, we have a common thread running through each culture, making up the great Indian culture. Moreover, each religion existing in India, also has its own cultural practices and heritage, like the Hindu culture, the Islamic culture, the Sikh culture and so on. Thus, India forms the land of 'unity in diversity', where a number of cultures coexist in harmony, each different, each unique, yet, each a part of a whole, each a part of India.

Similarly, in the world over, each nation or regional territory has different cultural norms and practices. The Eastern Oriental culture is totally different from the Western modern culture. The culture of the Arabian countries is different from the culture of the European countries. The African countries have their own cultures. Similarly, the 'Down-Under' countries like Australia with their ranches and cattleman, have their own cultural norms. Moreover, the industrially advanced countries of the world have their own culture (based on their industrial culture), which is different from the cultures of the developing or underdeveloped countries (which are primarily based on their agrarian culture). In the Western culture, values like independence, initiative, achievement are encouraged; whereas in Indian culture, values like modesty, cooperation, humility are appreciated.

G. Hofstede in 'Nationality & espoused values of managers' (1976), in the Journal of Applied Psychology and in 'Culture's Consequence: International differences in work-related values' (1980), Sage Publications, revealed that his empirical studies on work - related values across a number of countries and their comparisons have clearly indicated cultural differences among these values. Hofsted's studies found out that Americans scored high on values like recognition and achievement; and they scored low on conformity. On the other hand, Asians (including Indians) scored high on values like conformity and orderliness; but scored low on values like independence, individualism and leadership qualities.

Each culture of the world has its own ethical practices. The basic values of a society constitutes the core of its culture. Ethics, thus, has an intimate relationship with the culture of a place. Ethics is a normative science of the conduct of human beings living in societies. The study of human conduct leads us necessarily to the study of social life of man and consequently to its culture. It is not possible to study the moral values of man without studying the culture from which it originates. Man being a social animal, cannot live alone and hence his conduct has a direct or indirect reference to the culture he belongs to. His moral standards and value system is constructed by the customs and norms of his culture.

It is quite natural that like legal standards, ethical standards also differ among nations, societies and cultures. For example, in many countries, it is permissible for privately owned companies to make political contribution to political parties and candidates, during election time. In many other countries too, like Brazil, payments to government officials and other civil servants and bureaucratic personnel with political influence to 'get business done' i.e., to assure expedited or favourable handling of a business transaction, are not regarded as unethical bribes, but as proper payment for services rendered. In order to acquire a business contract from the government in many countries, the foreign company is expected to 'pay up', and payment of such commissions is regarded as a perfectly normal and acceptable way of doing business. People feel that governments set the salaries of such officials assuming that they would make a small percentage on the job. People from Brazil believe that it is morally acceptable to pay small bribes to get things done. People from the United States , on the other hand, find the practise of payment of petty bribes morally unacceptable. If the person from the US had to tell him American friends, 'I had to pay', they would be pretty shocked. On the other hand , if the Brazillian person feels, 'He does not want to pay', he would be shocked and probably also disgusted that a foreigner wants to break an accepted normal practice and both of them would think that they were right, based on their ethical standards. However, there is a difference between **believing** that something is right and that something is **actually** right. But the fact remains that both culture look upon something as 'right' and 'correct' in different ways. And no culture has the right to force its ethical views upon another. A person cannot impose American standards of bureaucratic integrity upon the Brazilian civil service. The social structure of Brazil could be such that it readily accepts the giving and taking of small bribes as part of its culture. For ultimately, business ethical behaviour consists of doing what is of greatest benefit to the society and the community.

The above discussion may point to bribary and corruption as being an indispensable part of international business, which unfortunately it is, and is difficult to avoid. It may also seem to indicate that bribary and corruption is a part of certain cultures in certain nations. However, this may not be the case and the issue lies somewhere else. As David Murray in his book, 'Ethics in Organisation', states - "In many countries where petty corruption is rampat, public officials at middle and junior levels have great difficult in supporting their families on their extremely low salaries and in many places even those low salaries may not have been paid for several months. The introduction of realistic pay scales for public officials, backed up by the assurance that they will be paid on time, would make a substantial difference. Many officials practise extortion not because they wish to do so, but, because it seems to be their own way of surviving. However, for governments to be able to pay their salary bills they must first receive their tax revenues. This means that the populace as a whole must pay its taxes".

The basic culture which forms the primary foundation of person's value system and ethical behaviour is the culture of the family he belongs to. Family culture has a tremendous impact and profoundly affects a person in building up his own ethical value structure. However, the moral conduct of a person is not confined only to his family culture. It transcends family culture and spills over to the culture of the society or the race he belong to.

Social Culture & Individual Ethics:-

The relationship between social culture and individual ethics can be considered from four different perspective. These four views are-

1. Social Contract Theory
2. Collectivism or Socialism Theory
3. Organic Theory
4. Idealistic or Group-Mind Theory

1. Social Contract Theory:

Hobbes, Locke and Rousseau put forward the 'Social Contract Theory', wherein it was stated that people established societies out of social contract. It was theoritised that previously each man was an independent unit by himself and a law unto himself. At that time the Jungle Rule that 'might is right' was prevalent. People lived in a 'state of nature', which was thought by Locke and Rousseau to have been peaceful. But with the growth of the number of men and the consequent conflicts arising out of the division and right to individual property, men felt the need for some rules for universal conduct. Hence, they all entered into a social contract and established their own ethical rules of conduct.

According this theory, men would seem to have consciously and collectively established rules and regulations, laws and ethics over themselves to govern social life. Though this theory is very simple and easy to understand, one only wishes that life was as simple as that. If upto that point man had no concept of what social life was like, it is difficult to accept that they were suddenly capable of making and entering into any form of contract to establish a society. Hence this theory does not seem very feasible and stands rejected. Moreover, it is difficult to explain the nature of culture and its impact on ethics from such a social set up.

2. Collection or Socialism Theory:

Plato and Aristotle propounded this theory which is the exact opposite of the Social Contract Theory. According to them, man had always lived in societies and it is impossible to imagine man existing without a society. This theory states that it is impossible for a man to develop, either intellectually or ethically, without participating in social life. This theory also states that man cannot exist without society, though society can exist without the man. Society makes it obligatory for the man to follow its rules, regulations, norms and ethics, which he cannot afford to ignore. This view would seem to suggest that cultural norms of the society makes it imperative for the individual to follow its norms and standards of behaviour. Thus, ethics is not a matter of individual or collective contract, rather ethics of a culture develops slowly and over time, to make up the ethics of that society. Thus, according to this theory, society or social norms and values control a man, but the man(i.e. an individual) has no control over societal norms and values.

This theory also appears to take an extreme view. A society is a collection of individuals. Without the individuals, the society too would cease to exist. Morever, the moral values of the individuals also affect society in the same way as the ethical standards of the society affect the individuals. The higher the moral values of the individuals, higher is the ethical standard of the society. In conclusion, it seems appropriate to say that individuals and their ethical standards affect society as much as societal ethics affect individuals.

3. Organic Theory:

Leslie Stephen and Herbert Spencer states that the relation between individuals and society is organic and not mechanical. The individuals belonging to the society are interdependent among themselves and in turn to the society. Hence, individuals cannot exist without a society and the society cannot exist if there are no individuals Social process and social rules, regulations, norms and values are organic in nature, forever changing, forever evolving. Just like living organisms, social cultures also pass through stages of birth, growth, maturity, and decay.

Though society resembles a living organism in many respects, an individual is not controlled by the society in many areas. An individual has his independent existence, and his actions are guided by his free will. His mental faculties can never be controlled or guided by the society. Though social values and ethics may compell a man to think and evaluate them, his own free will guide him in choosing his own moral standards and ethical behaviour. Though difficult, a man can live without society, unlike a cell which cannot live apart from the living organism. A man living without a society can still be ethical and practise high moral conduct. Morever, unlike an organism which decays, a society may just change and transform itself rather than decaying.

That people can exercise their own free will and not subscribe to the prevailing norms and rules of the society, can be illustrated with the example of Raja Ram Mohan Roy of Bengal. Though the practice of sati and child marriage were the norms at that time, he opposed both these norms of society, stating that they were unethical practices, got them abolished thought laws and also introduced the concept of widow remarriage. Similarly many people opposed, at various periods of time, the concept to the caste system, introducing inter- caste marriages in the Hindu society. Many people opposed the concept of untouchability of the Indian Hindu Culture, terming these practices as unethical and oppressive, notable amongst them being Mohandas K. Gandhi. Thus, people's individual concept of morality and ethics may differ widely from that of the society.

4. Idealistic or Group-Mind Theory:

Propounded by many philosophers, including Plato, this theory states that the relation between society and an individual as spiritual. A man living outside society cannot strive for and attain excellence. Without the society, man cannot develop his moral character or ethical value system. Without society, he cannot be termed as a complete man, and remains only as a fragment of humanity.

This group mind theory can be accepted only as metaphor, since it is difficult to practically apply this theory in relation to social culture and individual ethics. Perhaps it is important to keep in mind the saying of Gisbert who stated that 'social values are in the last resort personal values. Even those qualities or powers which belong to society as such are realised only in its members, present or future, for the life of society has no meaning except as an expression of the lives of the individuals'.

It is understood and accepted that the value system and the moral standards of the society affects the value system and moral standards of the individuals of the society and the value systems of the individuals make up the moral standard of the society.

The culture of a particular society is intimately linked to the individual ethical values of the people in the society. Some cultures consider certain acts to be highly unethical, while some other cultures may accept these very acts to be a part and parcel of daily living and an acceptable practice. However, there are certain immoral acts which are universally condemned as unethical, irrespective of the culture involved. For example all cultural systems deplore the practice of fraud, dishonesty and so on, as unethical; while all cultural systems recognise the need for equality, honesty, truth and so on. Even the earliest written book on ethics, called 'The Dialogues of Plato', mentions bribery and corruption as unethical acts. Today, all the world over, irrespective of the cultures involved, people accept bribery and corruption as unethical acts.

Morality refers to the standards of behaviour by which people are judged in their relationship with others. Any behaviour which has no impact upon others, cannot logically be termed as ethical or unethical. Hence, it is in the context of other people's welfare that morality is defined. Since this is possible only within a social set up, the culture of that group of people has a bearing upon the morality or immorality off the act. Ethics, thus, encompasses the entire system of beliefs and values that support a particular view of morality. The reason why Ethics is used in the plural term is because it encompasses a system of interrelated beliefs and values of the culture in question. Thus, we may speak of **moral standards of behaviour**, but **ethical systems of values**.

Similarity of Ethical Values in Different Cultures - The Principles;

Moral standards and values differ between different cultures, different societies, different ages and sometimes between different groups within the same culture. However, there are certain principles that govern the foundation of all ethical systems in all cultures, and through all the ages. One such principle is that it is unethical and even downright immoral to cause other members of the society some harm in the pursuit of one's own happiness and material success. We are all free to pursue our own happiness and success, but, it is also our duty to see and ensure that our individual pursuit of happiness and success does not result in collective harm for the society.

In the olden times, if an individual having his own drinking water supply, washes his clothes and his herd of cattle in the community drinking water tank of the village, and thereby poisons the water, it was considered to be an unethical act, whether it was a village of Hindu culture or Muslim culture; In India or in Africa. Similarly, today if a particular industry emits lethal gases and industrial fumes into the air and water of the society, and causes poisonous pollution, it is considered an unethical and immoral, apart from being an illegal act, irrespective of the culture and irrespective of the country.

The **second** principle underlying all cultures, even the most primitive is that people do not act solely for their own self interest and there lies a responsibility on each member of the group for the welfare of the other members of the group. Cooperation among group members is considered to be essential to ensure the welfare of the group.

The **third** principle, found common among may cultures, is that just as man takes from society, so also is man indebted to society in the same measure. There exists an universal recognition that we owe something to other members of the society, and to society as a whole, and we are bound by a concept of right and wrong in our behaviour with others in the society.

The **fourth** principle is the Principle of Fairness. This principle is the foundation of the concept of equality and justice in a culture. Different cultures may define and achieve fairness in different ways, their meaning and concept may change over time, but the principles of fairness is found as an ethical value on all cultures.

The **fifth** principle is the Principle of Integrity and Honesty. It has been stated before that every society, every culture requires people to cooperate amongst themselves to live in harmony. Without the principles of integrity and honesty, people cannot create the foundation of trust amongst themselves which is essential for cooperation and long-term personal and interpersonal growth.

The **last** principle is the principle of Human Dignity. Almost every culture believes that man is superior to animals, by virtue of not only his superior intellect, but by his superior conscience which can differentiate between right and wrong. Thus, every human being has the right to live a life of dignity and privacy, without encroaching on the dignity and privacy of others.

These principles are found again and again, when different culture are examined, throughout their social history. It has also been seen that the ability of the people of a culture to recognise and live with harmony with these principles steers their culture and their society either towards survival and stability or towards disintegration and destruction. These principles are a part of every major religion, social philosophies and ethical systems. These principles are almost like natural laws of human survival and development; and they are a part of the human consciousness.

Conclusion:

The concept of ethics is culture - specific. The bounds of ethics is relative to the culture of the social group. While the individual is affected and influenced by the level of moral standards of behaviour and the ethical systems of values and beliefs of the society, the society too can only be the sum total of the moral standards of the individuals who make up the society. The higher the moral standards and ethical values of the individuals of the society, higher is the moral standards and ethical values of the society.

Though there may be differences in their implementation or in the relative importance given to them, values like honesty, respect for life and freedom, fairness and loyalty are admired and sought after worldwide. Inspite of ethics being culture specific, yet there are certain principles which run like a common thread among all cultures, all religions and among all ages in history. These principles are unchangeable, immortal and remain valid, transcending time, space and distance. They are deep fundamental truths that have universal appeal and application. When these truths are internalised by individuals in a culture, that culture rises to a higher level of ethical conscience.

Reference:

1. 'The Ethics of management' - Larue Tone Hosmer; Universal Book Stall (UBS), New Delhi, 1987.
2. 'Ethics in Organisations'; David Murray; Kogan Page, The Fast Track MBA Series, 1997

Case Study :

M/s ABC Manufacturing Ltd. is a large multinational engineering company dealing with electronic goods. They have various industrial units and factories all over India. One of its department in India, is the Hospital Equipment Division (HED), which produces medical gadgets and equipments that are supplied to both government and private hospitals within the country and abroad. The HED of the company strives to keep up very good relation with doctors, since in this business, word of mouth publicity and reputation plays a far more important role than either advertising or personal selling. In fact, the company has a policy of retaining particularly influential and well - connected doctors with a 'retainer' fee who acts, unknown to competitors and other doctors, as their consultants and publicity agents. The company 'pays' these doctors Rs 25,000/- per sale if the customer can be directly attributed to their recommendation.

One such doctor was Dr. Kumar, who had acted as a go-between, confidentially, between the company and many a doctor and has resulted in many a sales. One day, when Mr. Sumant, a Sales Engineer of the company paid a visit to Dr. Kumar, to know whether there was any prospective customer at that moment, Dr. Kumar mentioned the name of one Dr. Khanna. Dr. Khanna was a very close friend of Dr. Kumar and Dr. Kumar informed Mr. Sumant that he was casually enquiring about a CT Scanner for his Sewa Trust, where he rendered voluntary work and of which he was one of the trustees. Apart from this voluntary work, Dr. Khanna had a roaring private practice. Dr. Kumar also informed Mr. Sumant that Dr. Khanna had given a Console to be repaired, to ABC Manufacturing Ltd. and was expecting some discount on its servicing cost. Dr. Kumar informed Mr. Sumant that when Dr. Khanna had mentioned his company's name in connection with the repairing job, Dr. Kumar, had suggested to Dr. Khanna to buy the CT Scanner from that company itself, and Dr. Khanna appeared to be quite agreeable to the proposal. Then Dr. Khanna had said that he would like to see the quality of service of the company before making a final commitment to buy such an expensive machine from them. So he said that he himself would go to collect the repaired Console, so that he could 'look around' and get a feel of the company before making up his mind. At that point, Dr. Kumar had also volunteered to go to the company with Dr. Khanna. Having given all this information to Mr. Sumant, Dr. Kumar said that he believed that with a discount on the repairing work of the Console, and a good servicing of it would clinch the order.

Thanking Dr. Kumar, and armed with this valuable information, Mr. Sumant approached his boss Mr. Basu and told him the story. Mr. Basu immediately called the Accounts Officer Mr. Mittal and asked him what was the bill of servicing the Console. Mr. Mittal, after checking up, informed that it was Rs. 8,000/ -. Mr. Basu immediately told Mr. Mittal to mention some more repairs to it and inflate the bill to Rs. 12,000/-, so that they could offer a discount of Rs. 2,000/- initially and if Dr. Khanna was not happy even then, then they would go down to Rs. 8,000/-, saying that they have given him a special discount. It was indeed a fact that no other company in the marketplace, other than M/s ABC Manufacturing Ltd., would service a Console for anything lower than Rs 10,000/-. But, since this company does not believe in keeping a huge margin and was satisfied with earning controlled profits, its prices were lower than most other players in the marketplace. Moreover, given the very good quality of its products-conforming to international standards - and its low prices, made the company quite popular in the market.

On the appointed day, as Dr. Kumar and Dr. Khanna were coming to the office building of the company, tragedy struck. Just as they were entering their car into the building, the security guards of the company prevented their entry, saying visitors cars were not allowed inside the building premises.

'What do you mean visitors ?', asked Dr. Khanna, 'we're customers'.

'You may be customers, Sirs, but we have instructions not to allow anyone in', replied the guard firmly.

'How dare you treat us like this,' thundered Dr. Kumar. 'Let us go in at once, or we shall complain'.

'You can do what you like, Sir', said the Guard, more stubborn now, 'but I refuse to let you in. This is the rule of the company'.

'You ignorant fool', said Dr. Kumar, speaking in a rage, 'don't you know whom you're talking to ? We 'are two doctors you're insulting'.

'I'm not insulting you Sir' replied the Guard hotly, 'You're insulting me. I'm only doing my duty and I don't care even if you are doctors'.

'We 're going to be here only for 15 minutes. Can't you allow our car in even for that amount of time ?', asked Mr. Khanna

'I can't break the rule even for 1 minute, leave alone 15 minutes', the Guard stuck to his position.

'Very well, get Mr. Sumant on the telephone' demanded Dr. Kumar.

'OK Sir, please come this way', said the Guard.

The Guard led the two doctors to the intercom in his booth and connected them with HED upstairs. Mr. Basu took the call, informed Dr. Kumar that Mr. Sumant was away on a sales call and would they please come up. When Dr. Kumar related what had transpired with the Guard, Mr. Basu was apologetic, but said he too was helpless as he could do nothing about the matter, as it was indeed a company rule. 'This indeed is our rule and we are extremely sorry, but you see, I would need to approach the Regional Manager for such a request. Please try to understand our position', Mr. Basu tried to explain the situation.

Finally, finding no other solution in sight, the two doctors took their car into the street and finding no parking place nearby, they had to walk down a long way in the hot blazing sun, after parking their car. By the time they were in Mr. Basu's cabin, they were hot and sweating, and boiling with rage and were in extremely bad humour. Sitting down Dr. Khanna said at once-

'I've come for my Console'.

'Of Course, it is absolutely ready', replied Mr. Basu

'Where is the bill ?', asked Dr. Khanna

Mr. Basu rang the bell and asked Mr. Mittal to come to his cabin. When Mr. Mittal came in, Mr. Basu said -

'This is Dr. Khanna. Dr. Kumar you already know. Please bring Dr. Khanna's bill."

Mr. Mittal then brought in the bill and handed it to Dr. Khanna. Dr. Khanna just gave a look at the amount of Rs. 12,000/-, took out his cheque book and wrote out a cheque for the entire amount, and handed it to Mr. Basu without a word. Mr. Basu, took the cheque and uncertain of what to do next, asked whether they would like coffee or a cold drink.

'We haven't the time. Please bring the Console', said Dr. Kumar.

The Console was brought and handed over to Dr. Khanna Dr. Khanna took it and both the doctors went out without as word.

As Mr. Mittal and Mr. Basu were discussing the incident in Mr. Basu's cabin, Dr. Khanna rang up Mr. Basu from the Security Guard's intercom. He reported that the Security Guard was not allowing them to go out with the Console without a Gate Pass.

'But I thought you'd put the Console in your hand bag. Your bag was big enough for you to put the Console in', said Mr. Basu helplessly.

'No it is in my hand, and the Security Guard is demanding a Gate Pass for it', replied Dr. Khanna.

'Oh, we're very sorry, I'm sending you a Gate Pass immediately', replied Mr. Basu urgently.

A Gate pass was immediately written out and another Sales Engineer took the pass and rushed out to the lift to go down with it. But just as he got near the lift, he saw both the doctors coming out of it. Dr. Kumar just grabbed the Gate Pass from the engineer's hand, and without a word both of them went down the lift again.

That evening when Mr. Sumant returned back to the office and heard about the entire episode, he hastily telephoned Dr. Kumar to apologise and to enquire how badly Dr. Khanna had taken the incident. To his horror he found not only had Dr. Khanna taken it very badly, but Dr. Kumar was also very upset about the supposed 'insult', and would hardly talk to Dr. Sumant.

'Not only did we receive sordid treatment at the hands of your security guard, but we were also highly insulted by your company's behaviour. I've never felt more humiliated before, and just when I'd taken along a new customer with me and was singing your praises all along', said Dr. Kumar.

Mr. Sumant then knew that the problem had gone beyond his hands and it had to be settled only at the level of his boss. He went to Mr. Basu and requested him to refund the Rs. 12,000/- as a measure of goodwill and as compensation for the 'insult' that they had felt. But Mr. Basu had an even better idea. He thought of visiting Dr. Khanna himself and to personally apologise and then tell him that he had come to return the money, but if Dr. Khanna still felt like buying the machine from them, then that money could be taken as an advance against his order for the CT Scanner . Mr. Sumant also approved of the idea, but felt that it would be better to tell Dr. Kumar first about it, or else he might feel offended that the company had bypassed him. Mr. Basu agreed and telephoned Dr. Kumar.

Dr. Kumar was cold and aloof in his manner at first, but cheered up considerably when he heard Dr. Basu's proposal. But he had one request. He asked Mr. Basu to tell Dr. Khanna that this was being done at Dr. Kumar's request. Mr. Basu readily agreed.

The next day, Mr. Basu and Mr. Sumant found out the time when Dr. Khanna would be free and available, made an appointment and landed of at his clinic in time. They were made to wait for half an hour before Dr. Khanna would see them. Finally, when they were allowed in, Mr. Basue placed his proposal before Dr. Khanna. Dr. Khanna had thawed a little at the profuse apology that both Mr. Basu and Mr. Sumant offered and then became quite amiable when the proposal was put before him.

'But how will you change the servicing charge to sales advance ?', enquired Dr. Khanna immediately.

'Oh, we have many government transactions, and we can show that we have given free servicing to one of them in our books of accounts', replies Mr. basu confidently.

'But is it quite possible'. Dr. Khanna wanted to be sure.

'Well, it is difficult, but possible', admitted Mr. Basu. 'We wouldn't have done it for anyone else, except for Dr. Kumar. It was he who insisted that we do this for you', said Dr. Basu smoothly.

'Oh, is that so?', said Dr. Khanna, quite pleased.

Later Dr. Khanna readily and immediately wrote out an order to M/s ABC Manufacturing Ltd. placing an order for the most expensive CT Scanner of the company.

Early next morning, Mr. Basu received a telephone call from Dr. Kumar 'I'm glad the deal has been clinched. Dr. Khanna phoned me last night to tell me that he really appreciated my request to you to put forward that proposal to him. I am also happy that his doubt about my influence over your company has been removed. Remember me whenever you need me next.'

Then he added- 'Oh, by the way, can you send my commission soon this time ? I am planning to go to Delhi with my family for a holiday next month'.

Later Mr. Basu told his people in the department 'Had we returned the money as Sumant wanted to do, we should have been left only with a free servicing bill. Now, instead we have an order for an expensive CT Scanner. One should know how to play by the rules of the business'.

Questions of the Case Study :

1. How, according to your opinion, ethical are the 'rules of the business' that Mr. Basu professed to play by ?
2. Discuss the stand taken by the security guard and how ethical or unethical you find his behaviour with respect to increasing business for his company.
3. Discuss the ethical role of Dr. Kumar.
4. Discuss the ethical conduct of this company, taking into account its policies, its standard of moral conduct and the rules of doing business.
5. Has the behaviour of Dr. Kumar, Mr. Basu, Mr. Mittal and Mr. Sumant been out side the realms of ethical conduct, as far as this incident is concerned ?
6. What would you have done, had you been in Mr. Basu's place? In Mr. Sumant's place?

Summary of the Chapter in brief :

* Different cultures of the world has their own ethical practices. The basic values of a society constitutes the core of its culture.
* It is not possible to study the moral values of man without studying the culture from which it originates.
* Man's moral standards and value system is constructed by the customs and norms of his culture.

* It is quite natural that like legal standards, ethical standards also differ among nations, societies and cultures.
* There is a difference between believing that something is right and that something is actually right.
* Business ethical behaviour consists of doing what is of greatest benefit to the society and to the community.
* The relationship between social culture and individual ethics can be considered from four different perspectives, which are-
  1. Social - Contract Theory
  2. Collectivism or Socialism Theory
  3. Organic Theory
  4. Idealistic or Group-Mind Theory.
* The Social Contract Theory stated that people established societies out of social contract, and established rules and regulations, laws and ethics to govern themselves.
* According to the Collective or Socialism Theory, man had always lived in societies, and the cultural norms of the society make it imperative for the individual to follow its rules and regulations, norms and moral standards of behaviour.
* The Organic Theory states that the individuals belonging to the society are interdependent amongst themselves and in turn to the society. Social norms, values and ethics are organic in nature, forever changing, forever evolving.
* The Idealistic or Group - Mind Theory states that the relation between society and an individual is spiritual and only through a social structure can man develop his moral character and ethical values and strive for excellence.
* Ethical values are culture specific, yet there are may be values which are common to all cultures all over the world.
* Morality refers to the standards of behaviour by which people are judged in their relationships with others.
* The concept of ethics arises only in relation to others in the society. Any behaviour which has no impact upon others, cannot be termed ethical or unethical.
* The reason why ethics is used in the plural term is because it encompasses a system of interrelated beliefs and values of the culture in question.
* Certain principles are common to all cultures. **First**, among them is that it is unethical and downright immoral to cause other members of the society some harm in the pursuit of one's happiness and material success. **Secondly**, people do not act solely for their own self interest and there lies a responsibility on each member of the group for the welfare of the other members of the group. **Thirdly**, just as a man takes from society, so also is man indebted to society in the same measure. **Fourthly,** is the principle of Fairness. **Fifthly,** is the principle of Integrity and Honesty. **Finally,** is the principle of Human Dignity.
* While the individual is affected and influenced by the level of moral standards of behaviour and the ethical systems of values and beliefs of the society, the society

too can only be the sum total of the moral standards of the individuals who make up the society.

* The higher the moral standards and ethical values of the individuals of the society, higher is the moral standards and ethical values of the society.

EXPECTED QUESTIONS:

1. Discuss how cultural imperatives determine the ethical standards of a society.
2. Does the ethical standards of the society affect the individual or is it verse versa ? Discuss.
3. Explain the relationship between social culture and individual ethics.
4. Can an individual exhibit ethical behaviour in isolation, away from the social setup? Why or why not ?
5. Discuss certain values and principles that are common to almost all cultures.

Chapter 5

Role of Legislation & Other Bodies in Ethical Business Behaviour

The legal system, with all its laws and regulations should ideally form a framework to regulate and to ensure ethical business behaviour. Since the law is an universally accepted, consistent and enforceable set of rules and regulations, established by the highest body of the society to govern behaviour within that society, it stands to reason that the Law should decide upon the question of ethics in the society. Moreover, if the law represents collective moral standards and judgements of the society, then the legal system should be a fit body to be the ultimate authority and the last say in ethical behaviour. But is it really so ?

Let us take an example. During the Indian Freedom Struggle, Mahatma Gandhi gave a call to his coutrymen to come out and march with him to break the Salt Law. In 621 B.C., an Athenian legislator designed some extremely harsh, cruel laws, which came to be known as the Draconian Laws. Even today, we have many nations of the world, and indeed some states of our country also, protesting against Draconian Laws and 'black laws', which are considered to be inhuman and unfair. Until 1962, the United States of America legally enforced racial discrimination. Considering the above examples, can it truly be left upon the legal system to determine the ethical conduct of a society, a community or a nation ?

Majority of the laws all over the world, do indeed, reflect collective moral judgements. Most laws are just, fair and aimed at human welfare and it is in fact a minuscule number of laws which are debatable. However, the fact remains that we are not sure as to how far we can use the legal system to form ethical decisions when faced with managerial dilemmas.

Many people may agree that if some laws are indeed found to be immoral of at least unfair, they could always be changes and new laws can be enacted to take their place. However, the contention is that if laws can be changed and interchanged so readily and easily, then 'good' and 'moral' laws may also be changed in the event of a corrupt and evil government coming to power, sometimes, somewhere; and moral and fair laws may get converted to immoral and unfair laws. This is only a hypothetical situation and the possibility of it occurring in reality is remote; but the point is that this situation may be possible in theory. The fact remains that laws are changeable, whereas ethics is **not**. But, the above discussion should not lead one to misinterpret that laws are usually unethical, or can be changed very easily to make them unethical. Laws **are** , by and large, fair and moral. But it is not easy to accept that laws can be the foundation of ethics, or even that laws can ensure ethical behaviour. We shall elaborate this point a little later.

There are many situations in life, where just following the law does not make one ethical. For example, it you knew that your neighbour's son is crying to sleep on an empty stomach, there is no law on earth that says that you must share your dinner with him. If you do so, you are doing it not because of some legal compulsion, but by the compulsion of your value system- because your ethics, your sense of compassion, compels you to share your dinner with a hungry child. If your next door neighbour has just today lost their only son in a motorcycle accident, just when you wanted to celebrate the birthday of your only son with gaiety, music, guests, enjoyment and much merry-making, there is no law to prohibit you from doing so. If you decide not to, it is because of the dictates of your conscience, not because of the dictates of the law. Your conscience, your ethical value system and your principles forbids you to rejoice when someone else nearby is in sorrow. The law has no role to play in such a situation.

There is no law involved in all the actions mentioned above. What is involved is our values, morals and ethical conduct. You may logically explain to yourself that not celebrating your son's birthday is not going to bring back your neighbour's son to life. Moreover, it may have even provided you with the perception that life is too short to waste-one should enjoy whatever is left of life, the sheer joy of just being alive. You may also argue that giving one dinner to your neighbour's hungry child is not going to feed him forever or from preventing him from being hungry for the next meal. Many other logical arguments for and against the point can be raised. But fact remains that what is involved in all these situations is not logic - its psychology - your psychology.

Moreover, not all laws have moral choice. There are many laws which do not involve any ethicality questions - for example, we are required to walk on the left hand side of the road. This is done to ensure traffic control and traffic discipline, but a question of ethics is not involved here. You cannot assert that your value system compells you to walk on the right side of the road, without causing a road accident and subsequent traffic chaos.

Again, all moral and ethical actions do not involve the law. For example, it is ethical to love and respect your parents, but there is no law for it, except when they are deliberately mistreated by their children and cruelty treated. In a court room, a witness is required to take an oath that he or she would speak only the truth and nothing but the truth. The logical implication of this seems to be that everywhere else, except the courtroom, he is free to speak the false.

Thus, we see that there are certain requirements of law that reflect the moral standards of society, but not all laws have ethical implication nor can all laws be passed for all possible ethical behaviour. Law codifies human behaviour, but not all human behaviour can be codified. Human behaviour are enormous and infinite. Apart from the considerable challenge that it would provide in enforcing them, there would also be a lack of agreement in defining and interpreting such laws.

Thus, law represent the minimum standards of behaviour expected from people. Merely following the law, does not make one ethical. In fact, everyday heroism or even life time heroism comes through following a high standard of ethical behaviour and through high ideals; not through following the law. Beyond that minimum standard of behaviour enforceable by law lies ethical behaviour or value-based behaviour. Ethical and moral behaviour comes from individual initiative, and not from legal force. To be termed ethically 'right', one has to act much more beyond legal expectations.

Another aspect of the legal system is that it **prohibits** us of certain actions. It also spells out the negative consequences of our not following the law - that is legal punishment. However, ethical behaviour **encourages** us to do certain things and explains the benefits, i.e., the positive aspects of these ethical behaviour. For example, the law tells us **not** to steal, **not** to kill, but ethics tells us to **do** good, **speak** the truth, **help** others in distress. Thus, there is a **positive** aspect inherent in ethical behaviour, whereas the law is more concerned about **negative** behaviour.

Yet another aspect of the law is that ethics precedes the action, the law follows it. Ethics tells us what we should strive to develop in ourselves, so that we have a high moral standard and a developed value system. On the other hand, law tends to be more concerned with the consequences of the negative action - what punishment would follow, who is guilty and how shall justice be done. If ethics tells us to be honest, then the law is more concerned about the punishment to be given because one was dishonest under certain sections (Eg. Section 420) of the Indian Penal Code.

Moreover, the law is an universally accepted, published document, whereas ethics do be not yet have an universally accepted, consistent and published concept - it is abstract, culture specific and left to the individual for interpretation and action.

Finally, the law clearly specifies what action would be taken against a person if he or she violates the provisions of to legal system. But, in case of ethics, there is no specific outcome of an unethical action. What would be the consequences of an unethical action is not very clear, not always the same and not universally accepted. An unethical action may have many repercussions and widespread ramifications.

Let us now summarise the above discussion with the following points-

5.1 - Relationship between Law and Ethics :

1. All legal provisions may not be ethical and some are, at best, debatable.
2. All ethical actions are not governed by laws.
3. Not all laws have moral choice.
4. Laws are specific concepts, ethics is abstract.
5. Laws represent the minimum standards of human behaviour, ethical behaviour goes much beyond the legal expectations.
6. Ethics has a positive aspect, whereas the law is more concerned about negative behaviour.
7. Ethics precedes action; the law follows it.
8. The law is universally accepted within its jurisdiction, and is enforceable, whereas ethics is not always universally accepted and is not enforceable by force or pressure.
9. Law prescribes punishments for illegal acts, whereas ethics do not clearly prescribe specific punishment for an unethical act, since the outcome of an unethical act is not always clear.

Thus, in conclusion we may state that laws provide the human society with the minimum standards of behaviour, but laws do not duplicate the value system of the society. Laws are not a replica of the ethical system, nor are laws an expression of the moral standards of the society. Laws merely provide us with the guidelines of behaviour for a disciplines, peaceful and safe society.

The law can be considered as a guide to managerial decisions, but it is not enough to usher in ethical business behaviour. Since the law does not duplicate the ethical value system of the society, we cannot accept it as a representation of the complete collective moral values of the society. Hence, depending solely on the rules or on the law to solve our managerial ethical dilemma, is not sufficient. But, not behaving ethically in business, just because there exists no laws to force us to so behave, is no excuse.

Business, have, do and will resort to antisocial and corrupt malpractices, if there are no legal provisions to restraint them. One cannot expect every business to operate out of altruistic motives alone, or all managers to be self-directed. Hence, businesses cannot be left alone to regulate themselves. Rules, regulations and legislation, and their enforcement should be ensured to restrain the worst types of corporate malpractices and lawlessness. Even with the existence of a most elaborate system of legal practices, businesses do find the means to circumvent around the legal provisions, even while keeping within the law. Any growing and thriving economy requires the support of a well- integrated legal framework, which provides for individual initiative and enterprise, encourages private entrepreneurial efforts, but at the same time restrains business from malpractices and curbs excesses. However, this alone is not enough. There are many areas of fairplay which are beyond the purview of the law. Businesses in general must accept that, for ethical business practices to thrive and survive, there is a need for individual initiative by all businesses to play by the rules of ethics. These rules are founded on such shared values as honesty, integrity, transparency, concern for human life and welfare, among others.

In the case of India, Article 39-A of the Directive Principles of State Policy of the Indian Constitution, lays down in clear terms the role of the legal system in the society. It states that; "The State shall secure that the operation of the legal system promotes justice, on a basis of equal opportunity, and shall, in particular, provide for legal aid, by suitable legislation of schemes or in any other way, to ensure that opportunities for securing justice are not denied to any citizen by reason of economic or other disabilities".

The law is supported by framework of highly specialised social institutions. There are agencies to enforce the provisions of the law. The government has the Police to enforce the law. Advocates and lawyers exist to give justice to people according to the law, Law Courts exist to interpret and implement the law, and so on. But when in the court room, an individual experiences that the aim of lawyers is on winning the case and not on providing justice to the individual, his perception of the law changes. When the aim of the police is on keeping law and order situations peaceful, rather than on ensuring safety and security of human life and property, then people feel that the law is no good. When these social institutions do not meet people's expectations from them, then people generally conclude that it is the law which is not perfect. All these contribute to people feeling that the law is not an ideal concept of rules to guide ethical behaviour.

Laws do not deliberatly go about making a mockery of ethics and justice. In fact, all laws have some genuine concern for social welfare and high, moral foundation. The governments of the country also strives to ensure that laws and the legal system and their operations are fair and just.

True Marketplace Example 1:

That the law has the power and also the responsibility to enforce ethical behaviour within the work place, is also true. In its first-ever judgement on workplace harassment, an industrial court at Mumbai in February 1999, directed the company, Steelage Industries, to pay Rs. 40,000 to a woman employee for its failure to protect her from humiliation by her boss.

The female employee in question, a telephone operator, has put in 22 years of excellent service in the company, and had a very good record. Now being a cancer patient, she had sought permission to come late to office as she needed frequent medical treatment. Instead the company's General Manager (HRD), taking advantage of her helplessness, made sexual advances towards her, thereby causing her to suffer from hypertension. He even proposed her increments, off-hand monetary help and a transfer to the company's showroom, to enhance privacy to carry on his offensive behaviour towards her.

All these were not enough for the company's General Manager (HRD), and there was more to the story. After her written complaint about the sexual harassment by the GM (HRD), to the company's President & Executive Director, she was transferred by the GM (HRD) on October 27, 1995 from the company's corporate office to its factory. This affected her service conditions, as it was done without giving her notice under the Industrial Disputes Act, 1947.

Holding the company and its officer guilty of unfair labour practices the court quashed the order of October 27, 1995 and directed the company's GM (HRD), to pay an additional amount of Rs.10,000/-.

The judgement is considered significant in legal circles as this is the first instance that an industrial court has actually gone through evidence of sexual harassment (**Source**: The Telegraph, dated Jan. 18, 1999).

That a company could subject a woman employee to such harassment, is in itself loathsome and disgusting and calls for stringent punishment, but that it could be meted out to an employee, whether male or female, who had put in 22 years of dedicated service with an excellent track record, is even more repulsive. However, the fact that this was done to a woman suffering from a life - threatening illness like cancer, makes it inhuman, barbaric and unbelievable, That she received justice and relief from the law, is encouraging. In fact, it was only the law which could come to her rescue in her time of distress. This example is an evidence of how the legislature can enforce ethical business behaviour within the workplace and help employees receive fair and just treatment from the management. This is an example of the law controlling and regulating ethical business behaviour, and making organisations accountable for their acts of commission and commission.

True Marketplace Example 2

Sometimes examples such as this, of awarding legal punishment, to the organisation, can make other organisations more cautious, while encouraging and supporting those affected, i.e. consumers, employees, suppliers, dealers, etc. Organisations sometimes become so wary and cautious of legal action, that they take all measures possible, to avoid a legal suit.

Recently, The Consumer Products Safety Commission (CPSC) found multi-coloured children umbrellas and beverage mugs too dangerous to be in the American market.

So the US company, Gymboree Corporation, the manufacturers of beach and golf sun shaded had to withdraw from the market 6,500 children's umbrellas with colourful designs. The Reason ? The colours were found to contain a high level of lead. Poisoning by lead in children is associated with behavioural problems, learning disabilities and growth retardation. The moment Gymboree realised that its products had a defect, to avoid legal suit, it withdraw the entire consignment of umbrellas from shop shelves.

When four consumers in the US complained of being burnt from using the Java Lava brand of micro waveable beverage mugs, Vesture Company which manufactured them, recalled 44,000, mugs off the supermarkets. When heated in a microwave, the mug could ignite, posing a fire hazard. Its plastic shell could also crack open. Recently in the UK, 'The Guardian' newspaper published a product recall of Chicken Tonight Sizzle & Stir Sauces. As a precautionary measure, the sauces were taken off the shelf, when a few packs were found defective.

In India, such prompt and decisive action against defective goods by manufacturers has not yet resulted. Inspite of the presence of all sorts of defective products in the market place, many consumers are unaware that they can approach the law for justice as consumers. Even if consumers are aware, seeking justice from consumer courts is a long drawn out process, painstaking efforts and loss of enormous time, involving umpteen harried visits to the court.

The recall of the umbrellas and mugs in the US was conducted by the industry in cooperation with the Consumer Products Safety Commission (CPSC), an independent regulatory agency. It is a safety triangle that combines the joint efforts of the industry, government and the consumers to ensure product safety. The commission's objectives are to make products used in homes, schools and places of recreation safe. While the Food & Drug Administration (FDA) deals with only food and drugs, CPSC was established to protect the public against unreasonable risks of injuries and deaths associated with consumer products.

According to CPSC data, there are 15,000 different types of consumer products in the market place and the estimated annual losses associated with consumer products in the US are 21,400 deaths, 30 million injuries and 200 billion dollars in societal costs. It is to reduce this colossal loss that the Commission seeks to reduce unreasonable risks associated with products. A product apparently safe - but bearing unsafe characteristics - threatens to infringe on consumer's right to safety. The CPSC enjoys immense clout and muscle power as they work closely with federal governments in the USA. When an industry is aware of a defect in a product it is mandatory to immediately inform the CPSC. Erring manufacturers have to face stringent laws and hefty fines. Enforcement is very strict. There is no way a manufacturer can escape if found guilty.

(**Source** : The Telegraph, Feb. 11, 1999, page-18.)

This is another example of ethical behaviour being legally enforced by a legal body. In India, we have the Consumer Protection Act, where from, consumers can get relief from unethical behaviour by companies.

5.2 Role of the Government of Indian in Enforcing Ethical Behaviour

In India, the government, state or central, has a great inpact on how businesses conduct their affairs. In fact, there is hardly any country in the world, the business of which are not influenced by state activities, in one way or the other. Even in market economies, the government owns and controls certain industries, which it considered critical. This is true even of the members of the European Economist Community (EEC), Canada, Sweden, etc.

Marshal E. Dimock, in his book, 'Business & Government ', states that taken together, the central activities of the government cut across all the broad categories of economic enterprises, namely entry into business, conduct of the enterprise, results and relationships.

First, the government may determine the conditions under which persons or associations may **enter** certain lines of business as in the granting of a Charter, a Franchise, or a Licence.

Secondly, the government may regulate or assist the **conduct** of economic ventures of many kinds, once they are under way. This includes controls that merely lay down general standards and prohibitions and those that interfere with matters that maybe considered managerial.

Third, public control may extend to the **results** of business operation as in the limitation of public - utility profits, ceiling on dividends and the imposition of excess - profits taxes on business generally.

Finally, the government **controls** the relationships between the various segments of the economy, the purpose being to settle conflicts of interests or of legal rights and to prevent an undue concentration of economic power in one place.

All these activities in principle, are, no doubt, highly moral and ethical . The goals are lofty and the concern is, undoubtedly for the welfare of the society, so that social imbalances does not result from economic activities. Consider what a World Bank Working Paper 'State Intervention in the Industrialisation of Developing Countries: Selected Issues', (Washington: World Bank, July, 1979), had to say -

> "It points out that the major justification for the industrial licensing system is the belief that the market mechanism is unable to allocate the scarce resources in the **socially optimal way**. The common presumption of this is that the State is omniscient and there resulting allocation of resources will be the socially optimal or desirable one".

With such genuine concern for social welfare, what then goes wrong ? Obviously, the fault lies in the discretionary nature of its implementation.

Not only limited to mere principles and visions, the government also takes upon itself to initiate actions for public good . For example, when private enterprises fail, the government takes over such enterprises so that their services continue to reach people and that their employees do not become unemployed. The government also take over private enterprises when there is a pronounced and blatant wastage of national resources; and more significantly when the private enterprises fail to consider themselves as trustees of public good and above all abuses its power, specially where these enterprises operate in a monopoly or semi-monopoly market.

The modern state is a custodian of the welfare of the society. The welfare government has the responsibility to bring about all-round prosperity in the society. To this end, the

Indian Constitution incorporates a number of welfare measures that earmarks the economic responsibilities of the Central and the state governments.

5.3 The Indian Constitution

The Preamble of the Indian Constitution conveys the general objective and intention of the legislature in enacting it. Among others, it also expresses the socio-economic **value** it envisages to promote. The Preamble of the Indian Constitution States that attainment of social, economic and political **justice,** and **equality** of status and of opportunity should be among the most important basic guiding principles of the functioning of the state.

The Fundamental Rights to citizens, laid down in the Indian Constitution aims at preventing the government and the legislature from becoming totalitarian. This is, again, very noble in principle. But in reality, it has been experienced that there is much more to be desired.

The Right to Equality prohibited discrimination against any citizen and ensures equality of opportunity to all citizens. On the other hand, in public employment, the enterprises are required to reserve posts for backward classes, and caste, not merit, forms the criterion for appointment. This is done in the guise of providing justice to a section of the society which is not adequately represented in employment and elsewhere. However, in most cases it is highly exploited, the benefits not going to those who really need them. Moreover, the debate remains as to whether one section of the society can be provided justice at the expense of another section, like say, a poverty-striken educated youth, but of a high caste.

The Constitution assures citizens as their fundamental right, the freedom to practice any profession, carry on any occupation, trade or business. In this connection, the government is empowered to make laws relating to professional or technical qualifications necessary for practising any profession or for carrying on any trade, business, industry or service, whether to the exclusion, complete or partial, of citizens of otherwise.

The Fundamental Rights against Exploitation prohibits traffic in human beings and beggars and other forms of forced labour, and any contravention of this provision shall be an offence punishable in accordance with the law.

The Directive Principles of State Policy of the Indian Constitution guides the state in making policies and their principles are taken into account in making laws. Some of the Directive Principles which promotes ethical behaviour are cited below.

1. The State shall strive to promote the welfare of people by securing and protecting as effectively as it may, a social order in which justice, social, economic or political, shall form all the institutions of national life. (Article 38(1)).
2. The State shall in particular, strive to minimise the inequalities in income and endeavour to eliminate inequalities in status, facilities and opportunities, not only among individuals but also amongst groups of people residing in different areas of engaged in different vocations. (Article 38 (2)).
3. The state shall, in particular, direct its policy towards securing –
   (i) that the citizen, men and women equally, have the right to an adequate means of livelihood;

(ii) that the ownership and control of the material resources of the community are so distributed as best to subserve the common good;

(ii) that the operation of the economic system does not result in the concentration of wealth and means of production to the common detriment;

(iv) that there is equal pay for equal work for both men and women;

(v) that the health and strength of workers, men and women, and the tender age of children are not abused and that citizens are not forced by economic necessity to enter a vocation unsuited to their age or strength; and

(vi) that children are given opportunities and facilities to develop in a healthy manner and in conditions of freedom and dignity and that children and youth are protected against exploitation and against moral and material abandonment. (Article 39).

4. The State shall secure that the operation of the legal system promotes justice, on a basis of equal opportunity, and shall in particular, provide for legal aid, by suitable legislation of schemes or in any other way, to ensure that opportunities for securing justice are not denied to any citizen by reason of economic or other disabilities. (Article 39-A).
5. The State shall, with the limits of its economic capacity and development make effective provision for securing the right to work, to education and to public assistance in cases of unemployment, old age, sickness and disablement, and in other cases of undeserved want (Article 41).
6. The State shall make provisions for securing just and humane conditions of work and for maternity relief. (Articles 42).
7. The State shall endeavour to secure, by suitable legislation or economic organisation or in another way, to all workers, agricultural, industrial of otherwise, a living wage, conditions of work ensuring a decent standard of life and full enjoyment of leisure and social and cultural opportunities and, in particular, the State shall endeavour to promote cottage industries on an individual or cooperative basis in rural area. (Article 43).
8. The State shall take steps, by suitable legislation or in any other way, to secure the participation of workers in the management of undertakings, establishment or other organisations engaged in any industry.(Article 43-A).
9. The State shall endeavour to protect and improve the environment and to safeguard the forests and wild life of the country (Articles 48).

The above mentioned Directive Principles clearly shows that the government has considerable influence upon business behaviour if it has to attain the egalitarian goals established by the Constitution. To carry out its responsibilities, the Constitution has provided for commensurate authority also, to the government. In Articles 43, 43-A of the Directive Principles, the Constitution has granted the authority to attain its goals, through 'suitable legislation's. Article 39-A of the Directive Principles is a clear indication of the role of legislation in the Indian society.

5.4 Indian Business Laws and Their Impact on Ethical Behaviour

Over the years, with a view to establishing control and to regulate business as also to achieve the lofty goals of a welfare state, as laid down in the Indian Constitution, the government has armed itself with numerous laws relating to business. The Directive Principles of State Policy of the Indian Constitution also provides enormous scope for government intervention in the functioning of businesses. All laws relating to businesses in India, can be broadly classified into two categories:

a) Business Laws
b) Labour Laws

(A) Business Laws

Some of the important business laws which aims to regulate ethical business behaviour are-

1. The Industries (Development & Regulation) Act

This Act, enacted in 1951 with the main objective of giving practical effect to the industrial policy, gave the government sweeping powers to control industries. It empowered the Central Government to develop and regulate the industrial sector in India, through suitable and appropriate means.

However, it was felt that the objectives of this Act was not being achieved and it has resulted in the distribution of the benefits of developments more for the richer sections than the poorer sections of society. A report on the operation of licensing under this Act by the Planning Commission, in 1966 (by Prof. Hazari who was appointed Honorary Consultant by the Planning Commission), stated that -

(i) the working of the planned economy had contributed to the growth of big companies;

(ii) the working of the industrial licensing system enabled the large industrial houses to obtain a disproportionately large share of the licences issued;

(iii) some of the large industrial bossed were guilty of non-implementation of licences and pre-emption or foreclosure of capacity;

(iv) the operation of the industrial licensing system was not successful in achieving the objective of regional dispersal of industries;

(v) the large industrial houses were the major beneficiaries of public financial institutions.

These points were once again more or less confirmed by the Industrial Licensing Policy Inquiry Committee (ILPIC), popularly known as the Dutt Committee, which was appointed in July 1967, and its report submitted in July 1969.

Thus, this Act, has not only failed to compel business to behave ethically, it has, on the other hand, encouraged unethical behaviour of big business houses.

In 'Industrial Change in India 1970-2000', George Rosan the American economist who carried out three studies of Indian Industrialisation during different decades, has this to say in his last study–

"The added restrictions or growth and entry by large and small firms have created new opportunities for private firms to earn monopoly rents or to enhance existing rents. Such rents arise from having first access to restricted or reserved productions areas. In many cases, the possibilities of gain from achieving such a position are more lucrative than from actually increasing production".

Thus, many controls of the government which were sought to be enforced through legislation, were, no doubt, introduced with good intentions, but they not only failed to achieve the avowed objectives fully, but in the process, resulted in much unethical behaviour particularly by the big business houses.

2. Foreign Exchange Regulation Act, 1973

The Foreign Exchange Regulation Act (FERA), 1973, which repealed the Foreign Exchange Regulation Act of 1947, applies to all citizens of India outside India and to branches of companies registered or incorporated in India. The main objective of the FERA is the conservation of the foreign exchange resources of the country and the proper utilisation thereof in the interests of the economic developments of the country.

Though the FERA was started with a noble objective and patriotic feelings, its implementation has not resulted in the desired effects. In case of foreign investment and collaboration, there are many instances of government approach and performance being totally different from the avowed policy. Foreign investment and collaboration have been sanctioned in many cases which have had no relevance to national priorities and development needs. On the other hand, foreign investment and collaboration desperately needed in critical sectors of the economy, like power, oil, transport, has either been delayed or shelved, for example, the Enron Power Project.

This Act, has come in for severe criticisms. It has resulted in a widening trade gap. It has also been said to have been a potent source of corruption, black money and major scams.

Thus, the FERA regulating and encouraging ethical business behaviour has remained a far cry. Instead of encouraging ethical business behaviour, its imposition has resulted in unethical behaviour not only in the case of companies, but also in the case of individuals.

3. The Companies Act, 1956

The Companies Act, 1956, provides for a greater governmental control over the formation and management of companies. Among its many objectives, the most significant ones, from the ethical point of view are that it seeks to provide a minimum standard of good behaviour and business honesty in company promotion and management; recognition of the legitimate interest of shareholders and creditors and the duty of management not to prejudice to jeopardise those interests; a fair and true disclosure of the affairs of the company; a higher standard of accounting and auditing; recognition of the rights of shareholders to receive reasonable information and facilities for exercising an intellectual judgment with reference to the management; a check on their transactions where there was a possibility of conflict of duty and interest; a provision for investigation into the affairs of any company managed in a manner oppressive to a minority of the shareholders or prejudicial to the interest of the company as a whole; and enforcement of the performance of duties by the management of the company.

In the 'Report of the High-Powered Expert Committee on Companies & MRTP Acts', Government of India, popularly known as the Sachar Committee, observes that 'although the present Act provides for the formation of unlimited companies, the latter have hardly had any useful career in the growth and development of the corporate sector'. It also said, 'In our view, the present position with regard to foreign companies...... .... is rather unsatisfactory'. There exists many provisions in the Companies Act, which are subject to manipulations. Companies resort to unfair practices while disclosing their affairs, and this Act has been helpless to detect and punish such offences.

4. The Monopolies & Restrictive Trade Practices Act, 1969

This Act was designed to regulate the functioning of the large industrial houses and dominant undertakings. Its objective is to control the concentration of economic power and monopolies and to prohibit monopolistic, restrictive and unfair trade practices.

As far as ethical business behaviour is concerned, this is a very significant piece of legislation, as most unethical business conduct results in unfair trade practices and the concentration of economic power. If this Act were to be strictly enforced, many unethical and corrupt business practices would automatically die out. But has this Act been effective in enforcing and encouraging ethical business behaviour ? Let's find out.

Let's take the example of educational institutes in our country. Advertisements in the field of academics can be as misleading as in all other products. Many moneymaking machines, going by the name of educational institutions, offer advertisements that are blatantly false and are aimed at capturing the gullible and unsuspecting student community. Specially in the months of March and April, at the beginning of the academic year, newspapers are bombarded with advertisements by various educational institutes offering numerous courses. These institutes, demanding steep course fees, make many exaggerated claims that student come to find out only after they have paid the advance fees and have committed themselves and have spend about 6-12 months in the institutes. And of course, by the time they find out, there is no turning back for the students. Firstly, because the student has already invested his time with the institute and stands to lose one academic year, if he withdraws now. Secondly, most institutes have an examination pattern consisting of internal marks and offending either the management or the teachers by way of questions about the credibility of the institute means that the student may lose out with his academic result. Thirdly, fees have to be paid in advance, however hafty they may be, and of courses, there is no refund.

And it is to stop such games with a student's career that the MRTP Act can be used. Ever since the MRTP Act was amended in 1984 bringing unfair trade practices under the preview of the Commission, the office of the Director General (Investigation & Registration), Department of Company Affairs and the Commission, have restricted and stopped many misleading and false advertisements.

However, in 1998, the Commission came out with a statement that it has no jurisdiction over matters pertaining to education and educational institutes. Hence even pending cases would now be dismissed. Since education has now been ousted from the preview of the MRTP Act, hence institutes would have a field day in offering advertisements as they like without anybody to control them.

The Sachar Committee Reported Thus

"It is a well-established principle of jurisprudence that for every wrong there must be a remedy. It is approved that prohibited practices, if indulged in, are likely to cause grave loss or damage to many consumers. But in the Act, there is no provision for awarding the damages .... This is a highly unsatisfactory state of affairs".

Francis Cherunilam, in 'Business & Government' analyses the impact the MRTP Act on the economy, in following terms–

There is considerable delay in disposal of cases under the MRTP Act. It has been seen that the MRTP Act has proved ineffective in controlling economic concentration. On the other hand, the MRTP Act also hinders economic growth and contrary to its objective, has in fact restricted competition to the common detriment, particularly in the large industrial sector. The MRTP Act designed to safeguard against monopolies and restrictive trade practices has in fact, guarded the large industrial houses in certain sectors from potential competition, from other large houses. Even after decades since its enactment, and despite major amendments, the MRTP Act still continues to be very controversial and perplexing, and has had a dubious impact on the control of the concentration of economic power. The restraints on the large companies have had an adverse effect on the industrial development in particular and on the economic development in general. There is no doubt, then, that such an ineffective piece of legislation had to ultimately be done away with.

5. The Essential Commodities Act, 1955

The Essential Commodities Act was established in 1955, to provide, in the interest of the general public, control of the production, supply and distribution of, and trade and commerce in, certain commodities. The government had listed specific commodities as 'Essential Commodities'.

The effect of this Act is that it had led to widespread unethical behaviour in the society. Shortage of essential commodities have led to blackmarketing and the generation of considerable sums of black money had led to the creation of a parallel economy. It also resulted in corruption in the bureaucracy which was invested with vast discretionary powers. It also resulted in abuse of shortages of commodities by trade, as it was difficult to control the actual price changed by the retailers.

All in all, this Act also led to unethical behaviour and hardly proved effective in controlling essential commodities.

Apart from these laws mentioned above, there exists a number of other pieces of legalisations which provide the government with sweeping powers to control business behaviour. Some of these are -

The Capital Issues Control Act; 1956

The Securities Contracts (Regulation) Act; 1956

The Prevention of Blackmarketing & Maintenance of Supplies of Essential Commodities Act; 1980

The Conservation of Foreign Exchange & Prevention of Smuggling Activities Act; 1947

The Imports & Exports (Control) Act; 1947

The Indian Patents Act; 1970

The Sick Industrial Companies (Special Provisions) Act; 1985

The Forward Contracts (Regulation) Act; 1952

The Partnership Act; 1932

The Sale of Goods Act; 1930

The Central Sales Tax Act, 1956

The Consumer Protection Act; 1986

The commercial banking sector is sought to be controlled by the Reserve Bank of India (RBI) through the enancment of the following laws -

The Banking Companies Act, 1949 & the Amendment Acts of 1956 & 1962

The Banking Laws (Miscellaneous Provisions) Acts of 1963

Though the government of India had enacted a number of laws to control business behaviour, they have not resulted in promoting ethical business behaviour. In fact, these laws have resulted in more unethical behaviour on the part of business as well as in individuals.

In a speech delivered by T. Thomas, the then Chairman, Hindustan Lever Limited, at the Annual General Meeting of the Company held at Bombay, on 20.2.1980, he remembered-

> "Government in India has such an all-pervasive and predominantly restrictive influence over various aspects of business, example, industrial licensing which decides location, capacity and process; import licensing for machinery and materials; size and price of capital issue; loan finance; pricing; managerial remuneration; expansion plans; distribution restrictions and a host of other enactments".

He further observed -

> "Trying to set up a new industrial unit in India is like running an obstacle race, except that in this case, as you go along, the obstacles are increased both in numbers and complexity without warning. We have estimated that it takes 7 years from the conceptual stage to the production stage for any significant investment to take place in India. Out of this, at least 50% of the time is spent in procedures to satisfy governmental regulations. In any 3-year period of such delay, the cost escalation in modern times will be almost 50%. In our protected economy, the Indian Consumer ultimately pays the price for this cost escalation. At the same time, our exports become less competitive. A further consequence of the delay is that in many cases, we are compelled to import or lose the potential for longer periods".

Thus, we see that there are many instances of meaningless business laws with loopholes that provide scope for nepotism and corruption on one hand, and hold the business or industry to ransom, on the other. Their injudicious and inefficient administration produces more unethical behaviour from business than ethical conduct.

(B) Labour Laws

The Constitution of India, in Article 43, directs the government to secure, by suitable legislation or economic organisation or in any other way to all workers, agricultural, industrial or otherwise, work, a living wage, conditions of work ensuring a decent standard of life, full enjoyment of leisure and social, cultural opportunities.

Labour Legislation represents a community's attitudes to the labour class. The basic philosophy of labour legislation is to ensure regulation of employee-employer relationship to prevent exploitation of employees and , more positively to ensure social justice, labour welfare, needs of national economy and international uniformity as far as possible without compromising national interest and ignoring special problems. Labour Legislation is, therefore, fundamentally based on the principle of social justice where the workman is not exploited. Justice to labour consists of meeting the needs of workmen at least to such an extent that the social good is adequately promoted. Justice requires that rewards, monetary or otherwise, shall be given, whenever and wherever it is due, and credit given wherever it rightly falls.

In the context of inequality of opportunity and economic power between the employer and employee, differences between labour laws exists, because different labour laws have been enacted to mitigate their effects in the evolution of employer-employee relation. Thus, it is clearly seen that considerable philosophy and values of a very high order have gone in inacting labour laws in India. With such lofty goals, business behaviour with respect to labour should have been considerably ethical and there should have been no conflicts between labour and management. Labour should have been protected from exploitation and all their grievances should have been mitigated. However, this has not been the case. Otherwise, why have strikes and lockouts, specially in the last couple of decades, become so rampant ? Why have labour courts numerous pending cases of conflict between labour and management? Why is labour still exploited in almost all industries? Why is child labour still prevalent ? Why do business still resort to unethical behaviour in relation to labour ? Let us examine why.

Sri V.V. Giri, in his book, 'Labour Problems in Indian Industry' (Bombay : Asia Publishing House, 1972), has classified labour legislation in India under the following categories -

I LAWS RELATING TO WEAKER SECTIONS (i.e., CHILDREN & WOMEN)

The legislations under this category includes :

1. The Factories Act, 1948;
2. The Mines Act, 1952;
3. The Plantation Labour Act, 1951;
4. The Employment of Children Act, 1938;
5. Maternity Benefit Act, 1961.

II LAWS RELATING TO SPECIFIC INDUSTRIES

The legislations under this category includes -

1. The Factories Act, 1948;
2. The Industrial Employment (Standing) Orders Act, 1946;
3. The Mines Act, 1952;
4. The Coal Mines (Conservation & Safety) Act, 1952;
5. The Iron Ore Mines Labour Welfare Cess Act, 1961;
6. The Coal Mines Labour Fund Act, 1947;
7. The Coal Mines Provident Fund & Bonus Schemes Act, 1948;

8. The Plantation Labour Act, 1951;
9. The Indian Railways Act, 1930;
10. The Indian Merchant Shipping Act, 1973;
11. The Indian Dock Labourer's Act, 1934;
12. The Dock Workers (Regulation of Employment) Act, 1984;
13. The Marking of Heavy Packages Act, 1951;
14. The Motor Vehicles Act, 1939;
15. The Motor Transport Workers Act, 1961;
16. The Contract Labour (Regulation & Abolition) Act, 1970;
17. The Workmen's Compensation Act, 1923;
18. The Employee's State Insurance Act, 1948;
19. The Working Journalists & other Newspaper Employees (Conditions of Service) & Miscellaneous Provisions Act, 1955;
20. The Bidi & Cigar Workers (Conditions of Employment) Act, 1966; and many, more such Acts.

III Laws relating to specific Matters

(a) Wages

1. The Payment of Wages Act, 1963;
2. The Minimum Wages Act, 1948;
3. The Equal Remuneration Act, 1976.

(b) Social Security

1. Workmen's Compensation Act, 1923;
2. Retrenchment Benefits Act
3. The Provident Fund & Miscellaneous Provision Act, 1952;
4. The Payment of Bonus Act, 1965;
5. Employees state Insurance Act, 1948;
6. Employee's Liability Act, 1938;
7. Fatal Accidents Act, 1955;
8. The Payment of Gratuity Act, 1972

(c) Bonded Labour

1. Bonded Labour System (Abolition) Act, 1976

IV Laws relating to

(a) Trade Unions-

1. The Trade Union Act, 1926;

(b) Industrial Relations–

1. The Industrial Disputes Act, 1947;
2. The Workmen's Compensation Act, 1923.

Despite the existence of such a numerous amount of labour laws, industrial unrest or labour disputes and conflicts are widespread in India. S. Nagaraju in 'Industrial Relations Systems in India', rightly stated thus–

> "Since industrial unrest involves questions of right or wrong and also affect every section of society, it thrusts upon itself the attention of the community and becomes a social problem"

One important cause of conflict among Indian workers is the rate and payment of bonus. Despite the Payment of Bonus Act, disputes over bonus is common. Psychological factors such as denial of opportunity to the worker for satisfying his basic urge for self-expression, personal achievement and betterment are also the causes for many labour unrest in India.

C.B. Mamoria & S, Mamoria, in 'Dynamics of Industrial Relations in India' rightly commented–

> "If a close observation of the IR scene in India is made, the immediate impression would be that here relationship between labour and management are rather strained. The relationships are plagued by such factors as the existing wage structure-which has often been chaotic, confusing and full of anomalies and inadequate - the bonus, which is wild cancer, made more complicated by a zig-zag policy of the government; the laxity on the part of the employers to fully and speedily implement the award and settlements pertaining to conditions against any wages; and the lengthy procedure needed in getting grievances redressed and the industrial disputes settied".

Dr. K.C. Sethi, in 'Workers Participation & IR in India: Some Reflection's, Decision, No. 3, July 1978, states –

> "The central values of our country's IR system appears to be competition, class struggle and compromise. The 'key' parties finding themselves in opposition endeavour to maximise their gains often at the cost of the other by making the best possible use of their relative strength and power. The employer and their managers, by and large, consider Trade Union and Trade Union leaders as 'nuisance' or 'hurdle' or at best 'unavoidable nuisance' or 'unavoidable hurdle'. The Trade Union, on the other hand, consider employers and their managers as 'exploiter obscurantist'. Workers are often mislead by their union leaders who make use of the collective strength of the Trade Unions for their vested interests. Collective Bargaining has proved to be coercive bargaining in many cases."

In India, a tripartite Study Group was formed by the National Commission on Labour to study the sociological aspects of labour-management relationship. An important observation of the Study Group was that an important aspect of the labour relationship is the extent to which labour and management accept the way of life and value system of modern technology. The Director of IR should develop for his company a 'Code of Ethics' and a 'Management philosophy for IR' in general and for labour relationship in particular that will meet the test of being firm but fair, tough but tender and hard but humane.

Conclusion of the chapter

This discussion on legislation regulating and controlling ethical business behaviour shows that business is as ethical as the laws 'allow' them it be. It the laws are faulty and full of loopholes, if people can get away with committing unethical acts very easily and if laws themselves are not based on any ethical value system, rather they encourage business firms to manipulate the provisions of the laws to their benefit and to serve their vested interests, then these laws can do very little to influence and encourage ethical business behaviour.

The USA today has very little unemployment, compared to not only underdeveloped and developing nations, but also to most European Countries. This welcome means of securing social welfare is possible due to the structure of its labour laws. Jobs in the USA do not come with a 'lifetime' guarantee. So American companies are able to move human resources far more quickly from one industry to another. People are, therefore, far less likely to be sticking to jobs and to industries in which they no longer have a competitive advantage. More productive capital means more jobs. Moreover, since companies know they can easily shed workers when business is down, they are more willing to hire them when business is looking up even a little.

Thus, it is the legal system of the country that provides the incentive to behave ethically or unethically. When, a few decades ago, the highest rate of income tax in India was proposed to be a mind-boggling 94%, do you suppose, even for a moment, that this would have provided the incentive to people to be morally upright and ethical and quietly pay up? If that piece of legislation had really come into force, it would have resulted in either of two consequences - either (a) people would have striven even harder to conceal incomes and thus evade taxes by resorting to all sorts of unethical means that the human mind can conjure up, or (b) it would have provided us with a fantastic disincentive to work and would have turned us into a nation of idlers. At that time, implementation was not rigid and a large proportion of economic activity remained unofficial. But the after-effects of this proposal was that it became a socially acceptable norm to evade taxes, to even laugh it off and brag about it as a smart move; it induced in Indians' an attitude and a sense of dishonesty and a lack of ethics.

Though corruption, at any level, cannot be excused or accepted, most low salaried people resort to corruption only to compensate for their meagre pay. Even a high salaried person when he is at the helm of affairs, has enormous powers. But, once out of his job, not only does he lose his power, but he also loses his ability to afford many things which he accepted then as a matter of daily affordable commodities. Knowing this, the temptation to parley that power, while in office, into lining his nest with golden feathers is great, and few managers and executives can resist it.

It is not that Indians enjoy being corrupt. Given half a chance and a choice, they would rather conduct their affairs ethically. But the laws not only encourage them to be unethical, they provide no incentive to stay ethical. Sometimes the system too encourages one to resort to unethical activities to further one's personal gains. When the system provides no incentive for a person to remain ethical, when salaries and pays forces a person to make a fast buck on the side, when a person knows he will never be caught; and even if be is caught, he can always bribe his way out or else the legal process will take such a long time, sometimes as long as 15-20 years, that he can safely enjoy his ill-gotten wealth before justice is done, that many people give in to the temptation of amassing huge material possessions in a consumerist society. Laws, to regulate and encourage ethical behaviour, must be practical and retain an element of fairness and justice. Otherwise people will continue to disregard and disrespect iniquitous laws. Coming from specific business areas to general, from laws to law courts, consider the following article reported in 'The Telegraph', 17 February, Wednesday, 1999, page 18, titled- 'Bypassed by justice', by Swati Bhattacharjee-

> "When the Superintendent of a psychiatric hospital in the city got an order from a magistrate to admit an eight-year old mentally retarded child, he was nonplussed. Mental retardation, according to law, is not 'mental illness' and cannot be treated in a psychiatric hospital. So if he complied to the order, he would be breaking the law. If he didn't comply, he would be pulled up for contempt of court".

Consider, another example, reported in 'The Telegraph', 10 February, Wednesday, 1999, in 'After the doctor and the bank ....', by Aniruddha Bose, "Can an insurance company arbitrarily refuse to renew the policy of its subscriber ? Are insurance contracts purely private arrangements, free of any constitutional obligations ?

Recently, when an insurance company argued in favour of such untramelled powers (Biman Krishna Basu vs United India Insurance Co. Ltd.), Justice Satyabrata Sinha of Calcutta High Court rejected its claim. The public sector insurance company, observed Justice Sinha in his judgement, falls within the meaning of 'state' as mentioned in Article 12 of the Constitution. Therefore, 'all its actions, including a matter relating to contract must be fair and reasonable', he ruled".

Mr. Basu and his wife had taken out a joint Mediclaim policy with United India Insurance (UII) in 1990. When UII rejected a claim he made under this policy, he approached the Consumer Court. The dispute ultimately reached the Supreme Court.

When Mr. Basu in 1996 sent a cheque to renew his insurance policy, UII informed him that it was unable to do so. Basu then approached the Calcutta High Court with a writ, seeking a direction upon the UII for renewal of his Mediclaim Policy. He complained before the Court that such refusal was malafied, since it was based on his past litigation with the company.

Justice Sinha's judgement was based on an earlier decision of the Supreme Court in the case 'Life Insurance Cooperation vs Consumer Education & Research Centre', where the apex court had struck down certain discriminatory clauses in the Life Insurance Policy.

The action of the UII in this case was not only inconsistent with constitutional ideals, it also did not satisfy business ethics. Insurance Companies have a constitutional duty to be 'fair and reasonable' to their subscribers and an ethical obligation not to be vindictive if subscriber makes use of his right to seek redressal.

Discussion Problem : An Ethical Dilemma

A celebrated Lawyer had taken a Junior Lawyer under him and groomed him for one year, under the agreement that after the one year period, the Junior would pay half the fees that he received from his first successful case, to his Senior. However, after the one year period was over, the Junior deliberately neglected to take up any case to avoid paying his Senior. This infuriated the Senior and he started a suit in the Court to sue Junior for his fees. Thus, dramatically, this became the first case of the Junior.

The Senior Lawyer was greatly thrilled as he felt that the case was already under his belt. Because, if he was successful, Junior would have to pay up, as this would he ordered by the Judges. Even if he was unsuccessful, this would mean that Junior was successful; which would mean that by virtue of their original agreement, Junior would have to pay up.

However, Junior soon dashed his hopes. He told Senior, 'If I win, it means you lose your claim by virtue of the sentence of these righteous Judges. If I pay up then, I may be held up for contempt of court. However, if I lose, it means that my first case was unsuccessful, and by virtue of our earlier agreement, I will not have to pay. Hence, whether I win or lose the case, I shall not have to pay you'.

All throughout the case, the Senior Lawyer argued before the Judge that whether he wins or loses, Junior shall have to pay; and all throughout, Junior argued that successful or not, he shall never have to pay.

Leaving aside all considerations, except the legal one, can you settle the Case?

Expected Questions

1. Write an essay on the role of Legislation in enforcing Ethical Business Behaviour.
2. Explain, giving relevant examples, the relationship between Law and Ethics.
3. "The Law can be considered as a guide to managerial decisions, but it is not enough to usher in ethical business behaviour", Is this statement true? Explain with illustrations.
4. Discussion the role of the Government of India in enforcing ethical business behaviour.
5. What role does the Indian Constitution play as far as ethical business behaviour is concerned ? Explain.
6. Discuss the Indian Business Laws and their impact on ethical business behaviour.

Chapter 6

Relationship Between Ethics & Corporate Excellence

Many organisations exist and operate in the marketplace not just to survive and get by, but to **'excel'**, become centres of excellence, become market leaders, release zero-defect products in the market and so on. All these are ethical pursuits; in fact, striving to achieve perfection and excellence in any field, in itself, can be termed as the basis of ethics. Delivering the keynote address at the 9th. Shankara Darshana Management Conference (19th Nov. 1998), Dr. M.B. Atherya, the renowned Management Guru, emphasised that our values of ***'Atithi Devo Bhava'*** (the customer is the God), our extreme stress on ***'Guna'*** (Quality) and the concept of ***'Atmanirbharta'*** (Self-reliance) are the three basic tenets that can take us a long way in not only surviving competition caused by Globalisation and Liberalisation, but can also lead us on to the way to corporate excellence. He also stressed on the values of ***'Kanashah artham saadhayet'***, which says that one should earn wealth by saving every bit possible, and this is vital to increase organisational productivity. This value is as true for organisation as it is for individuals. Not only do we owe it to the company to utilise its resources optimally, we also morally owe it to the country to put to best possible use, its scarce and dwindling natural resources.

Companies can achieve excellence through ethical means, by drawing inspiration from the Shloka, ***'Udyogam purusha lakshnam'*** (industriousness is the hallmark of a person). Companies also achieve excellence through the attitude of **'Seva'** or service to the community and to the customer. The 'Seva' attitude is strengthened and reinforced by a **'rini bhava'**, i.e., a feeling of indebtedness to the customer for patronising the company and its products, and for giving it an opportunity to serve them. These attitudes and feelings for the customer helps in providing satisfactory service to him.

Companies can achieve corporate excellence, also by following the Bhagavad Gita value of ***'parasparam bhavayantah'***, which means mutual concern – oriented actions.

In the same conference, Mr. Anil Sachdeva, Managing Director of Eicher Consultancy Services, in his speech, said that it is possible to become a leading company if we excel in quality in all respects and do more with less. He remarked "knowing our unlimited potential is the essence of Indian Ethos".

Today, the era of globalisation has ushered in a wage boom and an age of heightened cultural acceptance and exchange. The customer today is more exposed to the increasing number of new products daily flooding the marketplace through the numerous TV channels and the Internet. This has led to a shift from customer-creation to customer-retention, making companies resort to relationship building with existing customers and even with prospective customers. In such a scenario, a critical requirement for success is to ensure harmonisation with the social environment, trust and loyalty, transparency, competitive advantage and reliability.

Business ethics is the inspirational source behind quality products, smooth production processes, fair employment practices, operational transparency, concern for customers as well as for shareholders and for social welfare. All these factors, more often than not, are found together in the same organisation, leading to its corporate excellence. For example, quality products are almost always impossible to produce without dedicated and loyal workers, committed to the cause of quality in the organisation. Similarly fair employment policies and practices are impossible without the organisation having an internal ethical system and moral culture.

Business Ethics helps the organisation to achieve corporate excellence in many ways. It results in organisations establishing distinctive cultures for individual companies. When such distinctive cultures are established, they promote creativity and innovations within the organisations.

When an individual is in a position of responsibility and authority and when others rely upon his knowledge, ability and guidance to perform their tasks effectively, the pursuit of excellence has an ethical dimension. Making mistakes or being less than excellent, is certainly not unethical, but individuals in the seat of authority and responsibility do have a moral obligation to perform to the best of their capacity and capability, and avoid making costly mistakes.

There are many ways in which an organisation can achieve corporate excellence. The first instrument for achieving such excellence is the **Corporate Mission Statement**.

1. Corporate Mission Statement

An organisation's mission consists of its long term vision of what it seeks to achieve and the reasons for its existence. Usually this mission of the organisation is denoted through its mission statement and it contains an account of how it wishes to serve the society and contribute to social welfare. The mission statement has to be guided by a set of core values and moral integrity of every employee, particularly of those in the management cadre and who exemplifies the corporate value system. It incorporates the ethical values that the organisation strives to use in order to achieve corporate excellence. This mission statement acts like the *Constitution of the company*, the solid expression of the company's vision and values. It becomes the *criterion* by which the company measures its activities and achievements. The process of writing out the mission statement is as important as having the mission statement, because it forces the company to think about its priorities deeply, carefully and to integrate its activities with its beliefs. The company thinks with more clarity about its long term goals and how to go about achieving these goals. The mission statement helps the company to focus on its position in the marketplace and to find out where it wants to stand in the society. If these goals are the extension of a mission statement based on correct principles, then they would reflect the organisation's deepest values, its unique talents and potential, its sense of mission and would be a foundation for achieving corporate excellence.

An organisational mission statement that truly reflects the visions and values shared by everyone within the organisation not only creates tremendous commitment from the employees, but also creates a great bond of unity among them. Employees themselves create a frame of reference, a set of criteria or guidelines by which they govern themselves. If that kind of a situation is truly created, then there is no need for others to direct, control or criticize employees, for they create the ultimate corporate excellence, where employees govern their own *activities, performance* and *behaviour.*

An effective goal focuses primarily on **results** rather than on **activity.** It identifies where the organisation wants to be, and in the process, helps to determine *where it is now.* It unifies all the efforts and energies of the organisation, of the various people of the organisation, and of the various departments of the organisation, to achieve its ultimate goal.

Some companies, like IBM, believes in the dignity of its employees and has incorporated that dignity of the individual into their mission statement. Some other organisations, create a culture where all employees value deeply, the standard and quality of customer service. The central value of the mission statement of such companies could be – **'Uncompromising personalised service'.**

The mission statement really depicts the organisation's business character and the kind of organisation it strives to be. For the mission statement to become more meaningful, *everyone* in the organisation should participate in its formulation and not just its strategy planners or the top management. Only then can the mission statement of an organisation be truly effective. Once everyone in the organisation becomes fully aware of the significance of the mission statement, it becomes a basis for corporate excellence.

However, for the vision of corporate excellence to turn into reality, the organisation would need to 'balance' both its ethical *values and missions* with its *commercial considerations.* The organisation would need to be clear-eyed on both its ethical behaviour as well as its commercial goals. The excellent way to achieve this is, of course, to combine or incorporate an organisation's commercial and economic goals in its mission statement itself. Any organisation which concentrates solely on its mission statement about how to behave ethically, but is vague about what it wants to achieve commercially runs the risk of achieving very little for itself. Conversely an organisation which focuses only on commercial performance in its mission statement and is not clear about, or chooses to ignore, how it will conduct itself when faced with an ethical dilemma, runs the risk of becoming inhuman and socially irresponsible. Hence it is highly desirable to incorporate social responsibility with commercial viability. This alone will allow companies to demonstrate responsible corporate citizenship to the society in which it exists and thrives. This allows the company to undertake activities which results in benefits to both the company and the community. Prosperity is achieved and sustained into the long term only when a company tries to infuse **economic, social, technological, environmental** and **human** goals and objectives into the mission statement.

David Packard, in his book, 'The HP Way: How Bill Hewlett and I built our Company', 1995, demonstrates how values and commercial objectives could be closely linked together. As David Murray, in his book, 'Ethics in Organisations', says–

"The objectives of the company were heavily and explicitly value-laden. Growth was 'a measure of strength and a requirement for survival'. Products and services to customers should be 'useful'. Corporate citizenship was emphasized. Profit was 'the best measure of our contribution to society, to be pursued and indeed maximised, but consistent with our other objectives'. Creativity, personal satisfaction and ensuring that employees shared in the success of the company were further important components of the value mix which has been at the heart of this outstandingly successful company".

Prof. L.M. Prasad has cited the ethical practices of Tata Iron & Steel Company Limited (TISCO) and ITC, through their mission statements, with the remark–

"TISCO has defined its mission incorporating the interests of various groups in its decision - making process. Various programmes are taken according to this mission".

TISCO was also the first company in India to conduct social audit to find out the extent to which it is discharging its social obligations.

Mission of Tisco

The fundamental mission of TISCO is to strengthen India's industrial base through increased productivity, effective utilisation of manpower and material resources, and continued application of modern scientific managerial methods as well as through systematic growth in keeping with national aspirations. The company recognises that while honesty and integrity are the essential ingredients of a strong and stable enterprise, profitability provides the main spark for economic activity. It affirms its faith in democratic values and in the importance of success of individuals, collective, and corporate enterprise for the economic emancipation and prosperity of the country. Guided by its basic philosophy, the company believes in discharging its responsibilities towards:

1. Shareholders

(i) by protecting and safeguarding their investment; and

(ii) by ensuring to them a fair return.

2. Employees

(i) by a realistic and general understanding and acceptance of their needs and right and enlightened awareness of the social responsibilities of industry;

(ii) by providing adequate wages,- good working conditions, job security, effective machinery for speedy redressal of grievances, and suitable opportunities for promotion and self- development;

(iii) by promoting feelings of trust and loyalty through a human and purposeful awareness of their needs and aspirations; and

(iv) by creating a sense of belongingness and team-spirit through their closer association with management at various levels.

3. Customers

(i) by products of proven quality at a fair price;

(ii) by fulfilling its commitments impartially and courteously in accordance with sound and straightforward business principles; and

(iii) by bearing their counting confidence in its productive ability and its technical competence to keep improving the quality of its products.

4. Community

(i) by respecting the dignity of the individual and acting according to the ideas of social justice;

(ii) by encouraging talent and promoting civic sense among members of the community;

(iii) by availing of opportunities to develop the democratic qualities involved in collective

(iv) work undertaken in the interest of the community; and

(v) by assuming its proper share of social responsibilities in the community in which the company operates.

These missions of the company are directed towards making the company:

The best company to *buy* from;

A sound company to *invest* in;

A good company to *work* for;

A reliable company to *sell* to;

A *leading* company in the corporate field of the country.

In order to fulfill its mission, TISCO has taken a number of programmes. Such programmes are in the following directions –

The City Development: The company has developed the plant site, that is, Jamshedpur into a full-fledged city with adequate provisions of housing, health and conservancy medical services and related amenities.

Pollution Control: This is of very high order so that there is no pollution problem in any part of the work place or in the city.

Employer-Employee Relations: Workers are given every opportunity to voice their concern through the recognised union. In fact, the union is encouraged to take up the cause of improving employer-employee relationships.

Consumers: The company has adopted the policy of fair pricing and distribution of steel. Though there has been continuous shortage of steel, the company never indulged in unfair practices. To ensure quality, the company has very rigid quality control system.

Shareholders: An attempt is made to reward shareholders. Dividends could not be distributed when there was control over it, but later shareholders were given their due.

Community Development and Social Welfare Programme: To undertake various programmes for community development and social welfare, the company has created a separate department under the charge of Chief Social Services Manager.

Rural Development Programme: Under this category, the company has undertaken three programmes – agricultural and crop extension; setting up of training centres of allied vocations such as dairy, poultry farming, piggery and goat breeding; establishment of village industries and imparting training in those industries.

Obligations to Society: The company has undertaken programmes like smallpox eradication, flood relief, drought and cyclone relief and similar other activities.

Management Philosophy of ITC Limited

The Management philosophy of ITC Limited consists of the following concerns–

(i) Concern for their ultimate customers - millions of customers.

(ii) Concern for their intermediate customers - the trade.

(iii) Concern for their suppliers - their source of raw materials and ancillaries.

(iv) Concern for their employees – their most valued asset.

(v) Concern for their competitors whom they wish well - for healthy competition ultimately benefits the customer.

(vi) Concern for their shareholders - the investing public.

(vii) Concern for national aspiration - India's future.

The company undertakes various programmes to fulfil its obligations to various constituents of its business.

(Source : 'Principles and Practice of Management; L.M. Prasad; S. Chand & Sons; 1992)

The second instrument for corporate excellence is the **Code of Ethics.**

2. Code of Ethics

Managers of all organisations have a responsibility for creating a conducive organisational environment that encourages ethical decision making by institutionalizing ethics. The most common way of institutionalizing ethics in the organisation, apart from the Mission Statement, is to establish a Code of Ethics.

A Code of Ethics is a statement of the norms and beliefs of an organisation. Norms are the standards of behaviour, expected from everyone in the organisation when confronted with a particular situation consisting of ethical dilemmas. The norms of behaviour in the Code of Ethics are a series of 'do's' and don'ts' detailing the expected standard of behaviour from everyone in the organisation. It encourages people to think in *particular ways* which leads to **positive attitudes** and consequently to the **wanted behaviour.** They are usually written in general terms, to give people an idea of what sort of mental makeup the organisation expects from them.

Code of Ethics can generally make an employee of the organisation aware of his or her obligation and the moral duties towards the organisation, but these codes cannot help to solve managerial dilemmas between economic and social performance.

In 1996-97, the Union Government of India declared that it would set a reasonable standard for all services provided by Central Government Departments and Public Sector Undertakings (PSUs). Accordingly, the government directed them to prepare a **Charter of Citizens Rights** vis-a-vis the service (something like a Consumer's Bill of Rights). The government also clarified at that time that initially it does not intent to set very high standards for the services, but these standards would be raised gradually. These Charters are also statements of good intentions and commitments to the improvement of services provided to consumers.

The Charter down up by Dr. Ram Manohar Lohia Hospital in New Delhi, promises, among others, to –

* promptly attend to emergency cases;
* to settle genuine complaints within 10 working days of its receipt.

The Department of Administrative Reforms & Public Grievances of the Union Government of India has been co-ordinating with various government agencies for the implementation of the Charter Scheme and with the Consumer Co-ordination Council (CCC), a coalition of 40 consumer organisations in the country, which initiated the process. As per the guidelines issued by the Department of Administrative Reforms & Public Grievances, this Chapter should incorporate standards of performance, assured quality of service, access to information, simplified and convenient procedures for receipt and acknowledgement of complaints, besides time-bound redressal of grievances.

A Charter in line with these guidelines requires certain amount of commitment to understand the problems of users and improving the services on the basis of feedback received from them. The Consumer Co-ordination Council (CCC), on the basis of consumer surveys conducted in different parts of the country, is critically reviewing the charters and suggesting improvements.

However, for the Charter scheme to succeed, the government should play a more active role in its implementation. For a start, it should set up in every government department, independent cells that would regularly call for suggestions from users, set decent performance standards on the basis of feedback received, publicise the Charter widely and evaluate performance against these standards.

If all the above measures are taken, then these Charters of the Government departments and PSUs will function like Codes of Ethics of the private sector companies. This in turn will lead ethical business behaviour into corporate excellence.

(Source: 'Check Out', Pushpa Girimaji, The Telegraph, 11.2.99)

The Ethics Code of Johnson & Johnson, which they call their 'Credo', also tries to live up to the expectations of all concerned with the company. This Credo is based on the philosophy of the founder of the company, Mr. Robert Johnson. This company believes that their first responsibility is to the doctors, nurses, mothers, patients and all others who use their products and services. Then they list out their responsibilities to their employees, to the communities in which they live and work, and their responsibilities to be good citizens.

However, it is their attitude towards profits that deserves special mention, because it seeks to resolve the dilemma between profits and social welfare. 'Our final responsibility is to our stockholders. Business must make a sound profit', they assert. 'Reserves must be created to provide for adverse times', they add. At the end of the Credo, they confirm, 'When we operate according to these principles, the stockholders should realise a fair return', reinforcing the attitude that high financial returns could be earned only if they operate according to their ethical principles. Their concern for others profits is also expressed when they affirm, 'Our Suppliers and distributors must have an opportunity to make a fair profit'.

The Ethics Code of Johnson and Johnson, 'Our Credo'

We believe our first responsibility is to the doctors, nurses and patients, to mothers and all others who use our products and services.

In meeting their needs everything we do must be of high quality.

We must constantly strive to reduce our costs in order to maintain reasonable prices.

Customers orders must be serviced promptly and accurately.

Our suppliers and distributors must have an opportunity to make a fair profit.

We are responsible to our employees, the men and women who work with us throughout the world.

Everyone must be considered as an individual.

We must respect their dignity and recognize their merit.

They must have a sense of security in their jobs.

Compensation must be fair and adequate, and working conditions clean, orderly and safe.

Employees must feel free to make suggestions and complaints.

There must be equal opportunity for employment, development and advancement for those qualified.

We must provide competent management, and their actions must be just and ethical.

We are responsible to the communities in which we live and work and to the world community as well.

We must be good citizens-support good work and charities and bear our fair share of taxes.

We must encourage civic improvements and better health and education.

We must maintain in good order the property we are privileged to use, protecting the environment and natural resources.

Our final responsibility is to our stockholders.

Business must make a sound profit.

We must experiment with new ideas.

Research must be carried on, innovative programs developed and mistakes paid for.

New equipment must be purchased, new facilities provided and new products launched.

Reserves must be created to provide for adverse times.

When we operate according to these principles, the stockholders should realize a fair return.

Similarly, the Code of Conduct of All India Management Association (AIMA), reminds professional managers that they are responsible to the Investors of the company (that means surplus should be generated), as much as to their Employees, the Suppliers, Customers, the Government and the Community (which means social welfare).

All India Management Association
Code of Conduct for Professional Managers

1. The Basic Code:

A Member of a management association affiliated to the All India Management

Association (AIMA) shall:

* try his best to organise the resources available to him with a view to optimise their use in attaining the objectives of his organisation.
* consider the guide to good management practices conveyed by AIMA from time to time in carrying out his tasks.
* comply with the Indian laws relating to the management of his organisation and do his best to operate within the spirit of these laws.
* so order his conduct as to uphold and further the reputation of professional management and management movement.

2. Guide to Good Management Practices:

A professional manager is primarily responsible to his organisation. He is thereafter responsible to the following six stakeholders of his organisation –

(i) Investors

(ii) Employees

(iii) Suppliers

(iv) Customers

(v) Government

(vi) Community

1. As regard his ORGANISATION, a professional manager should:
   * Act both with loyalty and honesty in carrying out the lawful policy and instructions of his organisation and not undermine its image or reputation.
   * Plan, establish and review objectives, tasks and organisation structures for himself and his subordinates which are compatible with the Codes and Practice of other professionals in the enterprise and will help to meet the enterprise's overall objectives, and, by his own work and through leadership and coordination direct all available effort towards the success of the enterprise rather than of himself.
   * Provide a working climate in which innovation and free exchange of ideas are encouraged.
   * Fully respect the confidentiality of information which comes to him in the course of his duties, and not use confidential information for personal gain or in a manner which may be detrimental to the organisation for which he works or has worked.
   * In his contacts and dealings with other people, demonstrate his personal integrity and humanity and when called upon to give an opinion in his professional capacity shall, to the best of his ability, give an opinion that is objective and reliable.
2. As regards the INVESTORS in his organisation, a professional manager should:
   * Ensure that surplus generated in the operations of the company is divided fairly amongst investors, employees and for further growth opportunities.
   * Ensure that the investors are given fairly accurate financial and other important operating information periodically.

3. As regards the EMPLOYEES, a professional manager should:

 * Set an example for his subordinates through his own work, capacity and performance, through his leadership and by taking into account of the needs and problems of his subordinates.
 * Train people as appropriate under him to become qualified for higher duties, including his own position.
 * Pay proper regard to the safety and well being of the personnel for whom he is responsible.

4. As regards the CUSTOMERS & SUPPLIERS, a professional manager should:

 * Ensure that the terms of all contracts and terms of business be stated clearly and unambiguously and honoured.
 * In no circumstances supply inherently unsafe goods or services.
 * Operate an organisation's policy or require one to be established, which exclude corrupt practice, with regard to the giving or receiving of gifts or benefits and not to tolerate any practice which could lead to commercial or other corruption.

5. As regards the GOVERNMENT, a professional manager should:

 * Conform to the national interest as expressed in Government policies.

6. As regards the COMMUNITY, a professional manager should:

 * Make the most effective use of all natural resources employed.
 * Be ready to give professional assistance in community affairs.

These examples of Ethical Codes of Corporate Bodies illustrate how companies perceive ethical business behaviour, and how they strive to incorporate these ethical aspirations into their day to day functioning. Finally, as David Murray in his book, 'Ethics in Organisations', says – 'Fundamental principles such as honesty, fairness, trust and respect for human dignity may be phrased differently to make them relevant to individual organisations, but are essential to a sustainable human society and must be present in some form'.

3. Organisational Culture

In the organisational context, culture refers to the set of values, dominant beliefs and guiding norms of behaviour for its employees. It denotes the climate, the atmosphere, the 'mental attitude' shared by the members of the organisation. A strong culture provides a basis for productive ethos and ethical behaviour of an organisation. Excellent companies rich in ethical legends, moral anecdotes, a great sense of pride, excitement in doing and creating something of value, an achievement orientation and an unique corporate folklore provide the basis for a strong corporate culture. Such a culture spearheads the company's commitment to creating excellence - through zero defect products, excellent customer support service, quality, reliability, employee welfare commitment, etc. When a company holds certain values in esteem, the concern for these values that the company holds dear, is diffused throughout the organisation, amongst all levels of its employees.

The organisational culture plays a dominant role in influencing employee's ethical behaviour. The organisational culture governs people's behaviour in the direction where they strive to achieve and create excellence in corporate life. An organisation where its culture consists of top management's commitment to good business practices, open communication, shared values, beliefs and norms for everyone within the organisation, stands to benefit from corporate excellence.

Values are the bedrock of any corporate culture. The corporate culture consciously created, must be value-based. Only a focused and committed leadership can help to create a value-based corporate culture. Top management must continuously communicate these values to the lower levels in the organisation, explaining how they benefit employees and create value-added products for customers and the society. Values produce a sense of direction for employees and help to guide their day-to-day behaviour. Fundamental to any corporate culture are the values embedded within the organisation - both *extrinsic* as well as *intrinsic*.

Extrinsic values specify what the company stands for, its beliefs and attitudes and describe the ethical perspective of those who are at the helm of the organisation. Such extrinsic values are found in Company Mission Statements and Code of Ethics.

However, intrinsic values are actually found displayed within organisational context. There may exist a vast disparity between ideally expected extrinsic values and intrinsic values existing in reality. Morally excellent companies try to narrow down, if not totally eliminate, the gap between expectations from the company and the existing reality. Such morally excellent companies try to ensure that their ethical values are reflected in their consciously created corporate culture. They ensure that their basic ethical beliefs are reflected and earned through their objectives, policies, strategies and systems.

The need of the hour is to develop, within all organisations, a corporate culture whose ultimate objective is moral excellence. The corporate culture should be amenable and suitable for the pursuit of this moral excellence. The corporate culture should support and encourage ethical behaviour within the organisation. The company's Mission Statement and Code of Ethics should be supplemented by publicly stated expectations about employee behaviour.

The values expressed and practiced by organisations express its organisational character. To perpetuate such a corporate culture, management must clearly uphold and exemplify behaviour that will lead people to do the *right thing* when faced with a moral dilemma. By hiring and training people who share such corporate values, the company can build a strong **corporate character.**

However, one thing that is very important to remember is that these corporate values must arise from the *personal* values of the individuals and from the philosophies that everyone personally believe in. For, just like personal values, corporate values too cannot be imposed from the outside.

It is not necessary that all these corporate values must be altruistic or idealistic. Practical values like, Focus on Cost Control, a fierce desire to produce Zero-Defect Products, Quality Control or Innovations can be accepted as corporate values by companies and they can guide companies to corporate excellence. As David Packard, co-founder of Hewlett Packard Company, once remarked - 'I think many people assume, wrongly, that a company exist to make money. While this is an important result of a company's existence, we have to go deeper to find the real reasons for our being'.

True Blue Values

Can a company manage by values, and still be profitable ? At Levi Strauss & Co., a closely held family-owned company, values and profit go hand in hand.

Robert D. Hass, great-great-grandnephew of Levi Strauss & Co. and Chairman and CEO of the company that bears the family name, espouses 'responsible commercial success'. He believes the corporation should be an ethical being capable of both making money and making the world a better place. In practice, this combines liberal ideas such as diversity with management precepts such as empowerment.

Levi's is guided by an 'Aspiration Statement' written by top management, that lists the company's value-based goals. Printed on paper made from recycled denim, the statement hangs on office and factory walls throughout Levi's.

And it is not just an empty promise; its enforced. One-third of an employee's evaluation is based on "aspirational" behaviour. For failing to follow corporate values, an employee risks receiving a raise or promotion. (Source: Business Week, August 1, 1994)

Survival of the Fit

Charles Darwin probably never dreamed his theory of evolution would be an appropriate model for corporate America in the 20th Century. Yet 3M's visionary approach to developing new products exemplifies Darwin's notion of natural selection.

3M's name is synonymous with innovation. It has grown and prospered for nearly a century with a religious-like dedication to continually experimenting with new processes and products. Employees have the flexibility and encouragement to be creative. Post-It Notes, Scotch Tape and other products actually are byproducts of other developments which led employees to new ideas.

For every Post-It Notes, 3M has many failures. But the company expects new ideas to fail; it keeps what works and quickly discards what doesn't. Like any surviving organisation, it has evolved over time. (Source: Industry Week, September 5, 1994)

Management can expect value-based conduct from employees, only when they exhibit it themselves. Once employees too start demanding value-based behaviour, they need less supervision to do their jobs. Thus employees become better empowered and do their jobs better.

Companies which are value-driven does necessarily also become **visionary companies**. Visionary people with core values give birth to visionary companies. Jim Collins and Jerry Porras of Stanford University in their book, 'Built To Last - Successful Habits of Visionary Companies', stated that visionary companies performed better financially in the long run than their less visionary competitors. "The key point is that a visionary company is an organisation, an institution. All individual leaders, no matter how charismatic a visionary, eventually die and all visionary products and services, all great ideas eventually become obsolete. Indeed, entire markets can become obsolete and disappear yet visionary companies prosper over long periods of time, through multiple product life cycles and multiple generations of active leaders" – they said.

Visionary companies are built to last. Amongst the millions of companies existing in the marketplace, there are only a few visionary companies. Visionary companies survive and last because their corporate culture is built upon a value system and moral ethics, they are guided by certain core ideologies.

Based on the distinction made by Alvin Toffler between first wave, second wave and third wave companies, visionary companies are mostly third wave companies which are motivated by an ideology, by the chance to change the world and the chance to grow. These companies stress on quality, not only on the products, but *throughout the organisation.* These companies make no compromises on quality, and their products, processes as well as the whole company structure, culture and climate can be taken as a *benchmark* for quality assurance and quality control.

In visionary companies, pursuit of excellence is a never-ending process. As Walt Disney had once remarked, 'Disneyland will never be completed as long as there is imagination left in the world'. Thus, companies in pursuit of corporate excellence treat quality not only as the end result, but also in the process of its activities. In visionary companies, the value of innovation is zealously pursued and these companies are continually changing, adjusting, transforming and adapting to respond to the changes in its environments - both internal as well as external. They do not sit and rest on their laurels, but are forever flexible and ready to re-invent themselves.

Management must also continue to reinforce values through *consistent actions* over time. It is not enough to just have vision or that vision to be articulated only by the top management. The corporate vision and values must be understood, accepted and pursued by all levels of employees within the organisation. For this to happen, management must -

COMMUNICATE - the vision and the corporate values to everyone in the organisation, explaining the consequent expectations and the strategies following the vision;

GUIDE - everyone in the organisation about the correct way to pursue the corporate values, by providing effective leadership and by investing their own time, energy and corporate resources to enable the vision to become a reality;

EMPOWER EMPLOYEES - by overcoming their resistance to change, changing systems and methods that undermine the vision and encouraging creativity, innovations, risk-taking and entrepreneurial behaviour.

4. Total Quality Management (TQM)

The Japanese companies have demonstrated that the technique of Total Quality Management (TQM) propounded by Crosby, when taken as a philosophy by a company, becomes an ethical tool to usher in corporate excellence. Many organisations worldwide are today adopting the techniques of quality management in different forms. For example, in Switzerland, the government has become so quality conscious that it has made it mandatory to introduce quality management schemes by higher educational institutions.

TQM is today no longer just a technique. *TQM is a systematic approach to guide an organisation towards excellence through superior quality products, services and processes.* TQM involves new approaches for leadership changes in an organisational culture and consists of unique tools, techniques and methods used by all levels of individuals in the organisation to meet and surpass the quality standards set by customers. TQM means an organisational culture to satisfy totally consumers' needs and desires through an integrated system of tools, techniques and training. TQM is rather a *corporate strategy.* Quality as everybody's responsibility in the organisation is the basic tenet of TQM. Quality improvements could be leveraged primarily based on organisational culture and core values. The ISO 9000 certification is an endorsement of total quality management.

Behind the TQM philosophy lies the effort, the attitude, an entire mindset of the employees of the company. In other words, it is only a committed, dedicated and ethical workforce that makes TQM a reality in the organisation. That is why organisations like Modi Xerox, Eicher Tractors, etc. equates TQM with the development of the human resource in the company. HRD and TQM are considered to be the two sides of the same coin as only by changing the attitudes of the employees towards values, can TQM result.

The term 'quality' today is no longer limited only to products and services, but is also measured in terms of *value for customers.* This concept of 'quality' has to be explained to the workmen who physically produce the product. Quality is taken to be that standard of perfection that more than meets the customers' margin of expectation and results in *customers ' delight.* The expectations of the company and its customers about the standard of the product quality and how to go about achieving it, has also to be emphasised. It is in this context that HRD intervention becomes crucial. One way to do this has been the introduction of Quality Circles by many Indian companies. Many companies like IOC, L&T, etc. have introduced Quality Circles amongst their workmen, who themselves monitor the quality of the products they produce.

Many other companies try to explain the concept of quality by first emphasising quality of life. Workers are helped to define what quality of life means to them and how to achieve it. Factors contributing to quality of life are also identified. Then quality of worklife is explained and how quality in work life contributes to their job satisfaction. Finally the concept of quality products and services is introduced and the need for quality products is explained. They are then helped to understand how quality products can be made possible and how it can lead to overall corporate excellence.

Many individuals and indeed many companies, suffer from the fallacy that providing quality increases cost. They consider costly raw materials and extensive quality checks adding to the cost of the product, but forget that basic improvements of quality in the work process could eliminate rework and inspections, reduce wasteful and unproductive habits and methods, eliminate or reduce customer complaints, lower warranty costs, repair costs scraps and defects; and instead increase customer loyalty, goodwill, marketshare and competitive advantage. In reality, costs associated with increased quality goes up only initially, but in the long run, costs starts falling while quality continue to go up. And eventually, increased quality and reduced costs go together hand in hand.

TQM involves a complete overhaul of the organisation's corporate culture and climate, including its management philosophy and an unwavering commitment toward continuous improvement in pursuit of excellence. Philosophies advocated by the India ethos proves to be of vital importance in a company's adoption of TQM. *A holistic value driven management and ethical value system plays a vital role in TQM.*

Adoption of the Kaizen method advocated and practised by Japanese companies like Toyota provides a foundation to an organisation in its quest for perfection and goodwill. Kaizen means continuous improvement, continuously taking small steps for improvement; it epitomises a never-ending search for perfection. **Total Quality Management and Value-based Management** are complementary and if both are integrated, then the result is corporate excellence.

A Value - Based Company

⇓

Value - Based Management

⇓

Value - Driven & Quality Conscious Workforce

(Loyal, committed, honest, ethical & wise workers)

Continuous R & D

(Innovation & Creativity, entrepreneurial spirit, continuous effort to solve new problems.

⇓

Strict Quality Control

(new products satisfying needs & wants better with zero-defects)

⇓

Greater Value for money (to provide customers with competitively priced reliable products).

⇓

DELIGHTED CUSTOMERS

⇓

More Goodwill, Loyal Customers & increased Market Share

⇓

Greater Revenue ⇒

Continuous elimination of wasteful and non-productive habits, small improvements (Kaizen), efficient method

⇓

Cost reduction & cost control

⇓

Higher Productivity

⇓

Lower Cost of Production

⇓

Higher product margins (Earning higher profits without increasing the selling price of prodcuts).

⇓

Better Competitive Market Position

⇓

Greater Revenue ⇒ DELIGHTED SHAREHOLDERS ⇐ Greater Revenue

HOW A VALUE-BASED COMPANY INCREASES ITS MARKET POSITION AS WELL AS ITS PROFITABILITY.

The TQM philosophy believes that an organisation can never achieve external quality until it has assured quality internally and within the organisation. Hence employees involved in each manufacturing process have to regard those working in the next process as their *internal customers.* Internal service quality is the pillar of TQM, because to produce a superior quality product, each process in the manufacturing line from the beginning to the end must be accurate. For TQM to survive, every employee as well as every executive and every manager has to believe that he is serving internal customers. Every activity in the organisation has an internal customer. This is in accordance with the **'seva bhav'** of Indian Ethos, wherein people are expected to believe that work is only a means of serving other people - a means of purifying one's mind and soul through selfless service. Thus, the core of TQM is value-based - *a value for inner upliftment and ethical activities.*

Team work and team spirit play a very important role in establishing the TQM philosophy in an organisation. *Only togetherness and unity of direction* will help to create and sustain an environment, where everyone in the organisation is self-motivated to achieve total satisfaction of customer's needs and expectations, leading to consumer delight, each employee contributing his or her own special talents, skills and abilities to the process. Mutual trust, mutual respect, personal pride and above all genuine team work, will lead to perfection and to excellence.

TQM relies on team work. In fact, total quality management does not result without the cooperation of everyone in the organisation. Only through the efforts of all concerned, can a perfect product or a zero-defect product result. Hence for TQM to be implemented, a **matrix organisation** is useful. Cross-functional teams made up from the different functional areas working together are essential for TQM. Such a small work group, where self-interest is subordinate to the larger interest of the group, where everyone is self motivated and where there exists unity of direction and goal, becomes an example of efficiency and productivity in the organisation and here TQM can be sustained. Such a team creates the *synergy effect* which proves helpful for TQM.

The most important aspect of TQM is to create and maintain a favourable quality environment within the organisation. The organisation culture itself should be quality oriented. *The mission of such an organisation should be to produce and offer in the marketplace products and services of excellent quality and reliability and also to uphold high quality in its ethical conduct and in discharging its social responsibilities.* ***Its endeavour should be to conduct itself, within and outside, with high standards of quality.*** Only then TQM in the true sense of the word, will be honestly implemented in the organisation. And when TQM, in the true sense is implemented within the organisation, it achieves high standards of corporate excellence and becomes a visionary company in the process

A Model for Total Quality Management

Mission: To offer products and services of excellent quality resulting in consumer delight, at a fair price consummate with quality, and to behave as a responsible corporate citizen.

Vision: To synonymies the organisation's identity with high quality, within and outside the organisation.

Values: The organisation's stated values are –

* That the individual shall be the focus of all our activities, for without quality human beings, no quality products can be produced;
* Team work and team spirit shall be encouraged, for only through cooperation, goodwill and a spirit of 'one for all and all for one' can harmony, industrial peace, efficiency and productivity result which are so indispensable for producing quality products;
* Quality of worklife shall be maintained at a very high level, for poor quality of work life cannot result in high quality products;
* Commitment of employees, executives and managers shall be created towards designing and sustaining a quality oriented corporate culture, so that all activities of the organisation, however small or insignificant, shall be of a high quality and that production of quality products is but a natural result of the high quality conscious environment of the organisation.
* Qualities like integrity, honesty, truthfulness, courage, openness are valued in the day-to-day operations of the business.

Quality Focus: The quality focus of the organisation shall be –

* Quality products shall not be the end, but only a means towards corporate excellence and business ethics;
* Constant improvements in quality, in accordance with the concept of 'Kaizen', shall be the endeveour of the organisation, both within the organisational climate and in the organisation's products, and no stone shall be left unturned in providing efforts not only to meet, but also to surpass, the needs and expectations of consumers, as far as quality is concerned;
* Utmost importance will be given to the growth and development of our human resource, not only as a skillful workforce, but also as ethical, value-oriented human beings, so that they are assured of both personal and organisational benefits simultaneously;
* TQM shall be so implemented within the rank and file, at all levels and in all activities of the organisation, that the organisation can usher in prosperity, happiness, harmony and quality to all concerned.

Summary of the Chapter in Brief

* Striving to achieve perfection and excellence in any field can be termed as the basis of ethics.
* The values of 'Atithi Devo Bhava', stress on 'Guna' and 'Atmanirbharta' can lead an organisation to corporate excellence.
* 'Kanashah artham saadhayet' is vital to increase organisational productivity.
* Organisations can also achieve excellence through the inspirations of 'Udyogam purusha lakshnam', 'seva bhava', 'rind bhava' and 'parasparam bhavayantah'.
* The Corporate Mission Statement is the **first** instrument for achieving corporate excellence through ethical means.

* The mission statement acts like the Constitution of the company, the solid expression of the company's vision and values. It is the criterion by which the company measures its activities and achievements.
* An effective goal focuses primarily on results rather than on activity.
* For the vision of corporate excellence to turn into reality, the organisation would need to 'balance' both its ethical values and missions with its commercial considerations.
* Prosperity is achieved and sustained into the long run only when a company tries to infuse economic, social, technological, environmental and human goals into the mission statement.
* The **second** instrument for achieving corporate excellence through ethical means is the Code of Excellence.
* A Code of Ethics is a statement of the norms and beliefs of an organisation.
* This code of ethics encourages people to think in particular ways which leads to positive attitudes and consequently to the wanted behaviour.
* The Organisational Culture is the **third** instrument for companies to achieve corporate excellence through ethical means.
* In the organisational context, culture refers to the set of values, dominant beliefs and guiding norms of behaviour for its employees. It denotes the climate, the atmosphere and the mental attitude shared by the members of the organisation.
* A strong culture provides a basis for productive ethos and ethical behaviour of an organisation.
* Fundamental to any corporate culture are the values embedded within the organisation - both extrinsic as well as intrinsic.
* The need of the hour is to develop, within all organisations, a corporate culture whose ultimate objective is moral excellence. The corporate culture should support and encourage ethical behaviour within the organisation.
* The values expressed and practised by organisations express its organisational character.
* Corporate values must arise from the personal values of the individuals and from the philosophies that everyone believes in. Like personal values, corporate values too cannot be imposed from outside.
* Companies which are value-driven does also become visionary companies.
* Visionary companies stress on quality, not only on the products, but throughout the organisation.
* Total Quality Management, as propounded by Crosby, when taken as a philosophy by a company, becomes an ethical tool to usher in corporate excellence.
* TQM is a systematic approach to guide an organisation towards excellence through superior quality products, services and processes.
* TQM is a corporate strategy.

* It is only a committed, dedicated and ethical workforce that can make TQM a reality in an organisation.
* The term 'quality' today is no longer limited only to products and services, but is also measured in terms of value for customers.
* Quality is taken to be that standard of perfection that more than meets the customers' margin of expectation and results in customers' delight.
* Ultimately, in the long run, increased quality and reduced costs go together hand in hand.
* A holistic value-driven management and an ethical value-system plays a vital role in TQM.
* Adoption of the Kaizen method provides a foundation for an organisation's quest for perfection and goodwill.
* Internal service quality is the pillar of TQM.
* The core of TQM is value-based: A value for inner upliftment and ethical activities.
* Team work and team spirit play an important role in establishing the TQM philosophy in an organisation.
* For TQM to be implemented, a Matrix Organisation is useful.
* To achieve corporate excellence, the very culture of an organisation should be quality oriented.

Expected Question

1. Describe the relationship between Ethics and Corporate Excellence.
2. Explain how an organisation can achieve corporate excellence through business ethics.

Chapter 7

Ethics & Individual Behaviour:

Moral Relationship between the Individual and the Organisation

All individuals as human beings, have some unique characteristics, which separate us from other animals of the animal kingdom, and help us to distinguish between reality and fantasy, and to transform the clock of life into a compass of life, guiding us towards the direction of our choice.

One of them is our **self-awareness**, knowing who we *really* are, not of our external identity like our names and designations; but of our internal characteristics like our dreams, our likes and dislikes, our thought processes, out attitudes, our perceptions, our paradigms and the direction towards which we are travelling in the path of life.

Next we have our **conscience**, which is an inner voice telling us whether we are correct in our actions, in our decisions and in our judgements. It puts us in touch with something deep within us, even more deeper than our thoughts and more reliable than our intuitions and values. It is an internal guidance system that troubles us when we act or even consider acting in a way that is contrary to our principles and moral righteousness. Someone once described the conscience as 'that darn thing that hurts when everything else is feeling great'.

Finally we are endowed with an **independent will** that helps us to act as we deem fit, to take independent counsel, make our own independent decisions and our own independent choices. It helps us to act on our principles rather than react on our emotions, moods or situations. The independent will allows us to choose our own responses and be morally responsible for them.

We begin our life at birth, being totally dependent on others - physically, emotionally and financially. We are nurtured and sustained by others; fed, clothed, held, attended to and even led to sleep by others. Without this nurturing, we would not be able to stay alive for more than a few days, if not a few hours, after birth. But thereafter, as we progress through life, we become independent and able to look after ourselves - first physically, then mentally and emotionally and finally financially - as we become more self-reliant and self-directed. However, self-reliance and independence should not be mistaken with existing alone, in isolation, by oneself. Even when we are physically independent, we are emotionally dependent on so many people. Similarly, when a person is financially independent, he may still be mentally dependent on many people close to him.

Conversely, when an individual becomes financially and physically dependent, say, as the result of an accident or some serious illness, it does not mean that the individual has also become mentally and emotionally dependent and immature. We go through life being dependent on, and seeking support from, so many people around us that it is not possible for anyone to be truly independent. No man is an island - nor can he remain so, aloof and cut off from human support. In fact, being independent does not mean being alone and staying away from people. Man is a social animal and he can grow and flourish only in a social setting. And there are many dimensions of growth, apart from physical growth.

Thus, in a social setting, most people become, neither dependent nor independent, but interdependent. People in a community or in an organisation, depend on each other for what they seek and want, and to get things done. Dependent people not only rely on others but also find it impossible to get things done on their own. Independent people do not need to rely on others, and get things done through their own efforts. Interdependent people both rely on others and are relied upon, to get things done. Interdependent people combine their own efforts with the efforts of others to achieve greater success through the synergistic effect.

A physically dependent person - handicapped or disabled in some way - needs other people to physically help him or her even with his or her physical needs and movements. An emotionally dependent person requires approval and appreciation from others to be sure that what he or she is doing is right and such a person's worth and security comes from other's approval and opinion of him or her. An intellectually dependent person seeks out others ideas and opinions to conform with them and rarely put in enough effort to think out issues and logically analyse them for himself, and goes along with what the current opinions and thoughts may be.

On the other hand, a physically independent person would require no help physically from others and can get along on his own physically. An emotionally independent person requires no approval or appreciation from others to feel valued and becomes inner-directed. Such a person does not dependent on others' opinion of him for his sense of worth and value. An intellectually independent person can analyse and think out issues for himself and he does not get swayed by others' opinions and ideas, irrespective of whatever the current opinions may be.

A physically interdependent person, on the other hand, is self-reliant and capable, but he also realises that much more can be achieved if two people put their efforts together. He realises the importance of synergy and team work and seeks to achieve it. An emotionally interdependent person's sense of self-worth does not come from others, but then, he also realises the joy of loving and being loved in return, of appreciating and of being appreciated, for sharing and giving of himself and his time to others. An intellectually interdependent person, analyses things for himself, but also appreciates the intellectual opinions and thoughts of other people, both living and dead. He borrows from the pool of thoughts that other people can give him, and sometimes, if necessary, modifies his own thoughts in the light of what he has learnt from others.

These concepts of dependence to independence to interdependence are absolutely essential to understand the relationship between ethics and individual behaviour. Let us suppose that you are just a junior executive of your company and you do not have the authority to take whatever action you believe to be just and fair. Suppose you were faced with an unethical decision, which you were being forced to take and which you believe to be deeply wrong according to your personal standards of ethics and morality. Let us assume that you looked for ethical alternatives and found none, you tried to explain your concerns to your immediate superior and your arguments and concerns were rejected. Supposing acting in an ethical way, as you look at it, would place your career in jeopardy. Would you still consider your action, ethical as you call it, worth your career ? And even if you do so, and leave the job, would that have solved the problem ? Because, the unethical decision which you faced in the organisation still remains there and your leaving the job, or being fired from it, does not make it go away. If you leave, someone else will have to take that unethical decision and the persons you were concerned about, will still be affected by the unethical decision. Moreover, you may face such a situation again in your next job. So how many jobs will you go on quitting ?

To answer the above, first of all, it is important to realise and accept that, since ethics is an abstract concept, people have different ways of looking at it and can legitimately differ in their views of what should be done to resolve an ethical dilemma. Rejection of your ethical arguments and concerns does not automatically mean that others in the organisation are wrong or unethical. People can differ on ethical concepts because the relative emphasis they place on the economic, legal and moral forms of analysis may differ. People can also differ because the value system and the ethical standards upon which their moral reasonings are based, are different. Moreover, people may also differ on their views about what constitutes an ethical dilemma. People within your own organisation may be more concerned with economic performance and less with social performance. Many people may also believe that economic performance is the only way through which a business can serve society.

Having realised this, the second factor on which your decision will be based is how dependent, independent or interdependent you are. If you are dependent on others and on the organisation, you will take whatever decision is expected of you, even if you feel guilty and unhappy inside. If you are independent, you will take a decision, after independent thought and analysis, which you are comfortable with, based on your own value system and on your own concept of right and wrong, irrespective of other people's opinions and expectations. On the other hand, if you are interdependent, you will try to find out a way of carrying the people of your organisation along with you, while you take a decision you are sure is the correct course of action. Such a course of action, apart from filling you with exhilaration and mental peace, will greatly increase your self-confidence and make you better equipped to deal with similar situations later on. Your handling of others in the organisation will help you to relate to others in a deeper, more meaningful way. Others, and more importantly, *you yourself* will come to know your depth of character, your nature, your deepest values and your unique contribution capacity. Your adherence to your values and your refusal to compromise will help to define yourself in a unique way. Then your values, your ethics, your integrity, your self-control and your honesty will help you to curve out your own unique identity rather than through other people's opinions or through comparisons with others. Then 'right conduct' will have little to do with being found out by others.

When a person has achieved such an identity for himself, it becomes easy for him to choose his options on how he will conduct himself as far as ethics and moral behaviour is concerned. Such a person has the freedom and power to choose the response that he wishes to exhibit to a given stimulus.

Hence, even when an individual finds himself in a situation within the organisation where he has to take a decision that deeply affects his ethical values, he still has the freedom to choose for himself what action he wants to take. It seldom, if ever, happens that a man finds himself with no options, except the unethical one, to choose from. Even in that case, even when he is surrounded by evil, he still has the option to decide within himself as to how all this evil is going to affect him. Even in the death camps of Nazi Germany during the Second World War, were people of unique identities who *choose* to remain upright and ethical and not to compromise on their values, in the midst of death and evil. Few company culture, if any at all, could be as bad as these !

It has been stated previously, that human beings are endowed with an ability of self-awareness, they are gifted with imagination and creativity, they have a conscience and an independent will. When people are aware of themselves and their value systems, when their conscience tell them deep down what is right and wrong, then they can use their imagination to evaluate the various options before them and ultimately exercise their independent will to choose what they consider to be the right option, irrespective of the circumstances.

Mahatma Gandhi had stated, 'They cannot take away our self-respect if we do not give it to them'. It just means that whatever the circumstances within the organisation are, if you do not allow them to affect you, they cannot. They need your consent to hurt you. We must learn to be pro-active, rather than reactive. Reactive people react to everything in the environment. Everything and everyone has the power to affect them. Something happens and they automatically react to it. Thus, they are tossed and turned by every incident of life, which ultimately make them topsy and turvy inside. Such people are driven by their moods, feelings and emotions on one hand, and by circumstances, conditions and the environment on the other. Pro-active people, on the other hand, are not affected by these factors and are not tossed and turned by the external environment, nor by their internal feelings. These people are driven by values - carefully selected and internalised values.

Many executives feel that they cannot win the battle of the conscience because expediencies require lies, cover-ups, deceit, game playing and manipulating. However, these are just rationalisations and not reality. Nothing in the world is just black and white. It is very rare to find a situation where an individual is forced to choose only the 'wrong' option. That is hardly ever the case. An individual always has a choice to either choose the 'right' and the good or the 'wrong' and the bad. It takes mature judgement to know what one should do under such circumstances. But the underlying understanding before making any choice is the acceptance of the fundamental truth that a life of total integrity is the only life worth striving for. And pro-active people chooses just that sort of life !

It is not what happens to us, but our *response* to that incident, that has the power to harm us. No incident, no circumstance on earth has the capacity, the ability, the power to harm us if we do not allow it to. Being pro-active does not mean being pushy, aggressive or obnoxious. It just means recognising our responsibility to make things happen, to act and not to be acted upon. Pro-active people have the ability and the confidence not only to act ethically in the midst of unethical circumstances, but they also have the capacity to explain and to exhibit to people who matter in the organisation, how acting ethically can help the organisation in the long run. They can even take specific problems that the organisation is facing at present and then develop an effective presentation to show how acting ethically can help solve the organisation's problems in the long run. The pro-active person himself must however, be absolutely sure of the effectiveness of the solutions he is advocating, otherwise he will not be able to convince others. Such confidence will come only if the person truly, honestly and absolutely believes that values and ethics triumphs in the long run.

When a superior manager gives an order to the subordinate like 'secure orders at any cost', it conveys a message to the subordinate that the company is concerned only with the result - i.e., orders - and not on how the orders are secured. It implies that the company would evaluate the subordinate's behaviour in terms of the result (i.e, the end) and is not concerned with the means. This gives a great leverage to the subordinate to indulge in unethical behaviour and later to abdicate moral responsibility for their actions with the refuge of 'I was only following orders', and thus shifting the responsibility to the superiors. When a senior manager encourages an attitude that anything goes, it probably *will.*

Moreover, experience shows that whenever a company gains 'orders' or business for wrong reasons and by unethical means, it runs the risk of being complacent about the quality of its products and services. If it no longer requires to cater to customer needs, or to respond to market changes or to the challenges of technological advancement, it is bound to lose its competitive edge and eventually collapse under the deadweight of carrying its own 'sins' and gets buried under its own unethical activities.

Thus a company stands to lose out, and eventually die, by resorting to unethical means to gain business. What it stands to gain in the short run is only a illusion, because it stands to *lose a lot* to gain a little. The loss of goodwill, reputation, customer loyalty, the faith and pride of employees, all these cannot be calculated in monetary terms only. Similarly, the peace of mind, mental contentment, sense of self-worth, inner satisfaction and fulfilment, the feeling of confidence and power that righteousness brings, all these too cannot be calculated in financial terms. All these are achieved only when one conducts oneself and the affairs of the organisation ethically.

Given half a chance, most organisations would prefer to conduct their affairs honestly and ethically. Organisations resort to unethical activities, if and when they do, only because they focus on the short run and are not aware of how they are harming themselves in the long run. If they are made aware that ethics and profits are not mutually exclusive, and in fact the more ethical and socially responsible the organisation is, the more it stands to gain in the long run, every organisation would choose ethical means and ways of doing business. The organisation can combine the creativity and integrity of pro-active individuals within itself to create an ethical corporate culture. Then the organisation does not have to remain at the mercy of the environment; it can group together the shared values and purposes of the individuals involved, and create an ethical culture which will spread slowly within the whole organisation.

7.1 Areas of Influece (or Areas of Authority) and Areas of Interest

Every person has a wide range of concerns - his financial position, his health, his job, his family, his community, his religion, his country, the world. However, out of all these concerns, some of them are his immediate concerns - like his health, his financial position, his job and his family, and others are just areas of passing concern, called his **Areas of Interest** - like his community, religion, country and the world. This is because the areas under his immediate concern are his **Areas of Influence**, his **Areas of Authority.** This means that he can influence the outcome in the areas of his immediate concern, he can exercise his authority over these areas, he can exercise his options, he can choose and he can control these areas of immediate concern. However, in case of the areas of passing concern, i.e.., his Areas of Interest, he has no direct influence or authority over them and he can exercise control over them only as far as he himself, and may be his family, is concerned. In the areas of immediate concern, the person has mental and emotional involvement, as changes in them affect him directly, immediately and in an intimate manner. This is not the case in the Areas of Interest.

Even if things in the Areas of Interest concern and affect him directly, he can do very little about them, since he has no real control or influence over them.

Similarly in an organisation also, a person has a wide range of concerns. Some of these concerns are under his influence and authority, and hence controllable by him. But others are not under his authority and hence cannot be controlled directly. They remain merely his Areas of Interest as opposed to his areas of immediate concern.

It is in the areas of immediate concern that a person should focus his time, energy and efforts to improve and change. It is futile, and indeed frustrating, to spend time and effort over the Areas of Interest, without being able to make any effective and lasting impact.

The areas of immediate concern are termed as Areas of Influence or Areas of Authority of the person within his Department, his Section or his organisation. It is in this Area of Influence or Authority that a person can make his real impact and his real contribution.

Every person in the organisation has his or her own areas of influence and authority. For each person these areas of influence and authority are different. But there are many people to be found within organisations whose activities and concerns are only aimed at the Areas of Interest, while a lot remains to be done in the Areas of Influence, which are dreadfully neglected.

Pro-active people concentrate their efforts and activities in the Areas of Influence, because they know that these are the areas in which they can do something, contribute something. Reactive people, however, disperse their efforts and activities in the Areas of

Interest, because then they can blame their problems on the external environment, on other people, and on circumstances over which they have no control. Not that they do so consciously. They often do this unconsciously, more out of habit and early learning. But, being human beings, they can modify their behaviour to focus more effectively on the Areas of Influence. It is only animals whose behaviour is based on early learning and training, because they have no power to think and analyse how that training will affect them - i.e., they have no independent will. Human beings, however, are endowed with an independent will, with a capacity to think and analyse, and the power to assert how earlier learning will affect them. Inspite of this, if people choose not to change their behaviour and rely only on past learning and experiences, then they would be living just as animals do, inspite of possessing a brain and mind that is intellectually much more superior than an animal.

Moreover, when people primarily keep focusing on the Areas of Interest, they allow these areas to affect and influence them, without having any control over them. Hence they feel frustrated, out of control, powerless and a sense of victimisation. They allow themselves to be controlled by circumstances and people over whom they themselves have no control.

What is even more important is that when people keep on concentrating and focusing on the Areas of Influence and Authority, they slowly but steadily, start exercising their influence over the Areas of Interest also. It is bound to happen. The concentrated and focused efforts of pro-active people on their Areas of Influence slowly penetrates and spreads over to the Areas of Interest over time. Thus, by working on the Areas of Influence, a person becomes more influential.

Now after an understanding of the Areas of Influence or the Areas of Authority, one can realise the relationship between ethics and individual behaviour within an organisation. Since every person in the organisation has an Area of Influence, however big or small it may be, where he has the freedom and the authority to take action, he can take ethical and value-based decisions within that Area of Influence.

For example, if a person is the Head of the Marketing Division, then his Area of Influence is the Marketing Division, over which he has his authority. Hence he can decide that any action or decision taken within the Marketing Division, will be ethical and moral.

He can see that no misleading or false advertisements are issued, no defective products are sold, after-sales servicing is done immediately, sales calls are attended to promptly, his salesmen show courtesy and respect to customers and prospective buyers, they neither give nor take bribes to secure orders, he himself makes ethical marketing policies, strategies and decisions and so on. All these are within his Area of Influence and Authority. He can enforce ethical practices in his Area of Influence; he can make things happen in his Area of Influence- the Marketing Division.

On the other hand, if he knows that the Managing Director of the organisation has given a bribe to secure an order, or the Personnel Manager has received a bribe to hire someone, apart from bringing them to the notice of those concerned, there is not much he can do about these. All these lie outside and beyond his Area of Influence. He has no legal authority to either take action or to change these decisions, because they lie beyond the purview of his Area of Influence. These lie only in his Area of Interest; he is interested in knowing and he is concerned about such going ons within his organisation; but there is nothing much he can do about them, apart from exposing such people to the higher up authorities. It is the higher authorities who can take action against such misdeeds because such deeds fall under the Area of Influence of the higher authority. However, if one of his own salesmen was caught giving or receiving a bribe, then he can take action against him, because the salesman's conduct falls under his Area of Influence.

If this Head of the Marketing Division, were to always remain concerned with giving and receiving of bribes by his bosses or people in other departments or divisions, then he could be a reactive person, forever frustrated and depressed. This is because he would remain concerned with events and incidents beyond his Area of Influence, over which he has no authority and which cannot be controlled by him. And to do this, if he were to ignore or neglect his own Division, then he would be neglecting that area over which he **does** have control, where he **can** make a difference.

This is basically how an individual can relate his or her behaviour to the organisation. The individual can be as ethical and morally upright as he wants to be in his Areas of Influence. He can also try to influence others to be ethical in his Areas of Interest, but he cannot directly control them in those areas, as they are beyond his authority. Yet, as he becomes more and more pro-active in his Areas of Influence, he will find that the effects of his actions will spread over to the Areas of Interest also, and he will become more and more influential in these areas too. This is the essence of the moral relationship between the individual and the organisation, and this is how an individual can retain his values and principles even in the midst of confusing and contrasting ethics within the organisation. If a person can assure himself that he has remained as ethically correct as he can be within his Areas of Influence, has never compromised his values within these areas, has upheld moral principles, then he can be satisfied and at peace with himself and his organisation.

Summary of the Chapter in Brief

* What distinguishes human beings from other animals in the animal kingdom is that humans have self-awareness, they have a conscience and they have an independent will.
* We begin life at birth by being totally dependent on others, then we become independent and finally interdependent.
* These concepts of dependence to independence to interdependence helps us to understand the relationship between ethics and individual behaviour.
* Ethics is an abstract concept and people have different ways of looking at it and can legitimately differ in their views of what should be done to resolve an ethical dilemma. Rejection of your ethical arguments and concerns does not mean that others in the organisation are wrong or unethical.
* People can differ on ethical concepts because the relative emphasis they place on the economic, legal and moral forms of analysis may differ.
* People also differ because the value system and the ethical standards upon which their moral reasonings are based are different. People also differ on their views about what constitute an ethical dilemma.
* Many people also believe that economic performance is the only way through which a business can serve society.

* A dependent person takes whatever decision is expected of him, even if he feels guilty and unhappy inside.
* An independent person takes a decision after independent thought and analysis, one which he is comfortable with, based on his own value system and his concept of right and wrong, irrespective of other peoples opinions and expectations.
* An interdependent person tries to carry along with him the people of his organisation also while he takes a decision which he is sure is the correct course of action.
* Adherence to one's values and refusal to compromise on unethical dealings helps to define oneself in a unique way. Then one's values, ethics, integrity, self-control and honesty help one to curve out his own unique identity rather than through other people's opinions or comparisons with others.
* Being pro-active helps us to be more ethical than being reactive to situations and circumstances.
* It is not what happens to us, but our response to that incident that has the power to harm us.
* Organisations resort to unethical activities, if and when they do, only because they focus on the short run and are not aware of how they are harming themselves in the long run.
* A person's areas of immediate concern are his Areas of Influence or Areas of Authority, over which he has direct influence and can exercise his control over them.
* In the Areas of Interest, a person has no direct influence or authority and cannot exercise his control over them.
* It is in the Areas of Influence that a person should focus his time, energy and efforts to improve and change. It is futile, and indeed frustrating, to spend time and effort over the Areas of Interest, without being able to make any effective and lasting impact.
* When people concentrate and focus on the Areas of Influence and Authority, they slowly but steadily, start exercising their influence over the Areas of Interest also.

Expected Questions

1. Explain the moral relationship between an individual and his organisation.
2. Do you believe that it is possible to remain ethical within an organisation which resorts to unethical practice in its business? Explain why and how.
3. Is there, according to your view, any difference between personal ethics and ethics in the work place? Can a person remain ethical in his personal life while going along with the unethical activities in the organisation? Discuss.
4. Discuss how ethical individual behaviour of a person is affected by the ethics of his organisation and his workplace.

CHAPTER 8

GANDHIAN PHILOSOPHY OF WEALTH MANAGEMENT

Mohandas Karamchand Gandhi was one of the greatest Indians who ever lived. People understood him partly, misunderstood him vastly, yet took him to be the only leader who could influence all his countrymen, irrespective of caste, creed, language or religion, across the length and breadth of the country. His philosophy, today known as Gandhian Philosophy, still inspires, and at the very least, affects various spheres of social and commercial lives in India. Gandhiji's life was an amazing adventure of morality and ethics. He could, through his revival of Gautam Buddha's ethics of non-violence, shake the mighty British Empire in India. Albert Einstein, another great soul who ever lived, had this to say about Gandhiji-

"Generations to come will scarce believe that such a one as this ever in flesh and blood walked upon this earth".

For Gandhiji, morality or ethics was the very foundation of life. The moral conscience, according to him, should be man's inner guide to his actions. Truth and non-violence were the basic philosophy of Gandhiji's life. These two concepts are the essence of morality.

Gandhian philosophy of wealth management is based on the 'Servodaya' principles of Truth, Non-violence and Trusteeship; wherein class harmony between labour and management reigns supreme. According to Gandhiji, managers and proprietors of business firms are only the trustees of the wealth of the society.

The trusteeship slogan is to enjoy one's wealth in the true spiritual sense, by renouncing it. The view of trusteeship advocates that one should retain for one's personal use, as much as is necessary to make an honourable, but simple and dignified living, no better than that of the average people of the society, and to utilise the rest of one's wealth for the welfare of the community and for social good. The view of trusteeship has the fundamental ideal that even if one earns enormous wealth through one's productive activities, and with honest means, yet that wealth is not one's own, it belongs to the people of the community.

The idea of trusteeship advocated by Gandhiji, is based on and has its origin in the Bhagaved Gita-in the principles of 'aparigraha' (non-possession) and 'sambhawa' (equalism) which were ardently followed by Mahatma Gandhi. These two principles of the Bhagavad Gita took a strong root in Gandhiji's mind. Gandhiji believed that according to these principles, in reality, all men are trustees, for every man is required to use his wealth for the welfare of all in the community. Trusteeship involves a code of ethical behaviour as well as a principle of accountability.

Unlike the Utilitarian motto of 'greatest good of the greatest number', Known as

Teleology, Gandhiji's motto was 'greatest good of all'. According to Gandhiji, even an **attempt** made at achieving the greatest good for all is a matter of satisfaction.

Gandhiji dreamt of an economic order where labour and management existed in peaceful cooperation, supplementing each other efforts and activities. In his own words, he stated-

> "My ideal is that capital and labour should supplement and help each other. They should be a great family living in unity and harmony; capital not only looking to the material welfare of the labourers, but their moral welfare also-capitalists being trustees of the welfare of the labouring classes under them".

Thus, Gandhiji's philosophy implied that management was the trustees of, not only the wealth of the organisation and of the society and consequently of the nation, but also of the material and moral welfare of the labour class working in their organisation. Thus Gandhiji tended to assign a paternalist role to management in their dealings with labour.

Gandhiji encouraged workers to form trade unions and actively participate in them. He insisted that, 'The working class would never feel secure or develop a sense of self- assurance and strength unless its members are armed with unfailing subsidiary means of subsistence to serve as a second string to their bow in crises'.

Gandhiji considered trade unions to be a means of workmen's material and moral development. He remarked thus-

> "It is not anti-capitalist. The idea is to take from capital labour's due share and no more, and this, not by paralysing capital but by reform among labourers from within and by their own self-consciousness; not again through the cleverness of non-labour leaders, but by educating labour to evolve its own leadership and its own self -restraint, self-existing organisation. Its direct aim is not in the least degree political. Its aim is internal reform and evolution of internal strength. The indirect result of this evolution when, and if, it ever becomes complete, will naturally be tremendously political."

Gandhiji further said, '.........while it is quite proper to insist upon (workers') rights and principles, it is imperative that they should recognise the obligation that every right carries with it ....The workers should treat the business of their employers as if it were their own business and give it their honest and undivided attention ......fight it they must, on the path of righteousness'.

Gandhiji himself led and participated in a number of strikes. He declared that a 'strike is an inherent right of the working man for the purpose of securing justice, but they must be considered a crime immediately the capitalists accepts the principle of arbitration'. Thus, Gandhiji insisted that the ethical way to go on a strike was after giving 'fair notice' and after 'every other legitimate means has been adopted and failed', and only for a just cause. Every worker, during the period of the strike should be peaceful and non-violent. He also believed that laying down conditions of services by workmen was not an absolute right. Even if such an absolute right was granted to labours by management, Gandhiji felt it would not be proper and ethical to use it. Moreover, Gandhiji did not advocate strikes for workmen engaged in essential duties for it disrupted peaceful social order and created chaos in society. People were victimised for no fault of theirs and life was held at ransom.

Gandhiji also believed that while all men should have equal opportunity, yet not men have the same capacity. In the nature of things, some people will have the ability to earn more. If those who have talents, use their talents wisely and well, than they will be performing the work of the society. Gandhiji viewed social responsibility of business from the point of self-control and voluntary discipline.

Gandhiji's philosophy of Wealth Management also included non-possession or Aparigraha. From the principles of Aparigraha, truth and non-violence, evolved the concept of trusteeship, which was the foundation of Gandhiji's principle of wealth management.

According to Gandhiji, the principle of non-violence and truth in the business sense, meant a peaceful co-existence of capital and labour. However, if conflicts do arises, between labour and management, then also Gandhiji proposed non-violent means to resolve these conflicts. The weapon proposed for this purpose is the means of non violent non-cooperation, termed in Gandhiji's language as Satyagraha. Gandhiji declared that labours had a right to have their grievances redressed through Satyagraha, which should be absolutely peaceful and non-violent, resorted to for a just cause and only after management fails to respond to their moral appeals.

Gandhiji's Pprincipal of Trusteeship:

Gandhiji's principal of Trusteeship is the foundation of his philosophy of Wealth Management. Gandhiji believed that each capitalist and industrialist should consider himself to be a trustee of the wealth that he possesses. He should consider himself to be a custodian of the industry, resources, labour and wealth that he uses for his business purpose. If all capitalists and all industrialists begin to believe themselves as such custodians of their own wealth, then collectively, they would become the custodian of the wealth of the society. And that would transform the capitalist order of society into an egalitarian one, where the 'greatest good of all' could be achieved. Gandhiji also reminded management that they should consider themselves to be the trustees not only of the wealth of their business but also of the labour class who works for their industry. And not only were management responsible for the material well-being of the workmen, they were also responsible for their moral and spiritual upliftment, just as if they were their own children.

Trusteeship management and consequently wealth management does not recognise the right to individual property. All property should belong to the society and should be utilised for the welfare of the whole society, so that the division between the 'haves' and 'have nots' are narrowed down as far as possible. Our Constitution of India, also does not guarantee the right to private property as a fundamental right. Initially, the constitution had included, under Article 19 (1) (f), the Fundamental Right to Property and Article 31 had prohibited the deprivation or property of any person save as when authorised by the law and compensation is to be paid to any individual for the loss of or for the deprivation of property. However, in 1978, by the 44th Amendment, the Constitution abolished the fundamental right to property by abolishing Articles 19 (1) (f) and Article (31). But, Article 300A of the new 4th Chapter (Chapter IV) added to part XII of the Constitution provides that 'no person shall be deprived of his property save by authority of law'. Thus, now, the right of property of an individual is no longer a Fundamental Right, but is has been retained as a Constitutional right.

In Trusteeship management and Wealth Management, the right to individual and private property is abolished and is permitted by the society only to the extent where it is needed for one's own welfare. The society does not permit any right to an individual to hold or to use wealth beyond and in disregard to the welfare and interest of the society. Moreover this private wealth should not be of disproportionate extend and to the detrimental of the society. In case of industrialists, what they produce in their industries and release in the society, should be determined by social necessity with the optimum utilisaiton of the scarce resources of the society. What they produce should not be determined by personal whims or personal greed. During the process of production and later, management is expected to hold the industry as a trust for the society and the community. If workers are to work in harmony and in collaboration with the management, as envised by Gandhiji, then that makes the workers also co-trustees with the management. Thus, the responsibilities of trusteeship falls on the shoulders of the workers also, though to a lesser extent, as on the management of the enterprise.

In this sense, labour and management both being partners in the production process and both being co-trustees of their enterprise, should work together in harmony and peaceful co-existence. Then there exists no room for conflict of interest between management and labour, because the interest of both labour and management exists in the welfare of their industry and their enterprise. According to Trusteeship philosophy in Wealth management, though legally wealth belongs to the owners and proprietors of business, morally it belongs to the society, to the community.

Gandhiji also wanted labour to be organised and united amongst themselves. Gandhiji wanted there to be an awakening among the workers of their own strength and confidence in their own abilities and capacities. Gandhiji wanted moral growth and spiritual development on the part of the workers, so that they do not remain ignorant, unlightened and immature. He wanted workers to realise and utilise their moral strength and develop their conscience about righteousness and ethical means of behaviour as also the consciousness about their existence and their just position in the industry. Gandhiji wanted workers to develop a sense of pride in their own strength, in the face of which the question of management's exploitation of labour does not arise.

In 'Dynamics of Industrial Relations', C.B. Mamoria and S. Mamoria cited the ethical rules advocated by Gandhiji, to be used by labour in the process of resolving disputes between management and labour.

1. Workers should seek redressal of reasonable demand only through collective action;
2. If they have to organise a strike, trade unions should seek by ballot authority from all workers to do so, remain peaceful and use non-violent methods;
3. Workers should avoid strikes as far as possible in the industries of essential services;
4. Workers should avoid formation of unions in philanthropical organisations.
5. Strikes should be resorted to only as a last resort after all other legitimate measures have failed; and
6. As far as possible, workers should take recourse to voluntary arbitrattion where direct settlement has not succeeded.

Gandhiji believed that only with these preconditions, it was possible to avoid bitterness between labour and management, even when they are in conflict. Even though there may be some differences between management and labour on day-to-day matters and routine issues, there should never be any doubt that the interest of management and labour as far as the welfare of the organisation was concerned, is totally convergent. Only when this is the case, can ethical behaviour from both management and labour be expected.

Valid for both management and workers alike is the belief of Gandhiji about ends and means. Gandhiji believed that even if they were pursuing ethical and praiseworthy goals, the means for achieving the same should be equally justified. Gandhiji strongly believed that ends and means cannot be separated. Both need to be equally moral to achieve moral results. Even good motives or ends do not justify one resorting to just any means. Similarly, a good end can never be achieved through foul and evil means. According to Gandhiji, ends and means are equally important. Hence, even for securing their righteous demands and just rights, Gandhiji advised labour not to resort to any means, but to follow the path of **satyagraha**. Here the end-righteous demands and the means - Satyagraha are both highly ethical, and one will definitely lead to the other. Similarly, to the management, Gandhiji advocated the philosophy of trusteeship, with which means, management can arrive at the end - welfare for the labour and consequently welfare for themselves and their organisations.

Conclusion:-

It would be appropriate to conclude this discussion with a reference to the 7 greatest sins that Gandhiji believed could wreck the moral and ethical fabric of society. Let us find out their relevance to the modern business society-

1. Politics Without Principles--

Needles to say, this sin is the foundation of all things unethical in society. Corrupt political practices ultimately corrupt business and industry. When people resort to principle-less politics only to cling to power and wealth, not only do they themselves become morally corrupt and unethical, but they also leave behind them a trail of destruction of all moral and ethical values held sacred by the society. And business too gets sucked into this whirlpool of corruption and destruction of the society and all things ethical in it, gets shaken and ultimately shattered. The ethical value system gets eroded and all morality stands crumpled. Such a society, where value-less and principle -less politics is practised, cannot stand on its feet after a while; and moral and ethical decadence sets in.

2. Education without character:

The main aim of education is character-building. If students feel that the aim of education is only securing more and more marks through cut-throat competition, then there is something lacking in the focus of the education system, as is happening at present. When students rely heavily on the results and not on the learning process, character-building takes a back seat and later on in adult life, the student finds himself or herself ill-equipped to meet the challenges of life. Moreover, education should be a life long process. Those who stop learning as soon as the academic life is over, are those whose character had not been fully developed in the initially formative years. Such people, sometimes with numerous degrees to their names, remain literate but uneducated in the true meaning of life. Their degrees, without their character, does them no good in their pursuit of the really meaningful things in life.

3. Commerce without Morality:

Even before it became fashionable to talk about ethics in business, Gandhiji considered conducting business without morality and ethics as a great sin. What happens when business is conducted without morality, has been the running theme of all the topics of this book.

4. Pleasure without Conscience:

All over the world today, in every society and every country, people are seen primarily obsessed with securing and with pursuing pleasure. Most of these people confuse happiness with pleasure. Happiness in not pleasure and neither do all pleasures result in happiness. Happiness is spiritual gladness, a quiet contentment and inner joy. Whereas for many people, pleasure is merely vulger sense gratification. Peole today go to any length to gratify their senses and that too immediately and instantaneously. Like instant coffee, senses must be gratified instantly as and when the need, or more specifically the want, arises. That is why we see incidents like pre-martial sex , where it is asking for too much to wait for after the wedding, and more commonly, without the wedding; killing of innocent and defenceless animals to gain hunting 'pleasure'; eating and drinking of intoxicating things to get oneself a 'high', drug abusing to excite the senses; and so on. Pleasure of the senses, without the sanction of one's conscience are futile and meaningless, it degrates human dignity and generally brings about all-round destruction for all concerned.

5. Wealth without Work

This sin is spreading like wild cancer in today's society, and has given rise to may a get-rich-fast, high risk half-baked schemes. The fact is, there cannot be wealth without hard work, and even if there is, one is not entitled to use it as one has not earned it throughout his own efforts. One has no right to spend someone else's wealth not earned through his own hard work, even if that wealth belonged to one's father or grandfather. Gandhiji believed that one is entitled to spend, in adult life, only that much wealth as has been earned through his own efforts and hard work. Today's crimes are mostly committed because one wants to get rich quickly, without investing the time and efforts of earn it. People desire to get into certain professions, including politics, because then wealth can be made without working for it. Militants start revolutions and then resort to extortions, because then wealth can be made without working for it. Youths spend their most productive years dreaming about schemes, business or otherwise, to get rich quickly, because then wealth can be made without working for it. It can only be said that wealth generated without work can only come thought dishonest means; and one has no moral or legal right to such wealth.

6. Science without Humanity

Science is a wonderful and tremendous force at the service of humanity. Science has the capacity to alter human life drastically and beyond one's wildest imagination. It can serve human beings in so many different ways and make his life as comfortable and as luxurious as he wishes it to. The quality of human life has been tremendously uplifted, by using the fruits of science. Truly, scientists are to be as revered as great saints !

However, science also has the potential for great destruction. It can destroy people's peace of mind, ways of thinking, his position in society, and in fact, his whole life. When technology-the application of science, is used haphazadly and indiscriminately, it results in wide spread destructions in society, the Bhopal gas tragedy on December 3, 1984, killing some 2,000 people and injuring another 2,00,000 people is a case in point. The methyl isocyanate gas used by the Union Carbide Company plant in Bhopal, was used to manufacture sevin, a plant pesticide, the use of which increased the harvest of the food crops by over 10%, enough to feed 70 million people. However, the carelessness of the company resulted in wide speed destruction.

When Alfred Bernard Nobel (1838 - 1896), invented the dynamite, he did not do so that it could be used in making Atom Bombs for mass massacre of people and animals. Yet it was used for this very purpose in the Second World War. When technology upgraded the means of production, it was done for the welfare of society in general, and not to reduce workmen to becoming mere cogs in machines. Yet this is exactly what it has resulted in. Indiscriminate automation has resulted in wide spread changes, some so drastic, baffling and bewildering, that the human mind, unable to cope with the rate and pace of change, has quietly gone insane. This frantic pace of change has induced many employees to such an extremed state of stress, that insanity is the resultant phenomenon.

This is certainly not what science, and its child-technology, had set out to do. Hence, science must be more humane, dedicated to the welfare of all sections of society, and more particularly dedicated to those sections of society, to whom the benefits of science has till date, remain elusive. Business firms have a major role to play in this scenerio. And the by-product of science-technology, must be applied with more caution and even more consideration to suit the needs and the temperaments of human beings. And here too, business firms have a significant obligation to society in general, and its employees in particular. Technology must be applied in such a way that it reaches those sections of society to whom the benefits and fruits of technology has not yet reached. Much more important than that is that both science and technology continue to be more humane and for humanity.

7. Worship without Sacrifice

Finally, Gandhiji, believed in sacrifice during worship. It is important to understand the meaning and significance of he term 'sacrifice' here. A man deeply committed to non-violence could never have talked about animal sacrifice, against which Gandhi fought, anyway. Sacrifice here implies destroying all evil qualities and tendencies in a human being. Worshipping God, without sacrificing one's evil intentions, one's immoral character, one's unethical conduct, can never lead us to inner peace and contentment. Sacrifice here means doing away with one's ego, one's selfish motives, one's jealousies, one's envy, one's passion and replacing them with compassion, generosity, helpfulness, truth and basic goodness of character. Thus, Gandhiji believed that it was a sin to worship God without sacrificing something evil in oneself and replacing that with genuine goodness. Even fasting, which basically means sacrificing one's meals, held great meaning for Gandhiji.

Reference:

Quotes of Gandhiji taken from 'The Ahmedabad Experiment in Labour Management Relations', International Labour Review, 1959.

Summary of the Chapter in Brief:

* Gandhian Philosophy of wealth management is based on the 'Sarvodaya' principles of Truth, Non-Violence and Trusteeship; wherein class harmony between labour and management reigns supreme.

* According to Ghandiji, Managers and Proprietors of business firms are only the trustees of the wealth of the society.
* The trusteeship slogan is to enjoy one's wealth in the true spiritual sense, by renouncing it.
* Gandhiji's idea of trusteeship had its origin in the Bhagavad Gita, in the principles of 'aparigraha' (nonpossession) and 'sambhawa' (equalism).
* Ghandhiji's philosophy implied that management was the trustees of, not only the wealth of the organisation and of the society and consequently of the nation, but also of the material and moral welfare of the labour class working in their organisations.
* Gandhiji assigned a paternalist role to management in their dealings with labour.
* Gandhiji encouraged workers to form Trade Unions and actively participate in them, because it would increase their sense of security and self-assurance.
* Gandhiji viewed social responsibility of business from the point of self-control and voluntary discipline.
* The principle of non-violence and truth in the business sense meant a peaceful co-existence of capital and labour.
* Gandhiji declared that labour had a right to have their grievances redressed through Satyagraha, which should be absolutely peaceful and non-violent, resorted to for a just cause and only after management fails to respond to their moral appeals.
* Gandhiji's philosophy of wealth management was based on the idea that all capitalists and industrialists should consider themselves to be the custodian of the industry, resources, labour and the wealth that they use for their business purposes.
* Gandhiji reminded management that they were responsible not only for the material well-being of the workmen, but also for their moral and spiritual upliftment, just like their own children.
* Trusteeship Management and consequently Wealth Management does not recognise the right to individual property.
* All property should belong to the society and should be utilised for the welfare of the whole society.
* What Industrialists produce in their industries and factories should be determined by social necessity with the optimum utilisation of the scarce resources of the society, and not by the personal whims or personal greed of the industrialists.
* During the process of production and later, management is expected to hold the industry as a trust for the society and the community.
* If workers are to work in harmony and in collaboration with the management, as envised by Gandhiji. then that makes workers also co-trustees with the management.
* Labour and management being partners in the production process, are also the co-trustees of their enterprise, and should both work together in harmony and peaceful co-existence.

* According to the Trusteeship Philosophy, though wealth legally belongs to the owners and proprietors of business, morally it belongs to the society and to the community.
* Gandhiji strongly believed that ends and means cannot be separated. Both need to be equally moral to achieve moral results.
* According to Gandhiji, the seven greatest sins that could wreck the moral and ethical fabric of society and which has great relevance to modern business society are -

Politics without Principles;
Education without Character;
Commerce without Mcrality;
Pleasure without Conscience;
Wealth without Work;
Science without Humanity;
Worship without Sacrifice.

EXPECTED QUESTION:

Discuss the Gandhian Philosophy of Wealth management.

Chapter 9

Social and Economic Responsibilities of Business

(A) Social Responsibilities of Business

Business organisations today, apart from being economic entities, are also considered to be social institutions, primarily for two reasons. **Firstly**, since business organisations exist and operate within a social structure, they must earn social sanction, without which they will collapse and die out. **Secondly** and more importantly, since business organizations exercise a definite and extensive influence on our social lifestyles, they must discharge social responsibilities.

Businesses today no longer exist only to maximise profits. They exist and operate for a number of reasons, one of which should be the welfare of the society in which they operate and grow. Hence, businesses should be socially responsible, socially conscious and they should carefully consider the social and ethical implications of their decisions, as they sometimes have irreversible impact on the society. If businesses exist to earn profits only, then profits can be earned in numerous ways - even through black-marketing, hoarding, adulteration, etc. But these acts degenerate business into swindling the public. Hence, profit motive of business must be tempered with service motive, to fulfil social obligations for social welfare.

No business can exist without the acceptance and sanction of the society in which it carries out its activities. The organisation is so dependent on its social environment that its very existence, survival and growth depends on its acceptance and approval by the society. No organisation can hope to exist and grow which has outlived its utility to the society. As early as in 1963, Peter F. Drucker, the renowned management guru, in his book titled - 'The Practice of Management', stated that the relationship between business and society "is like the relationship between a ship and the sea which engirds it and carries it, which threatens it with storm and shipwreck, which has to be crossed but which is yet alien and distant, the environment rather than the home of the ship. But society is not just the environment of the enterprise. Even the most private of private enterprises is an organ of society and serves a social function".

Moreover he goes on to add–

"The responsibility of management in our society is decisive not only for the enterprise itself. But for management's public standing, its success and status, for the very future of our economy and social system and the survival of the enterprise as an autonomous institution. The public responsibility of management must therefore underline all its behaviour. Basically it furnishes the **ethics of management**".

In a Seminar sponsored by the India International Centre, New Delhi, titled 'Social Responsibilities of Business', in 1966, our late Prime Minister Lal Bahadur Shastri said in his inaugural speech–

"Too often the community views the businessmen's aims as selfish gain rather than advancement of the general welfare. That impression can be removed only if business is fully alive to its social responsibilities and helps our society to function in harmony as one organic whole".

He further added–

"The benefits of development must accrue more and more to the relatively less-privileged class of society and there should be progressive reduction of the concentration of incomes, wealth and economic power. The importance of the role to be played by the businessmen in the establishment of this new order cannot be over-emphasised. It is, I venture to think even greater than that of the economist and the politician".

Organisations today can become, and is indeed required to become, agents of social change, if they want to play a more meaningful role within the social structure. Each decision of the organisation has an impact upon society. Hence management of an organisation is required to conduct a **Social Cost-Benefit Analysis** of its various decisions, taking into account their impact upon the society.

As a result of rising public expectations from business, many companies are incorporating social responsibility into their mission statements. Businesses today have a natural and intimate stake in the viability of society, in the stability and growth of its economy; in the orderly functioning of its free and democratic institutions under the Rule of Law. As an organ of society, business activities have a decisive impact on the social scenario. The first and foremost responsibility of a business is to operate at a profit for its continued survival and avoid making losses, which cause great hardship to the society and untold miseries to its people. But along with its survival, businesses also have the responsibility to grow and develop. Businesses are wealth creating and wealth producing organs of the society. Keeping these organic functions intact, businesses must, at the same time, strive to improve the well-being of the society.

The Committee for Economic Development, New York, in its report 'Social Responsibilities of Business Corporations', 1971, reported–

"It is in the enlightened self-interest of corporations to promote the public welfare in a positive way. Indeed, the corporate interest broadly defined by management can support involvement in helping to solve virtually any social problem, because people who have good environment, education and opportunity make better employees, customers and neighbours for business than those who are poor, ignorant and oppressed".

The first verse of Ishavashya Upanishad describes–

> "All that exists in this Universe is the abode of the Almighty. Therefore, enjoy the good things in life by sharing them with others. Do not covet the possessions of others".

Another Sanskrit sloka invites–

> "May we prosper together and enjoy our prosperity in common. Let our exploits be joint adventurers. May our studies be full of light. May we not quarrel with each other. Let there be peace, peace, peace".

These are the traditional thoughts of ancient India. They hold good even today and can guide the economic activities of organisations. It is in this spirit that businesses can integrate themselves with the social aspects of people's life and discharge their social responsibilities.

9.1 Social Responsibility Defined

Keith Davis in 'Can Business Afford to Ignore Social Responsibilities?', California Management Review, 1960, defines Social Responsibility as–

> "Social Responsibilities refer to the businessman's decisions and actions taken for reasons at least partially beyond the firm's direct economic or technical interest".

Keith Davis uses the term 'Social Responsibility' of business to refer to two types of business obligations, i.e.,– i) the Socio-Economic obligation, and ii) the Socio-Human obligation.

The **Socio-Economic** obligation of business refers to its obligation to prevent economic consequences of business from adversely affecting public welfare. To this end, businesses are required to promote employment opportunities to reduce the unemployment problem in the society, to maintain healthy competition so that consumers can enjoy its benefits in terms of high quality products and fair prices along with avoidance of monopolistic practices, curbing inflation, etc.

The **Socio-Human** obligation refers to the obligation of business to nurture and develop its human resource so that employees get every opportunity to grow and develop and advance through life and their careers; to make the organisation more humane and humanistic and to promote human values within the organisation.

Adolph A. Berle, in 'The American Economic Republic', New York, 1963, has defined Social Responsibility as the manager's responsiveness to public consensus. This public consensus would be determined in each country by its customs, religions, traditions, its level of industrialisation, norms, standards and various other aspects.

Kenneth R. Andrews, in 'The Concept of Corporate Strategy', Homewood, 1971, provides a broader definition of Social Responsibility–

> "By Social Responsibility, we mean the intelligent and objective concern for the welfare of society that restrains individual and corporate behaviour from ultimately destructive activities, no matter how immediately profitable, and leads in the direction of positive

contribution to human betterment, variously as the latter may be defined".

These definitions are very broad in scope and do not prescribe specific activities to be taken in the interest of the society or the organisation. L. M. Prasad, in 'Principles & Practice of Management', Sultan Chand & Sons, 1989, gives an operational definition of Social Responsibility, as–

> "Social Responsibility contends that management is responsible to the organisation itself and to all the interest groups with which it interacts. Other interest groups such as workers, customers, creditors, suppliers, government and society in general are placed essentially equal with shareholders".

V.B. Day, in 'The Social Relevance of Business', also observed that–

> "As a statement of purpose, maximising of profit is not only unsatisfying; it is not even accurate. A more realistic statement has to be more complicated. The corporation is a creation of society whose purpose is the production and distribution of needed goods and services, to profit of society and itself. Each element of that statement is needed if the whole is to be accurate; you cannot drop one element without doing violence to the facts".

Thus, taking into account all the above definitions, we see that today business consists of a well-blended mixture of altruism, self-interest and good citizenship. Today no business can survive in the long run in total disregard to its social concern. Business needs to make profits through the creation of utility for fulfilling needs and wants of consumers along with social benefit. Organisations today have learnt that discharging social responsibilities do not detract them from, or is counter to, profit making. Rather by discharging their social obligations and behaving in a socially responsible manner, they build a solid foundation to continue to make profits, not just in the short run, but also in the long run.

9.2 Why Business must be socially Responsible

According to the systems approach to business, both business and society interact with each other and are mutually dependent on each other. A business exists and operates within a social framework and thus requires social sanction. Society, on the other hand, requires business to fulfill its needs and for its economic and social well-being. A business receives inputs from the society. It offers its outputs to the society in terms of products and social service. Its outputs, i.e., its products and activities must be beneficial and acceptable to the society. All businesses need society's approval in order to function.

Interaction between Business and Society

1. **Growth-Responsibility Expectation**–Business must realise that the best way to survive and grow in the long run is to operate profitably by serving customers responsibly. The social expectation is that the bigger the organisation grows, greater are the responsibilities it is expected to assume. George A. Steiner, in 'Business & Society', New York, 1975, explains this expectation like this–

"The manager of the biggest companies know that as a business gets larger, the public takes more interest in it because it has a greater impact on the community. The antennae of these managers are tuned to public opinion and they react to it. They seek to maintain a proper image of their companies in the public mind. This leads to the assumption of greater social responsibilities".

SOCIETY

INPUTS		BUSINESS		OUTPUTS
Manpower 1. Raw materials 2. Social Infrastructure 3. Money (from financial institutions) 4. Machinery 5. Market 6. Information	⇒	Uses Physical, Human, Technical resources to manufacture & produce products & Services.	⇒	1. Satisfies needs and wants of consumers through quality products offered at fair price 2. Provides employment & thereby economic and social security. 3. Offers solutions to consumers problems. 4. Generates revenue for shareholders. 5. Educates society about market choice. 6. Social Service activites.

Interaction Between Business & Society

2. Long-term Orientation–If an organisation expects to conduct its business in the long-term, it will require a loyal brand of customers, repeat customers, customers with goodwill. This goodwill cannot be bought, begged or borrowed - it has to be *earned* ! And it can be earned only when organisations behave responsibly; when they discharge social responsibilities. Moreover, if they act in a socially irresponsible manner and society is harmed, it will harm them in the long run, because they have to operate in the same society which they have harmed. Business cannot remain immune while the rest of the society is being destroyed. It will get affected too, sooner or later.

3. Reputation of the company–Many organisations want to build up a reputation of a good, friendly company and what better way to do this then to engage in socially approved activities ? This is why many companies, build a company image of care and concern, by giving away scholarships to deserving students and donating products to the weaker sections of the society. This is specially true of the major Indian tea companies which are perceived as being exploitative by the people of the North Eastern states of India, where most of their tea gardens are located. To offset this image, they resort to community service and social activities.

4. Give-Take relationship–Since business exists and operates within the society, take so much from the society, need its sanction and approval to function, hence it also owes something to the society. To keep the balance even, it needs to give back something to the society, to do something for its benefit. And what it does for the society and its welfare restores the balance between the business and the society.

The S'vetas'vatara Upanishad in its peace invocation says–

"May the Divine protect us *both* together. May the Divine nourish us *both* together. May we *both work* together with great energy. May our study be vigorous and effective. May we not hate each other".

This seems to be an apt slogan for both business and society to function in harmony !

Business organisations are also social entities. Apart from the fact that they exist and operate within a social framework, various social relationships also develop within the workplace. Working within a group, a team or a department, becomes a social activity. Work is an indispensable part of a man's life (and now-a-days, in a woman's too!), not only because it provides him with purchasing power and all the necessities and luxuries of life, but also because it provides him with an opportunity for self actualisation and self development with fulfilling human relationships while working with others. Work is what provides a man with exciting possibilities and endless challenges to develop himself mentally, intellectually, emotionally and spiritually. It gives him his status and recognition in society. But most importantly, it provides him with an opportunity to work with others, to grow with others, to enrich his life through *building bonds* with others. And that is exactly why, work and business are termed as an extension of the social framework.

If an organisation can improve the quality of life of customers and help to solve their problems, then the operations, activities and relationships of the organisation will automatically grow. Then there is an integration of private and public good simultaneously. It is in the goal of serving society that the personal interest of a company and the interest of society meet. The more closely a company concentrates on solving a particular problem of the society or of its customers (who are members of the society), the better it is able to solve its own problems of growth and prosperity.

BUSINESS AND ITS INTEREST GROUPS

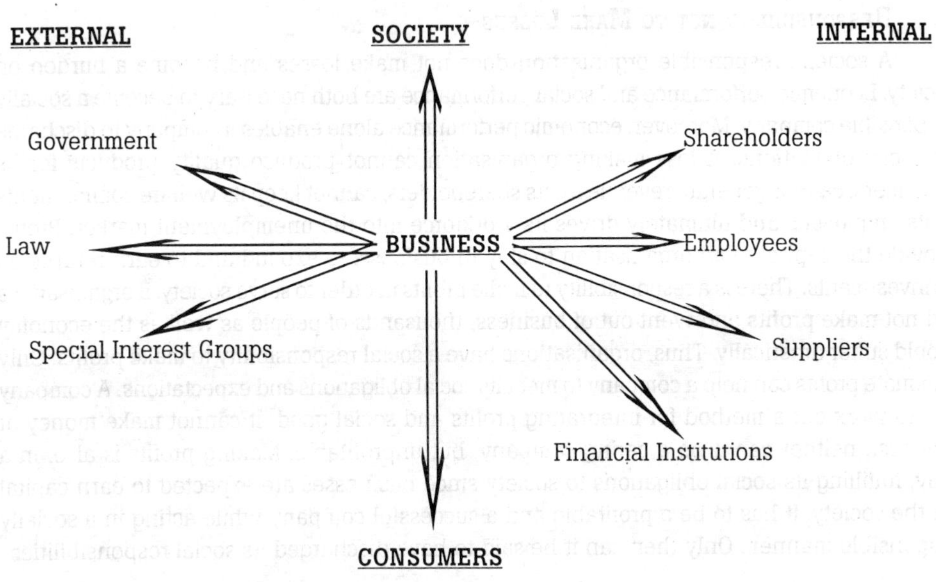

9.3 Major Social Responsibilities of Business

1. Optimum Utilisation of Scarce National Resources–

All business firms have the moral obligation to utilise the scarce national resources of the country in an optimum way and not to waste, misutilise, damage or cause to deteriorate the resources at its disposal. It is assumed that the natural resources of a country are always limited at a given period of time, and hence they must be utilised carefully and in a way to optimise their use. Since many uses can be made of the same natural resources, hence options must be carefully choosen to find out which uses will serve the country better and result in social welfare. There is always an opportunity cost associated with using scarce natural resources of the country. For example, take the case of wood. The given amount of wood that a country has at a particular time is limited, and can be utilised in various ways - it may be used to build houses, it may be used to produce paper, it may be utilised in wood-based industries and factories, it may be used to produce household goods and decorative items and so on. Hence it must be first ascertained as to which of these options are of crucial importance - whether it is better to use the wood for house building purpose, for producing paper or it is more important to make decorative items. Moreover what proportion of the wood should be used for what purpose, must also be ascertained. Because, whatever wood is used by one industry, that amount of wood is denied to other industries. That is where the concept of opportunity cost comes in. It is important to find out the cost to one industry for making alternative uses of the same material by another industry. Hence, the industry to which this scarce natural resource is being made available, must make a moral commitment to utilise this scarce resource to its optimum level, and not to waste or misutilise it in any way. It must remember at all times that what is being made available to it, is being denied to others. That is one of its major social responsibilities.

2. Responsibility not to Make Losses–

A socially responsible organisation does not make losses and become a burden on society. Economic performance and social performance are both necessary to become a socially responsible company. Moreover, economic performance alone enables a company to discharge its social obligations. A loss making organisation cannot produce quality products for its customers, cannot generate revenue for its shareholders, cannot keep its welfare commitments to its employees and ultimately drives its workforce into the unemployment market. Profits provide the capital to an organisation to stay in business, to expand and to earn returns on its investments. There is a responsibility to make profits in order to serve society. If organisations did not make profits and went out of business, thousands of people as well as the economy would suffer drastically. Thus, organisations have a social responsibility to make profits. Only adequate profits can help a company to meet its social obligations and expectations. A company has to work out a method for integrating profits and social good. It cannot make money at any cost, neither can it be a caring company, but unprofitable. Making profits is also, in a way, fulfilling its social obligations to society since businesses are expected to earn capital for the society. It has to be a profitable and a successful company while acting in a socially responsible manner.. Only then can it be said to have discharged its social responsibilities.

3. Improved Quality of Life–

Quality of life is not merely dependent on our standard of living, but also on our standard of life. Standard of living is based on one's financial power and is the indicator of the quality of life and one's material growth. Standard of life, on the other hand, is based on one's internal growth, the growth of one's character, growth of the mind and soul. Though standard of living is important as far as physiological and security needs are concerned, it is standard of life that provides the real quality of life, an enriched quality of life. Business firms also have the responsibility to provide for opportunities to the society and the members of the society (like its workers and its customers) to enrich their lives and to better the quality of life. Improvement of the quality of worklife of employees is a special area of focus. Moreover its products and services can be targeted to improving the quality of live of the people of the society.

4. Responsibility of Employment and Income–

Every business should make provisions for the payment of fair wages, satisfactory working conditions, steady employment and job security, prospects for promotion, growth and development of workers and also take adequate measures for employee welfare. Thus, a business must be just and humane and must provide for fair opportunities to all workers for their advancements. Business must create conditions which enable workers to put forward their best efforts to achieve the organisational goals. This includes recognition where due, appreciation for efforts put in, employee's right to justice, a right to participate in decisions affecting their work life, right to collectively bargain for their dues, right to form trade unions and assemble peacefully, and a right to be compensated fairly for the efforts of the workers. Moreover, business should offer employees the opportunity to develop their abilities, capacities and skills, help them in their personal and professional growth and development and offer them opportunities for advancement within the organisation through education and training. Moreover they should be treated as human beings, with due regard and respect for their thoughts, feelings and beliefs. As far as monetary compensation is concerned, every worker, apart from receiving a fair income, should be entitled to enjoy a percentage of his productivity and the profitability of the company. He should receive an income commensurate with his skills, abilities, talents and efforts. The compensation scheme of the organisation should be one which is not only fair and just, but also equitable and which encourages productivity and efforts from workers. And this must be accompanied by job security so that workers continue to receive their incomes without fear or forbidding of the future. If business does all these, then it shall be doing a great welfare for society and would have discharged one of its major social responsibilities.

5. Offering Quality Products at Fair Price–

Customer's satisfaction should be the ultimate aim of all business activities. Offering adulterated products, poor quality products and not abiding by the standards of measurements, lack of proper attention and courtesy to customers, inadequate after-sales service, misleading and false advertisements, etc. are examples of violations of business ethics and socially irresponsible behaviour on the part of business. Moreover, business firms should try to offer the best possible quality in its products. Consumers do not buy the product as an end in itself, but for the services it can give. If the service given by the product can meet consumers expectations, if not exceed it, then consumers will be satisfied with the product. However, the price of the product should also be *fair*. This means that the price of the product should be commensurate with the quality of the product. Just because the quality of the product is satisfactory or because the seller is operating in a monopolistic market, they should curb the temptation to fix exorbitant prices for their products. Moreover, it is not only unethical, but also morally wrong, to overcharge the price of a product or to supply lesser quality for a higher price. Providing quality products at fair prices is a major social responsibility of business organisations.

6. Environmental Protection–

Business organisations also have the social responsibility of taking serious steps to protect the environment from industrial pollution and destruction. The refrigerator companies cause the ozone layers of the atmosphere to deplete; the dust of the cement companies may cause lung cancers and other breathing problems; the fumes of many industrial houses pollute the atmosphere and cause various types of biological diseases; the waste and effluence of many manufacturing firms are thrown into lakes, rivers and ponds thereby polluting the water of the community; the high temperature and severe noises from many industries apart from polluting the atmosphere, causes innumerable damage not only to human population but also to others in the animal and plant kingdoms. Business does so much irreparable harm to the environment, that it becomes an obligation for them, not only morally, but also legally; to undo the damage by taking serious and responsible steps to protect the environment and keep it in a healthy condition. Planting of trees, avoiding polluting the atmosphere, water and greenery of the community as well as of the country and also taking active steps to protect the environment from further harm is what business organisations must do to conduct themselves as responsible corporate citizens. However that alone is not enough. Business firms must also provide for civic amenities so as not to destroy or damage its environment. It should provide for sanitation, public health, prevention of noise pollution and try to restrain bad effluent, chimney smoke and smog, ugly and dirty buildings and structures, poor housing and living conditions of workers, unhygienic and overflowing drainage, piling up of debris, etc. Taking measures for all these activities constitute a major social responsibility of business firms.

7. Fair Trade Practices–

Fair Trade Practices of business firms constitutes of:

(i) Avoidance of monopolistic and restrictive trade practices, by entering into secret combination agreements;

(ii) Charging fair and reasonable price from customers and not engaging in, or leading the entire market into, a price war;

(iii) Offering products and services of quality consistent with their claims and expectations;

(iv) Making goods and services easily available in the marketplace and not resorting to artificial scarcities;

(v) Not indulging in profiteering, hoarding or blackmarketing and thereby swindling the public;

(vi) Not making false, misleading and exaggerated claims in its advertisements;

(vii) Providing accurate, relevant and timely information to creditors and suppliers;

(viii) Making prompt repayment of loans and other borrowings;

(ix) Abiding by the rules, regulations and the laws of the country;

(x) Paying corporate taxes, duties and other dues; honestly and promptly without any cover-ups or cheatings;

(xi) Not bribing public servants and corrupting the democratic structure of the country;

(xii) Not buying political favours to sway decisions in its favour;

(xiii) Maintaining fair business policies, decisions and activities;

(xiv) Setting up desirable standards of living and avoiding ostentations and wasteful expenditures;

(xv) Playing a proper role in civic affairs and providing and promoting general amenities;

(xvi) Not selling rebuilt, secondhand or used products as new;

(xvii) Not resorting to planned obsolescence of products and spare parts, in order to gain a continuous market for its products;

(xviii) Not procuring business or trade secrets of competitors through espionage, bribery, coercion or in any other way;

(xx) Not deliberately make the organisation sick so as to avoid many of its obligations and escape from its responsibilities.

8. Fulfill All National Obligations Under Various National Laws–

Business organisations are considered to be corporate citizens of the country in which they operate and conduct their business. As citizens, they are required to fulfill certain obligations under various national laws and to perform certain duties towards the nation. Firstly, it has to fulfill its civic duties like avoiding pollution and keeping the environment clean. Then they must regularly and honestly pay all their taxes and duties to the concerned governments. They must make sure that they obey all the provisions of the various business and labour laws of the country in letter and spirit. Moreover, they must conduct their affairs as law-abiding citizens without creating any nuisance to the community or to the country in which they exist and operate. Above-all, they must have the national interest of the country in which they operate, at heart and uppermost in their mind, at all times. They must make an attempt to ensure national prosperity and reduce some of the country's national problems, like unemployment, corruption, blackmarketing, etc.

9. Safeguard the Health and Well-Being of Consumers

One of the vital social responsibilities of business is to safeguard the health and physical safety of consumers using the products of the company. Yet, how many manufacturers take adequate care to check and safeguard consumers' health and well-being ? Many pharmaceutical as well as cosmetic manufacturers neglect to take enough protection to uphold consumers' health. Let us take some examples in point - Recently a consumer found that a liquid medicine had gone bad even though it was well within the date of expiry. Had the consumer not paid heed to the foul smell and unpleasant taste and had gone on taking the medicine because the date of expiry had not expired, and because the medicine was expensive, one can well imagine the consequences, that too when the person was sick and his immune system was weak. The effectiveness of a drug not only depends on the quality of the product, but also on the seal, packaging, transporting and storage conditions. Most liquid medicines advice users to close the cap tightly after use. But the caps or closures provided on the bottles are usually of such a poor quality that once the seal is broken, it becomes almost impossible to close the bottle properly. Which means that the medicine deteriorates over time and during use, and gets spoilt even when it is well within the expiry date. The effectiveness of the medicine also goes down and sometimes the medicine itself may well become toxic. Sometimes the seals themselves are of such poor quality that the liquid is leaking by the time they reach the customer's home.

The Consumer Guidance Society of India (CGSI), Mumbai recently examined and found cases where the quality of pediatric multi-vitamin formulations deteriorate even during the period of their use, where the in-use stability of the products were not satisfactory. The colour and flavour of these liquid vitamins undergo perceptible changes even while they are being used. Thus, even though the bottle lasts only a month, it gets spoilt even during this period of time. The fact that these are pediatric medicines and are administrated to infants, makes the manufacturers of these medicines even more irresponsible and unethical.

Coming from drugs to cosmetic companies, the situation remains the same or gets even worse. Many cosmetics and toiletries contain a cocktail of chemicals which cause irreversible damage to the skin, nails, hair and eyes. Badly researched and poor quality cosmetic and toilet products cause irreparable damage and may sometimes cause skin diseases and even cancer.

Deodorants contain aluminium, zinc and zirconium salts, antiseptics, perfume, propellant or alcohol and formaldehyde and these may cause skin irritations and allergic reactions in sensitive skins. Aerosol sprays can cause irritations to the eyes, nose and skin. All aluminimum based sprays (especially those with zirconium) should be used cautiously. But manufacturers of the product hardly ever bother to issue such warnings with the product. Deodorants may cause rashes and infection of the sweat glands by blocking them by trapping bacteria deep in the fat layers under the skin surface. Unsuspecting public who are not informed about these health hazards continue to use deodorants excessively and indiscriminately in our hot and humid climate and cause a great deal of harm to themselves.

Soaps are an indispensable part of our daily cleaning. Its problems also stem from the potency of the antibacterial agent. There are no truly safe bactericides. The health hazards from them are allergic reactions, resulting in dermatitis. Bubble baths are more dangerous than bar soaps. They are made of synthetic detergents found in shampoos, laundry detergents and dish washing liquids. These detergents often cause severe irritations. A liquid bubble bath could be contaminated with nitrosomanines and expose the entire body to skin absorption of the proven animal carcinogen. They can strip away the mucous lining of the urinary tract, making that area susceptible to infection. The public is generally unaware of all these as manufacturers and business companies continue to act in socially irresponsible ways.

Shampoos commonly consist of detergents, perfumes, colours, germicides, thickeners, preservatives, opacifiers (turns clear liquids into cream lotions) and dispersants (to control formation of hard water scum). Strong shampoos damage hair and causes hair loss. It erodes hair, causing each strand to become thinner and weaker. Hair becomes more liable to drop off due to the presence of synthetic detergents - found in detergents for washing dishes and clothes. Prolonged exposure to these chemicals may cause dry, rough and badly cracked skin, itchiness, rashes, sores and retracted finger and toe nails. Undiluted hair conditioners can severely irritate the membranes around the eye or cloud the cornea. Though in normal use, they are safe enough not to endanger the eye, they are potent enough to be dangerous to careless handling like splashing undiluted conditioner into the eye. However, since the manufacturers of these products do not deem it fit to enlighten the public about these health hazards, these products in the hands of children could be very dangerous. Similarly, most hair dyes are harmful. Permanent hair dyes contain coal tar derivatives, while non-permanent hair dyes contain a mild acid. Even hair dyes claiming to be 'natural' contain toxic ingredients.

The ideal eye or face cosmetic should not affect the skin in any way. Unfortunately, most people suffer allergic reactions to many of the ingredients which appear in eye and face make-up. Among all cosmetics available in the market, mascara is the one which causes most medical problems. A major problem with mascara is bacterial contamination and conjunctivitis of the eyes. Lotions and moisturizers have the potential to cause acne and the fragrance cause more allergic reactions than many other ingredients. Moisturisers which contain formaldehyde as preservative may cause skin irritations.

Nail polishes are based on nitrocellulose, which is a highly inflammable synthetic substance, which is chemically related to gun cotton, an explosive. Colouring agents, plasticisers and perfume (usually camphor) are the other major components of a nail polish. Nail polish solvents are narcotic if inhaled at high concentrations and can act on the nervous system. It is dangerous to breathe in the vapours of the nail polish, specially under inadequate ventilation and also to touch the nail polish, while wet to the face. Inhalation of acetone found in nail polish removers can cause headache, fatigue or bronchial irritation. Acetone is a highly inflammable substance which is dangerous to bring in close contact with an open flame. The most dangerous health hazard associated with fragrance, found in most cosmetic products, is internal poisoning of the human body.

(**Source**: 'Insight', Consumer Education & Research Society, Ahmedabad)

Using scented products may have become a fashion statement, but strong perfumes are likely to affect your health, says a report published in the 'Environmental Health Perspectives'. Many people are reported to be suffering from the ill-effects of using strong fragrances. In the late nineteenth century, the first fragrance containing artificial ingredient was introduced. Since then, chemicals have been used extensively to mimic scents from nature. Cosmetics, lotions, soaps, oils, perfumes are some of the products in which aromatic chemicals are used to add smell. Recent reports have been attributing headaches, dizziness, nausea, fatigue, shortness of breath, difficulty in concentrating and even allergy to the usage of those chemicals. It has been seen that asthmatic patients and people who are allergic to several chemicals often fall ill after using scented products. Claudia Miller, an associated professor of environmental and occupational medicine at the University of Texas Health Science Centre, says that several studies indicate that 15 to 30 per cent of the general population suffer from the adverse effects of fragrances. 4 to 6 per cent report that chemical intolerance has a major impact on their quality of life. More than 80% of these people find exposure to chemicals bothersome'. When 31 selected brands of scented products were examined for a study published during the Air and Waste management Association's 84th Annual Meeting in 1991, the researchers found there were at least 150 chemicals in those products. Most of these chemicals cause irritations in skin, eyes, mucosa, nausea and dizziness. Nervous disturbances, palpitation and bronchitis are also not uncommon. Moreover, a few of these chemicals have actually been tested for carcinogenicity. Perhaps the most important aspect of the problem is the effect of these chemicals on children. Quite a large number of children's products are scented and several perfumed products are marketed specially for them. Children are more susceptible to the adverse effects of these products than adults because of their smaller size, higher respiratory rate and thinner skin. Little research on this has been done. It is difficult to regulate the use of chemicals as perfume manufacturers are nor required to obtain a pre-market clearance for their products. As per the rules of the trade, manufacturers are neither required to reveal fragrance ingredients nor do they disclose the chemicals used. Most products only have the term 'fragrance' written on them. Most manufacturers do not have their own safety tests. In the USA, the Research Institute for Fragrance Materials (RIFM) has been set up in 1996 to conduct studies on fragrance ingredients in order to ensure safety. The RIFM has tested more than 1,300 aromatic chemicals and published test results in international journals. In India, people are mostly unaware of the dangers of fragrances and perfumes, leave alone setting up research institutes in the line of the RIFM of the USA. Even though many companies have agreed to let their products be tested in the USA, there is no law which makes it compulsory. In India, as has been stated before, consumers as well as manufacturers are still unaware of the magnitude of the problem. Even in America, the RIFM only tests the raw materials and not the finished product which is marketed. Very soon when public awareness grows, there will be a need felt to use safe, chemical free perfumes by manufacturers. In the USA, messages asking people to refrain from using scented products are appearing frequently. Such messages are also urgently needed in countries like India to draw public attention to the dangers of such products.

(**Source**: The Telegraph KNOWHOW, 5 April, 1999, Calcutta, page 4)

Irresponsible and dangerous activities by business organisations 4 have a great adverse effect on the health and well-being of unsuspecting and unaware consumers. Here's another such real life example of irresponsible and irrational behaviour by a drug company–

During a rush hour at the Kalighat Metro station at Calcutta, recently, in the middle of a crowd stands a man busily distributing small packets and slips of paper among passengers. You would think that these were free samples of yet another shampoo, perhaps, or something similar. However, what passengers find in their palms are a pack of two metacin tablets and a coupon which, when presented to a chemist, promises two more free tablets in a 'customer-friendly pack'. The medicine, the coupon claims, 'Fills painful moments with joy'. Can a company induce consumers to try out a brand of medicine as one tries out a mint ? Ethically, and in responsible behaviour, there should stand a chit of paper between a consumer and a drug - the medical *prescription* ! Medicines often have toxicity and, when taken in wrong doses or for wrong reasons, may well aggravate the disease or trigger off new complications. Moreover, some drugs cannot be taken when a patient is already suffering from some other ailment. In case of the metacin tablets being handed out with such a carefree attitude, whether it is all right to take these tablets by a diabetic patient, a heart patient, a high-pressure patient, can only be ascertained by a qualified doctor. Apart from this real- life incident, one also sees advertisements of medicines freely prompting people to take one or two tablets for certain kinds of pain - for faster, longer-lasting relief from headaches, cold, backaches and so on. Physicians warn that every drug, whether herbal or chemical, can produce side-effects. The former Secretary of the Indian Medical Association feels that advertisements of drugs should be addressed only to medical practitioners. 'Lured by the promise of immediate relief, patients often use drugs which result in 'symptomatic relief' or 'placebo effect', but does not cure the underlying disease". What is worse, immediate relief delays proper diagnosis of a disease. He recalls one of his patients who had irregular bowel disorder and took a much-advertised indigenous drug regularly. When the symptoms aggravated, he had to get a colonoscopy done. The test revealed cancer. Another patient who took an aspirin preparation regularly developed acute gastric-ulcer. Persistent ads of a drug extolling its virtues, sans a single word about possible side effects, encourages the habit of self-medication which is potentially dangerous. A physician prescribes a drug after thorough clinical examination. No such logic operates behind self-medication. Often a self-prescribed medicine like an antacid interacts with prescribed drugs and renders them useless. Self-medicated drugs can also have the opposite effect - paracetamol tablets taken regularly for headaches can aggravate headaches and even lead to liver or kidney damage. Commonly advertised drugs often have side-effects. Crocin may cause gastritis while Coldarin, which is a brand name for aspirin, can cause allergy. Ayurvedic and Unani drugs are also advertised flouting all rules. The Drugs and Magic Remedies Act, 1954, has provisions to protect the public from objectionable drug advertisements. The crucial question however, is in the implementation of the Act. A personnel from the Drug Technical Advisory Board says, "While taking a medicine, the dosage, the time and the age of the patient has to be taken into account. It is unethical for the press or television ads to prescribe a dose or to promise relief within a set time".

(**Source**: Excerpts from 'Try another pill ?', Patralekha Sandilya, The Telegraph, 8 April, 1999, page 18)

Although dangerous ingredients associated with cosmetics are present in minute quantities to cause widespread harm, yet this does not absolve manufacturing companies of their social responsibility to inform and educate consumers about their potential health hazards. In the long run, what is good for society is good for business. Self-regulation by business is far more effective than compulsory or state regulation to assure consumer protection. Otherwise, a time will come when, like cigarettes and baby foods, cosmetics will also be compelled by the government to carry statutory warnings. Business today is required to provide products and services that not only satisfy consumer needs and desires, but, are also consistent with new social values like ecological protection and consumer safety. Products are required not only to cater to consumer demand, but must also be good for the consumer and the society, i.e., products must be socially desirable.

Manufacturing and marketing companies must learn to act responsibly where consumers health and security are concerned. And this cannot be truer than in the case of drug and cosmetic companies. Informing and educating the public may not result in consumers buying and using less cosmetics, but it will help them to be more careful and use them more cautiously and judiciously by increasing their awareness level.

9.4 A Look at Social Performance of Business

Many companies today have accepted social responsibility of business as part and parcel of their economic activities. Progressive and enlightened companies all over the world are taking up more and more social responsibilities. Many of these companies are determined to play the role of a responsible corporate citizen. International Business Machines (IBM), the giant computer transnational company has a world-wide policy of taking up social projects in the countries where it conducts its business. These projects included the renovation of the biggest Buddhist temple in Indonesia and help in saving a city in Italy which was threatened by sea erosion.

Public Sector companies have always given social service its due importance and have included social responsibilities as part of their activities, as they were set up with the intention of playing the role of change agents in society. However, some PSUs have been more active in this regard than others. Oil India Limited (OIL) is one such PSU. Oil India Limited, the Indian oil drilling company, is associated with community development and social projects like building schools, colleges, hospitals, roads, low-cost housing, as well as offering monetary help to financially weaker students in the form of scholarships and sponsorship, besides promoting games and sports in rural areas and spotting and training talented youths.

Many companies have promoted their own Universities to encourage higher learning. Notable among them are Motorola, Ford, GE, AT & T. In India too, efforts made by companies like IPCL, HLL, IOC, TATA and banks like SBI, to the cause of education and higher learning is notable.

MBB, the biggest German aerospace company has donated expensive equipments to a New Delhi hospital for bloodless surgery. Brown Boveri and Migros, two large Swiss companies have involved themselves in a massive programme of consumer education.

The Midland bank of England had spent about 3 crores in terms of Indian rupees to organise a Great Japan exhibition in London to promote Anglo-Japanese relations, a few years back.

Indian private companies have also not lagged behind in discharging their social responsibilities. Mention, of course, must be first made of the TATA group of companies whose corporate name is synonymous with ethical practices and their high standards of public duty. For Jamsetji Tata and JRD Tata, establishment of their industrial empire was more of a social duty than for private earnings, a duty to make India more industrialised and self-reliant. JRD Tata wanted to bring about an 'industrial revolution' to an economically backward India, so that the country could stand on its own. The result of his efforts was the establishment of a hydroelectric power project at Bombay, the Steel industry at Jamshedpur and the Indian Institute of Science at Bangalore. Thus the three specific goals of JRD Tata at that time - hydroelectric power as a cheap source of energy, a steel plant in India and the establishment of a technical school - had been responsible for sowing the seeds of industrial development of the country almost a century ago. JRD Tata conducted his business in a very socially responsible way. He set up a pension plan for his employees and introduced the eight-hour workday much before the law enforcing it (The Factories Act) came into being in 1948. Russy Mody, the able disciple of JRD Tata and who shaped Tata Steel for more than half-a-century, is said to have stated -"My values were fashioned by the House of Tatas. These were to so conduct your business that profit was not your only motive. The happiness of those who worked in your business; a fair deal to customers who bought your goods; and efficiency in your job". The same beliefs were echoed by Ratan Tata who said in an interview in 1993, "Ethics for Tatas means conducting business in a manner which is fair and just to employees, suppliers and shareholders; having a concern for the community in which one is operating. It would involve putting combined interests above personal gain or exploitation".

Associated Cement Companies (ACC) has been rendering social service for over 3 decades. It launched a village welfare scheme in 1952 and has been continuing with setting up schools, colleges, health centres, bunds, agro-based and local industries and cooperative societies with the sole aim of providing employment and improving the quality of rural life. From the help from ACC, farmers in Andhra Pradesh have doubled their per acre yield of rice whereas in Bihar, they have raised crops of protein-rich soyabeans as a matter of routine.

Another group of industries that have rendered important social service is the Hero Group. Brijmohan Lall Munjal, the patriarch of one of India's fastest growing and most modern automobile groups, is a true believer in Indian ethos. The company started at the time of the British Raj, before independence, and today it is a Rs. 2,600 crore enterprise. This company started with a mission, way back in the 1940's, to 'provide excellent transportation to the common man at a price he could easily afford'. One of the track records of the company included emerging as the world's largest manufacturer of bicycles, as early as in 1987, and getting an entry into the Guinness Book of World Records and maintaining it till 1996-97, when they manufactured 4.5 million bicycles. Another significant achievement is emerging as a leading player amidst stiff competition in the two-wheelers segment, consisting of mopeds, motorcycles and scooters. The company's constant refrain is that the triumph of the Hero group is not as much due to the business acumen of its founders as due to the undying spirit and commitment of the common workmen and the hundreds of skilled engineers of Punjab. This is hardly surprising as the company was way ahead of industry norms in rewarding their workers with a uniform allowance, House Rent Allowance (HRA) and Leave Travel Assistance (LTA), long before any other company in India did so. Further, the company organised regular medical check ups at company cost not only for their full time permanent workers, but also for migrant labourers working in the company and even for their parents.

Companies like Cadbury India, Glaxo and Richrdson Hindustan are also helping farmers with their crops.

The Mafatlal Group of industries is also engaged in rural welfare activities and in helping the poor. It has constructed homes for the homeless, provided drinking water, distributed books, stationary and scholarships to students in rural areas. In association with Bharatiya Agro Industries Foundations, it has developed a complete package of technology with facilities for breeding, testing and treatment of high yielding milch cattle which had been successfully extended to a number of villages in the backward districts of Gujarat, Maharastra, Uttar Pradesh, Madhya Pradash and Orissa. This Group had also carried on a food-for-work programme in collaboration with the Gujarat Government to grow superior varieties of fodder grass.

Bharat Heavy Electricals Limited (BHEL), also, for a long time have carried out numerous social welfare activities. They have implemented a number of welfare schemes not only for their employees, but also for people living in the townships where they have their operations. It has identified specific problems of its surrounding communities and have cooperated with local bodies, authorities and voluntary agencies in providing their solutions. BHEL has, in the past, implemented schemes for provision for drinking water facilities, construction of external sewerage, roads and culverts, providing health facilities, improving employee's quality of life through job redesign, job enrichment, etc.

The Cadbury family which pioneered and built up the chocolate and cocoa industries in Great Britain in the 19th century came from a strong religious tradition. The Cadbury company was always determined to be profit-makers, but along with making profits for the company, it was resolute to be practitioners of ethical standards of behaviour. Based on their corporate mission, they undertook several welfare measures for their employees, thereby improving the quality of their lives to a great extent. The factories and houses that they built for their staff at Bourneville in Birmingham remained as a model for others to emulate even today.

Another organisation which has been consciously discharging its social responsibilities is the Housing Development Finahce Corporation (HDFC). Its CEO was conferred the JRD Tata Corporate Leadership Award by All India Management Association (AIMA) for the year 1996, in recognition of their corporate excellence through socially responsible activities. Their responsible corporate philosophy coupled with good ethics catapulted HDFC into the leadership position in the home mortgage market in India, achieving a growth rate of 30% on an average per year and adding to shareholders wealth. Today, on an average, 5,000 new applicants for house building loans approach the organisation every day ! Thanks to this organisation, one million middle-class Indians till date have been able to build their own homes. This is an example of responsible social behaviour.

Maruti Udyog Limited (MUL) is another name associated with social responsibility. In the year 1997, of all the cars sold between January and April, this responsible company recalled about 50,000 of their most popular product, the Maruti 800 passenger cars from the market, because they suspected them to be made of inferior steel! This made newspaper headlines as it was the biggest ever recall of cars from the Indian marketplace. The story of this recall was that in January 1997, Sona Steering's raw material supplier, Mukand Limited, supplied low alloy steel dubbed as SCM 415 for manufacturing the pinions of the cars. But due to an error at Mukand's stockyard, the batch of raw material consignment dispatched to Sona Steering was of a different grade of steel, which was not meant for pinion manufacturing. This was detected during the grueling test drives that the cars are subjected to, and the whole batch of 50,000 cars was recalled at the company's expense.

Another company acting in a socially responsible manner is Infosys Technologies Limited. This company is a much sought after company by employees due to its personnel policies and welfare schemes like the Employee Stock Option Plan. According to this plan, every employee has the option to be made a partner in the common endeavour to achieve excellence in the software industry. In 5 years, this company's sales zoomed from about a modest 10 crore rupees in March 1992, to about 135 crores rupees in March 1997, a jump of a mind-boggling 1250%. The CEO of the company attributes this to its corporate philosophy. He 5 stated - "From day one, we recognised that, to succeed, we had to operate on certain principles, and having decided to go public, we made sure that wealth is created within the business". A very transparent organisation, this company became the first Indian company in 1997 to prepare its accounts in compliance with the US Generally Accepted Accounting Practices and Securities Exchange Commission disclosure norms, a massive step towards attaining global-level transparency !

Apart from those companies discussed above, mention must also be made of some more ethical and socially responsible organisations like the Aditya Birla Group of companies, Choksi's Asian Paints, NDDB, the TVS Group of companies and so on. These companies have been practising ethical business conduct in all their dealings with customers and the public at large. Moreover, they have been functioning as socially responsible corporate citizens and have taken business conduct as a whole, into new heights of ethical excellence.

(B) Economic Responsibilities of Business

A company can earn economic returns in more than one way. While it can, of course, earn profits in monetary terms or Return on Investment, it can also earn profits in terms of market goodwill and credibility, winning the trust of society and the loyalty of consumers.

These are much more difficult to earn, are more lasting and are definitely more valuable.

Earning profits only in terms of money ignores the social cost to the community, specially in terms of using up scarce natural resources and polluting the environment. A company can grow only when it acts in a manner that benefits not only consumers, but also the environment and the society it serves. Profits, merely in terms of money is a poor indicator of the health of a company. How the company is perceived by consumers and the society in which it operates, is a more reliable guide for long term existence, operation and growth.

There are many ways in which a business can be economically responsible. An organisation does not exist only to serve society. It must also make profits, generate surplus, while serving society. Hence it must always calculate its activities in economic terms and find out the cost of serving society. The ethical dilemma comes up when someone in the society, it does not matter whether this is an individual or a group, stands to lose something or gets to be harmed or hurt in some way while the company is on its way to making profits.

Economic responsibility of business, like social responsibility, is a means of striking a moral balance between the economic and social performance of business. Economic responsibility focuses on the efficient utilisation of the resources of the firm to satisfy consumer needs and wants. It means to produce those products and services which are desirable and are meant for the welfare and benefit of society. It means avoiding producing those products and offering those services which degenerates and degrades society, or some segments of the society, specially the vulnerable segments like the teenagers, the youth and the children of the society; even if it means that the company can make huge profits out of such products and by offering such services. Socially immoral and undesirable products and services offer business firms with endless opportunities to make immense profits. However, socially responsible and ethically aware companies would refrain from succumbing to such temptations to make quick money. They would consider social welfare and social benefits before personal greed and personal wealth. They would try to offer products and services which benefit society and would conduct their affairs in such a manner that the ultimate good is for society and the community in which they exist and operate. To do this and to achieve economic equilibrium, we need to achieve the condition of Pareto Optimality in the society.

Pareto Optimality refers to a condition of the marketplace, in which the scarce resources of society are being used so efficiently by the manufacturing firms, and products and services are being distributed so effectively by the competitive markets, that it would be impossible to make any single person better off without harming some other person. Thus, Pareto Optimality is an ethical concept aimed at equality of the society. Pareto Optimality dictates that firms produce the maximum economic benefits for society, recognizing the full personal and social costs of that production, and then broaden the receipt of those benefits, if necessary by political, if not economic actions. Without the concept of Pareto Optimality, the existence of organisations in the marketplace becomes only for individual gain and corporate profit. The concept of Pareto Optimality offers a means for achieving the social goal of maximum availability of goods and services produced at minimum cost for the benefit of the society and for the welfare of society.

The challenge before business firms is to generate enough revenue for itself and for the society, so that inspite of the stiff competition present and the globalisation of business activities, they can not only sustain themselves well, but also become market leaders in their own fields. However this generating of revenues and making of profits must be done in an ethical and socially responsible way, not only because it is desirable and morally correct, but also because this is the only way which will allow business firms to survive and grow in the long run. This is possible only if business firms start pursuing quality and excellence in a zealous manner and without compromise, not only externally, but also internally, within the organisation. Excellence and superior quality, in every aspect of business life, must be a committed way of conducting itself.

In conclusion, it must be again stated that business is an indispensable part of society. It is that organ of the society which creates wealth for the community. Business cannot exist on altruistic ideals alone. It needs to make profits. Indeed it is ethical to generate profits; rather it is *unethical* not to make profits, not to generate revenue for the shareholders of the business and for the society. Business today can play an important role to enable the people of the nation to lead a life of dignity and self-respect inspired by humanistic values of civic morality. In the coming millennium, business managers have a great role to play in regenerating our people socially and economically, and in reducing corruption from the country by adopting the value-oriented holistic management as found in our ancient culture and as taught by our saints and philosophers many many centuries ago. We already have a huge reservoir of ethnic ancient thoughts and beliefs on value-based ethical business conduct and on holistic management at our service. The only effort needed on our part, and on the part of the business houses, is to draw out sufficiently from this great reservoir of thoughts and beliefs and apply them for our own benefits and for the benefits of our business community.

Summary of the Chapter in Brief

* Business must discharge its social responsibility because of two reasons - one, since it exists and operates within a social structure, it must earn social sanction; and two, because it exercises a definite and extensive influence on our social lifestyles.
* The profit motive of business must be tempered with service motive, to fulfil social obligations for social welfare.
* No organisation can hope to exist and grow which has outlived its utility to the society.
* Organisations are required to conduct a Social Cost-Benefit Analysis of its various decisions, taking into account their impact upon the society.
* As a result of rising public expectations from business, many companies are incorporating social responsibility into their mission statements.
* The Socio-Economic obligation of business refers to its obligation to prevent economic consequences of business from adversely affecting public welfare.
* The Socio-Human obligation refers to the obligation of business to nurture and develop its human resource so that employees get every opportunity to grow and develop and advance through life and their careers; to make the organisation more humane and humanistic and to promote human values within the organisation.
* Business today consists of a well-blended mixture of altruism, self-interest and good citizenship.
* Business and society interact with each other and are mutually dependent on

each other. Business receives inputs from the society and requires social sanction to function; society needs business to fulfill its needs and for its economic and social well-being.

* Interaction between Business and Society takes place because of-Growth Responsibility Expectation, Long Term Orientation, Reputation of the Company and Give-Take relationship with each other.
* Work is an indispensable part of a man's life, not only because it provides him with purchasing power and all the necessities and luxuries of life, but also because it provides him with an opportunity for self actualisation and self development with fulfilling human relationships while working with others. Work is what provides a man with exciting possibilities and endless challenges to develop himself mentally, intellectually, emotionally and spiritually. It gives him his status and recognition in society. But most importantly, it provides him with an opportunity to work with others, to grow with others, to enrich his life through building bonds with others. And this is why work and business are termed as an extension of the social framework.
* The more closely a company concentrates on solving a particular problem of the society or of it customers, the better it is able to solve its own problem of growth and prosperity.
* The major social responsibilities of business are - Optimum Utilisation of Scarce National Resources; Responsibility not to make losses; Improved Quality of Life; Responsibility of Employment and Income; Offering quality products at fair price; Environmental protection; Fair trade practices; Fulfilling all national obligations under various national laws and Safeguarding the health and well-being of consumers .
* Self-regulation by business is far more effective than compulsory or state regulation to assure consumer protection.
* Earning profits only in terms of money ignores the social cost to the community, specially in terms of using up scarce natural resources and polluting the environment.
* Profits, merely in terms of money, is a poor indicator of the health of a company for the long run.
* Business firms must calculate its activities in economic terms and find out the cost of serving society.
* Economic responsibility of business is a means of striking a moral balance between the economic and social performance of business.
* Economic responsibility focuses on the efficient utilisation of the resources of the firm to satisfy consumer needs and wants.
* Economic responsibility compels a business firm not to make losses and drive its workforce into the unemployment market.
* Economic responsibility of business compels a business firm to generate revenues for itself, for its shareholders and for the community.

* Economic responsibility means avoiding producing those products and offering those services which degenerates and degrades society, even if it means that the company can make huge profits out of such products and services.
* Economically and socially responsible companies consider social welfare and social benefits before personal greed and personal wealth.
* Pareto Optimality refers to a condition of the marketplace, in which the scarce resources of the society are being used so efficiently by the manufacturing firms, and products and services are being distributed so effectively by the competitive markets, that it would be impossible to make any single person better off without harming some other person.
* Pareto Optimality dictates that firms produce the maximum economic benefits for society.
* Without the concept of Pareto Optimality, the existence of organisations in the marketplace becomes only for individual gain and corporate profit.
* Business today can play an important role to enable the people of the nation to lead a life of dignity and self-respect inspired by humanistic values of civic morality.

Expected Questions

1. Discuss why business must be socially responsible .
2. Explain the concept of Social Responsibility of Business.
3. What is Economic Responsibility of Business? How does it differ from Social Responsibility of Business?
4. Discuss the socially responsible activities of some of the companies known to you
5. Elaborate on the areas where business firms are expected to be socially responsible

Select Bibliography

Bases of Yoga, Sri Aurobindo; Sri Aurobindo Ashram Publication

Bhagawad Gita As It Is, A.C. Bhaktivedanta Swami Prabhupada; Bhaktivedanta Book Trust, 1995

Business & Society, George A. Steiner; New York: Random House, 1975

Capitalism & Freedom, Milton Friedman; Chicago, 1962

Encyclopaedia of Religion and Ethics (ed.), Hastings, J; NY, Scribner, 1920

Ethical Choices in Business, R.C. Sekhar

Ethics in Organisations, David Murray; Kogan Page, The Fast Track MBA Series, 1997

Ethics in Management, S.A. Sherlakar

Harvard Business Review, 1970 to 1990

"I'm OK - You're OK", Thomas A. Harris; Sterling Paperbacks, New Delhi, 1989

Indian Management, Journal of All India Management Association, 1980 to 1999

Journal of Applied Psychology, Sage Publications, 1976 to 1998

Labour Problems in Indian Industry, V.V. Giri; Bombay: Asia Publishing House, 1972

Principles & Practice of Management, L.M. Prasad; S. Chand & Sons, 1992

'The Tata Group: Profits with Responsibility'; World Executive Digest, 1989

The 7 Habits of Highly Effective People, Stephen R. Covey; Simon & Schuster, 1990

The Ethics of Management, Larue Tone Hosmer; Universal Book Stall (UBS), New Delhi, 1987

The Geeta and The Art of Successful Management, Ajanta E. Chakravarty

Values/Ethics in Management - Relevance and Application; Naresh B. Shah

3